IMPOSSIBLE DEMOCRACY?

Impossible Democracy?

The progress and problems of participation in the firm

GUIDO BAGLIONI

Avebury

Aldershot · Brookfield USA · Hong Kong · Singapore · Sydney

The English edition of this monograph was supported by the Department of Employment, Industrial Relations and Social Affairs of the European Commission, Consiglio Nazionale delle Ricerche (CNR), the European Trade Union Institute (ETUI) and Centro di Studi Economici Sociali e Sindacali (CESOS).

The translation is by David S. Giannoni

Published by
Avebury
Ashgate Publishing Ltd
Gower House
Croft Road
Aldershot
Hants GU11 3HR
England

Ashgate Publishing Company
Old Post Road
Brookfield
Vermont 05036
USA

British Library Cataloguing in Publication Data

Baglioni, Guido
    Impossible democracy? : the progress and problems of
    participation in the firm
    1. Management - Employee participation 2. Industrial
    management - Employee participation
    I. Title
    331 ' . 0112

    ISBN 1 85972 537 6

Library of Congress Catalog Card Number: 96-85902

Printed in Great Britain by Antony Rowe Ltd, Chippenham, Wiltshire

Contents

Preface

Participation is a matter of current concern but has been an open issue since subordinate employment first developed in the capitalist economy.

This investigation of the subject spans from past to more recent experiences, taking into account a large number of proposals and contributions by prominent or interesting authors, with reference to European countries as well as Japan and the United States, and considering that participation has always centred on manufacturing firms, though it is thought to be also applicable to other sectors.

The purpose of my approach to the subject is to retrace and describe the main realisations of participation (whether achieved or only envisaged) and to assess such evidence against with reference to a concept of participation capable of truly and realistically applicable solutions, i.e. those compatible with the firm's functioning.

This notion of participation differs significantly from traditional mainstream approaches and reflects the beliefs after an analysis of the employment relationship in the economic and political-institutional evolution of advanced capitalist countries. It also arises from my work in Rome at the CESOS (*Centro di Studi Economici Sociali e Sindacali*) institute for the study of industrial relations and trade-union action, and from my experience as director of a highly participatory cooperative venture of the Banca Popolare di Milano.

While researching and writing this book, I relied on the constant and valuable assistance of Gian Primo Cella, who first persuaded me to address the subject, and of Giancarlo Provasi.

I am also grateful to other friends who accepted to discuss specific topics or single chapters with me. In particular, my thanks go to: Aris Accornero, Giuseppe Bonazzi, Lorenzo Bordogna, Marco Carcano, Mimmo Carrieri, Colin Crouch, Giuseppe Della Rocca, Giorgio Del Mare, Serafino Negrelli,

Antonio Martelli, Alberto Martinelli, Domenico Paparella, Pippo Ranci, Michele Salvati, Paolo Santi, Gilberto Seravalli and Tiziano Treu.

On several occasions I have deeply missed the encouragement and contribution of Guido Romagnoli and Ettore Santi.

I am really grateful to Erminia Borra Vaghi, who carefully typed my minute scripts.

It may help the reader of this rather ponderous and complex work to know that: the overall features and models of participation are presented in Chapter 1; the problems involved are exposed with the author's views in the Introduction and in Chapters 7 and 8; the progress of participatory experience is discussed in Chapters 2-6; and current proposals are listed in the last paragraph of Chapter 8.

The book is dedicated to my family, and in particular to my wife Laura and my grandson Lorenzo.

University of Milan

G. B.

Introduction
A realistic and modern view of participation

1

The subject of this book is workers' participation, which concerns proposals and experiences seeking to alter or improve employment relationships, working conditions and often also workers' socio-economic standing in society. Participation was devised as a means for correcting to different degrees the imbalance inherent in employment relationships. Its context is generally the firm; on a wider scale it has revealed either direct or indirect connections with relations between actors in the firm. The subject is deeply rooted in past experience and has followed for over one hundred years the use of subordinate employment in capitalist economies and in countries whose political systems uphold representative democracy. After phases of varying intensity, with striking differences from one country to another, it has recently become a highly relevant subject and has changed in significant ways.

The need to correct this asymmetry and hence to uphold workers' rights, interests and hopes has often been viewed in a perspective that emphasises the ideal and actual opposition between employers and employees which aims to modify the typical condition of employees within the firm. For a long time proposals involved ideological assumptions, radical changes and predictions of non-capitalistic productive settings.

Some of these proposals led to real though short-lived experiences. While others never went beyond the theoretical phase. Difficulties in realising such proposals, coupled with an ongoing debate on their actual bearing on workers' interests, have contributed alongside other factors to highlight and stimulate participatory initiatives that postulate the decline or demise of opposition between employers and employees, although they envisage qualitative improvements in the use of labour. Among these factors a decisive role belongs to achievements due to union action and legal provisions for the protection of labour.

Recent and current participatory perspectives are characterised by motives and themes that assume interests and objectives common to the firm's actors. In particular various closely-related innovations are found: they receive consensus and more widespread applications, they are often accepted and supported by entrepreneurial and managerial groups, and they are considered consistent with the firm's needs and its organisational and cultural changes.

2

The research presented in this volume aims to: retrace the long development of participation, illustrating and assessing the main instances suggested or implemented; address the notion of participation with no ideological bias, over-idealised intentions or excessive expectations, focusing instead on relevant problems with a realistic and pragmatic outlook; outline which participatory forms appear adequate to our times and how they should be implemented.

Our approach preserves the central point in the participatory tradition, that is the notion of participation as an arrangement in favour of workers. This arrangement, however, is free of the (explicit and implicit) feelings and goals of opposition between the parties concerned: the opposition could be justified by structural and social conditions in the past, but now it does not seem justifiable. Today even more than in the past, participation appears sustainable and applicable only if its processes and outcomes are compatible with the firm's functioning and the constraints of economic enterprise.

Our approach assumes a total acceptance of the market economy and of rules favouring conditions of competitiveness and efficiency within the capitalist system; though in the beginning this system was spontaneously unfair, it eventually allowed a considerable rate of development and widespread wealth, in a greater and more civilised way than any alternative system; it has undergone and incorporated far-reaching changes, especially around the middle of our century as a result of political-institutional action and political and social movements – changes aimed at reducing social costs, structural imbalance and instances of inequality; to this day the system shows a need for actions that will bring about fairer social and economic relations and, at the same time, do not conflict with actual conditions of efficiency and competitiveness.

Though limited, participation offers an opportunity in this direction.

Our remarks are not entirely proved nor highly original but in this context serve to explain our *concept* of participation. This is introduced by five propositions that run through the research, whose implications will be addressed in the closing pages (Chapter 8). The propositions are as follows:

i   participation appears in conjunction with goals and institutes possessing distinct qualities and, despite later adjustments and considerable recent innovations, it prolongs a long tradition of labour protection and employment regulation;

ii participation does not constitute a strictly necessary and exhaustive arrangement for the use of subordinate employment within industrial relations systems. When the conditions for its implementation are met, participation can operate, providing that the requirement of converging intentions and mutual benefits for all parties concerned is satisfied: it cannot simply be an "acquisition" of workers or a response to the mere needs of the firm;

iii even if participation rests on the parties' belief that they are contributing to attain objectives that outlay their immediate interests, it acquires greater stability and continuity through mutual obligations and exchange devices that offer workers only material benefits;

iv in the presence of exchange devices, participation displays its consistency if the negotial method is employed, which tends to view workers in their (single or multiple) collective dimension and, accordingly, through their representative structures whose functions – even when they differ from trade-union tradition – are recognised and actually performed;

v   participation should be characterised by the attainment of a fair degree of equity – i.e. the distribution of recognition to individuals and groups in proportion to their contribution – by the actors' refusal to maximise their own benefits, by a moderate use of their institutional, organisational and market power, and thus by the existence of social and cultural preconditions for reaching common goals of productive efficiency.

Our concept is very different from the other two opposing interpretations often considered in this research.

The first of these – a well-rooted and recurring trait in the long road to participation, resulting in highly diversified proposals and experiences – seems prone to disregard or underestimate the need for employers' consensus and benefits, as well as the firm's reasons for efficiency and its difficulty to reconcile the use of entrepreneurial prerogatives and participation in decision-making processes (Chapters 1, 2 and 7). This interpretation used to deliberately promote goals and institutes antagonistic to the capitalist order;

although in more recent times this approach has been abandoned, it still seems to uphold forms of participation hardly in keeping with the firm's functions or the competitiveness of the economic system.

The second interpretation – easily found in management literature – adopts the latest prominent changes in participation and favours chiefly the firm's needs, offering a participatory "climate" that may favour the assessment of workers' qualities and contributions but restricts exchange implications and disregards the function of their representatives (Chapter 6). This interpretation is prone to reach beyond the protection and regulation of employment and envisages a firm where relations among actors take place without influence from the institutional setting and social trends.

3

The *object* of our research concerns two major dimensions, which in many ways are inseparable.

One embodies the "progress" of participation and regards its relations with other types of regulation of subordinate employment, past and present participatory forms and models, its overall development and that of single forms (Chapters 1-6).

The other embodies the "problematic" nature of participation and translates into various questions stemming from the recognition of two related key issues: the relationship of participation with political democracy and with the firm's functioning (Chapters 7 and 8).

4

Relations between participation and *other means of regulation* of employment involve economic democracy and collective bargaining: two distinct means that someone regards as alternative.

"Economic democracy" has usually been embodied in proposals and objectives that to some extent allow for change in capitalist settings – in macroeconomic terms and in the firm – under political conditions that positively influence employment relationships or with changes in such relationships that affect the political system itself. This picture of economic democracy tends to overlap with the first of the mentioned interpretations.

The success of the term "economic democracy" is emblematic of the fact that participation may be acted out in two areas: political rationale and the economic reality. Indeed the term has often been used to define an economic and social system ideally more equitable and provided with suitable institutional adjustments.

This duplicity seems to stem from many real situations, mostly of the past. We believe, however, that in the context of representative democracy the main domain of economic democracy lies within economic policy. Participatory forms and institutes – referred to as "participatory economic democracy" – can complete this domain as they are typified by being: normally initiated outside the political-institutional sphere, though often favoured and supported by it; due to the initiative of social groups and their representatives rather than the public actor; implementable at different levels, but mostly at the level of productive venues.

According to this approach, most participatory proposals and experiences fall within the confines of economic democracy: in certain cases in the area of economic policy itself, especially through concertation (Chapter 3); far more often by means of participatory economic democracy, as experienced in "industrial democracy" (Chapter 4).

Participation is an event that generally tends to enhance the value of subordinate employment and those who perform it. This has no doubt been the prevailing purpose not only of legal provisions but also of collective bargaining – two constant or cyclical ways of correcting criteria the governing the employment of labour.

Collective bargaining may be viewed as a body of negotial practices for the economic and formal protection of workers, which can improve their conditions periodically without challenging the position of whoever uses or offers subordinate labour.

Collective bargaining naturally differs from participation, chiefly because – using pluralistic schemata – it does not explicitly tend to diminish the sharp distinction of interests and objectives between the sides, unlike participation. In effect, if recent events are considered, it is notable that: the outcome of bargaining is collaborative in nature; contractual and participatory processes often integrate each other and, at any rate, are certainly not incompatible; the negotial-contractual method is often applied even in recent participatory forms accepted and supported by entrepreneurial and managerial groups.

Nevertheless, it must be observed that such forms are applied also to trade-union negotiation and mediation; accordingly, the most ambitious and idealised proposals of economic democracy have always assumed that the "natural" limits of bargaining institutes and practices would be overcome.

5

Participation appears from the start in a wide array of events: plans, proposals, major experiences, short-lived attempts, formalised institutes and customs – even if only a single period and country is taken into account.

This research classifies such events by placing participatory forms into *models* that illustrate the intentions and aims of those concerned, reveal their rationale and objectives, and highlight essential differences and potential agreement. Three models were found:

a *antagonistic* participation or participation with antagonistic components, which tends to *modify* the actual asymmetry in subordinate employment and often also the workers' social standing;

b *collaborative* participation, which allows for improvement in workers' socioeconomic position and a *correction* of the asymmetry, without altering the institutional arrangements of capitalism or the firm's corporate name;

c *integrative* participation, which aims to *involve* employees (not necessarily through they representatives) in the firm's functioning and/or *commit* them to its activity and prospects.

Within this framework we will describe and evaluate the *evidence* of participation; this includes, for instance, "workers' control" and the cooperative firm (model a), concertation and codetermination (model b), profit sharing and employee share ownership (model c).

The main differences between such models may be illustrated as follows: the antagonistic model conceives participation as a step for overcoming the traditional employment relationship in the capitalist firm; the collaborative model gives participation duties and institutes that envisage agreement between better conditions for workers and the needs of the firm or the economic system; the integrative model, which largely embodies recent forms of participation, relying on interests shared by the firm's actors or on the search for common objectives.

These models are defined with reference to their early features, when differences are greater. Their forms, however, have undergone considerable change in time; so that they often differ from their original appearance, with varying degrees of adjustment and combinations of forms belonging to different models.

If we shift our attention from these alterations to the overall evolutionary progress of participation, the following observations are warranted: antagonistic forms are essentially obsolete, in theory and practice; while collaborative participation is endorsed. After the substantial results of post-war years, the latter has retained its validity thanks to the spread of collaborative intentions and needs, although these do not appear only within the collaborative model; evidence of integrative participation lacks uniformity and, compared with its original conditions, is often implemented by the negotial method and trade-union mediation.

If interpreted, this progress points to several significant generalisations: the "weight" of changes expected in the productive and social setting is high during the first phase, in conjunction with harder working conditions for subordinate labour, but then it gradually decreases; the most solid and lasting (non-antagonistic) participatory events are found in settings where organised labour has both power and recognition, especially in contexts where trade-union action is an essential and consistent component alongside reformist actors and programmes in the political-institutional sphere; today as in the past, such experiences are complementary to consolidated and coordinated industrial relations systems; more recent participatory forms (integrative model) appear as decisions in favour of workers' expectations and dignity and at the same time as an opportunity due to economic and market conditions, to the firm's functional requirements and to the new composition of staff.

6

Since these different participatory perspectives aim to alter or correct the typical employment relationship in its relation to the structural and institutional features of capitalism, they have often encountered practical difficulties and always caused theoretical problems.

In the course of our research, we focused on both of these *issues*, with reference to single participatory proposals or events. As these are here considered in general terms, it may be claimed that they hinge on the two basic and interrelated issues mentioned above, namely the relationship between participation on one side and political democracy and its relations with the firm's functioning on the other.

The first issue is important because of the deep ties often assumed between participation and political democracy, especially as a legitimation of the motives and aims of participation through the political democracy method applied to relations between the firm's actors.

The second issue is unavoidable if participation is conceived as a range of opportunities to favour workers in accordance with the firm's objectives, functional needs and obligations.

This consideration advises the need to address three *questions*:

(i) is the political democracy method viable, as applied to the concept and implementation of participation?

(ii) if the political and social basis of participation is admitted, can an economic basis be found as well?

(iii) admitting that a "connection" between the two bases is achievable, what participatory forms and processes are really adequate at present?

7

The first question may appear less critical than the others. But this is not the case. The connection between participation and political democracy was clearly present in subordinate employment in the beginning and has extended to recent times: it has often remained an unclear element, similar to a flaw in approach hindering the success of participation. The title of this book (*Impossible democracy?*) embodies, in the author's intention, this consideration.

The above connection rests on the belief that the function of participation should be to assist the shift from formal democracy to substantial democracy, spreading democracy throughout production relations: indeed it is unacceptable that democracy should be absent from them as its absence can undermine the very existence and development of political democracy.

Our *thesis* is that this connection lacks a foundation. Many forms of participation contain several elements of democracy, as they are totally involved in the growth of "democratisation" processes (Chapter 7), yet the political democracy method is not applicable to them.

Limiting our references to "classical" theory, it may be seen that participation does not allow the application of democracy's essential components, namely: a condition of equality in the political rights of citizens, the selection by citizens of representatives legitimised to take decisions, in accordance with the will of the majority.

Subjects active in the firm do not dispose – formally or factually – of the same rights, they are not in a condition of equal rights. Workers are employees insofar as someone is allowed to use their services in exchange for remuneration or other assets. Many significant exceptions have been granted to this type of relationship, but they are all partial and do not cancel its nature.

Workers are not entitled to appoint those charged with decision-making. Unlike the political arena, the firm does not provide for the possibility that all those involved should contribute to its decision-making will. Workers have a legitimately established counterpart, which they cannot replace but only influence in its use of authority.

Decisions within the firm cannot be taken according to the majority principle. This states that, once the rules of the game have been fixed, the outcome of the competition normally entails the victory of one side and the defeat of the other. In the context of the firm – even admitting the presence of a similar form of competition – one of the sides cannot lose, without forfeiting its ownership rights and managerial duties.

If the connection mentioned above has no foundation, then what can be the political and social basis of participation?

This may be found in its capacity to act at different depths in the sphere of equality of relations between the firm's actors. This basis does not concern method; it concerns, instead, the motives and aims of participation,

8

which may differ greatly from political democracy as to method, but has strong tries and significant similarities to its values and components in the area of substantial democracy conceived as the reduction of social and economic inequality.

In time workers have secured both rights and recognition, but their condition in the firm is not equivalent to their citizenship in the political and institutional arena. This limit should not be seen as evidence of incomplete democracy, as it is due to the special nature of economic action, to the firm's organisational needs, and to the legitimate rights of other actors. Nevertheless, workers' interests and demands have a fair chance to succeed in reducing economic and social inequality, even if activated by methods other than political democracy.

The method and rules of participation are in fact heterogeneous because of its objectives and context. With forms that satisfy the requirement of convergence among actors involved, the action of participatory institutes and processes is ensured by the use of the negotial method; this is observed, for instance, in experiences of industrial democracy or often also in economic participation.

The negotial method has long been tested in industrial relations systems, above all with collective bargaining. At the same time, it has changed and become richer, passing from collective bargaining to participation; the use of the resource "conflict" is now less common; there has been a rise in the number of institutes (information and consultation, joint committees, reference to objective indices, etc.) which make negotiations more predictable and procedural; and notably the distinction of interests and objectives between the two sides has become weaker.

Though by far preferable, the negotial method is not the only one available. Other methods are applied to participation, in which the negotial rationale is surely not prominent. We have in mind the tradition of the cooperative firm, the only one that permits to choose the political democracy method (because its members are both workers and owners) and current forms of integration of workers without the presence of their representatives.

8

The second question concerns the possibility of finding an economic basis of participation, parallel and complementary to its political and social basis. The latter preserves a certain validity, even if its motives appear today less deep than in the past. Recent instances of participation rely on the opportunity to improve employees' conditions qualitatively, and to add new rewards (tangible and non-tangible) which tend to reduce exclusive traits in the subordinate employment relationship.

The validity of the political-social basis goes hand in hand, however, with its insufficiency. Under the current economic and institutional arrangements, in particular, this opportunity offers great potential if participation does not conflict with the firm's good running or rather if it displays compatible forms and means.

This statement calls for the need to define the economic basis of participation. We have tried to satisfy this requirement by referring to a successful line in theories of the firm and to authors who anticipate or develop the neo-institutionalist paradigm, which contains several peculiarities compared with the neo-classical paradigm. What we did was to compare some of the main findings of these theories in order to find out if they contained any explicit or implicit confirmation of participation.

For institutionalist as well as neo-classical economists, efficiency is the undisputed yardstick for measuring a firm's good functioning.

For neo-classicists the firm operates under conditions of perfect competition; it functions as a technical link between needs and resources, leaving its actors hardly any space for discretionary power in decisions; it is like a predetermined and necessarily efficient unit where actors pursue the maximisation of their advantage and are able to choose in terms of total rationality.

Institutionalists, instead, view the firm as a complex and imperfect "transformer". The role of competition is considered equally crucial, but should be viewed taking into account the institutional setting and the adjustment of economic operators to it. Thus a crucial issue is that of decision in the firm's governing structures, of what activities should be organised within it, and of why and how they are to be organised. This concerns the degree of efficiency attainable through possible *organisational forms,* since alternative organisational arrangements directly affect the firm's objectives and may influence its results no less than other important factors (e.g. technological factors).

The connection between the degree of efficiency and the response of the organisation is supported by the main analytic units provided by the above theories, such as: the deep uncertainty that typifies economic activity; the limited rationality available to subjects for decision making; transaction costs, which outline a type of coordination of economic activities preferable to the market's and assume their "internalisation" within firms with an organisational structure and hierarchy; and the incompleteness of the contracts on which the firm's actors build their relationships, which are such because they cannot be described *ex ante* in unequivocal and verifiable terms, as happens notably in the case of employment contracts (Chapter 8).

Using these analytic units, which enable us to look inside the firm, we are able to observe the significance of its actors' behaviour, especially of those who hold authority and take decisions.

These enjoy a considerable *margin of discretionary power,* related to the level of efficiency and the objectives established, which are not always focused merely on the maximisation of profit. Such actors operate in conditions that allow a choice in decisions on the nature of organisation, on hierarchical structures and relations, and on processes concerning the making and implementation of decisions.

The coordination of economic activities within the firm confirms that marked differences may occur in its functioning according to the character and quality of its organisation, which is typified primarily by the handling of transitions involving its actors as a whole. This type of coordination is definitely relevant to *employment contracts*. Apart from other considerations, these cannot be associated with market-led coordination, because after an initial relation between two market agents they turn into authority-based relations between the employer and his employees.

The employment contract contains special features different to other types of contract, especially a high degree of incompleteness: certain points are addressed in the contract's clauses, while others are a prerogative of the hierarchy and the employer, others again are left to the worker to decide during the performance of his tasks.

The structure that manages manpower has to act with great care, especially in the case of high professional skills and limited replaceability. It will have to introduce frequent adjustments to employment contracts; to allow for procedural safeguards offering a fair balance between services and rewards; and to favour continuity in the employment relationship (an additional source of value), considering that the contribution of labour is often far subtler than the mere account of work done.

The employee is granted the recognition of an active role in the firm's functioning, of which he is responsible: the degree of action, if not of freedom, employed in his service and the right to participate in the distribution of the firm's results.

With this recognition, authority-based relations – though fully legitimised – can be integrated by negotiation between the parties concerned and eventually take into account the role of representatives and of workers' organisations. These voice employees' needs and preferences and may become an essential component in the firm's governing structure. They restrain "opportunistic bargaining" (typical of small groups), rationalise wage systems according to the objective nature of services, and encourage commitment to cooperation.

This overview of some of the main propositions in recent theories of the firm seems to provide sufficient grounds for the economic basis of participation. Such a basis rests of course on assumptions and empirical evidence related to the firm's functioning and it also confirms the legitimation of essential components of the political-social basis.

In this light, one of the many concerns associated with the implementation of the efficiency criterion is the search for conditions and institutes that foster effort and commitment within the firm's community. They point to the need to realise this aim by furthering conditions of balance in relations between resources and incentives offered by the organisation on one side, and the participants' contribution to its demands on the other side; such conditions reach beyond the original terms of the contract and are guaranteed by negotiation between the firm's actors, whether individuals or their representatives.

9

The third question regards participatory forms and processes which at present can be considered actually viable. Such *forms* and their implementational *processes* depend on agreement between the above-mentioned bases, whose convergence may be imagined as an area where the qualities of participation (as a conveyor of equity) meet the firm's need for coordination (in particular the need to improve individual commitment). This approach eventually establishes equal (ideal and practical) dignity between the element of participation that meets workers' interests and expectations, and the element that favours the firm and its need to actively involve workers.

In our view the following *forms* deserve attention, ranging from the latest experiences to significant past experiences:

a   cultural and organisational participation (workers' involvement in the firm's of objectives, mission and constant need for adjustment, applied primarily by total quality schemes and means);

b   economic participation in the firm's results (embodied in profit sharing institutes and practices);

c   participation concerning employees' access to share ownership of the firm's capital;

d   collaborative participation, which dates from the industrial democracy tradition and through codetermination is applied to decisions taken by the firm and workers' representatives in its institutional bodies.

Alongside these forms, adequate attention should be given to an issue (normally ignored in participatory proposals) that involves a major sensitive point affecting workers' conditions, namely: the chances of recognising their "voice" or rights within the "firm market" (lifetime and allocation of firms, ownership allocation and control).

This issue is surely among the most difficult as regards the search for arrangements and adjustments applicable jointly in the workers' interest and yet adequate to the firm's economic activity. In our view, this is the least legitimised area of labour employment in the capitalistic firm at present, as it leaves workers unprotected (despite the presence of welfare provisions) in events that deeply alter their lives and often also their occupational and professional prospects.

The forms listed include, in different degrees, workers' rights, interests, objectives and expectations which influence the firm's functioning. Thus reference to its governing structure is necessary if we are to define the venues and processes required by participation.

The *venues* are strategic control (the right to make "political" decisions in the firm) and hierarchical control (managing the organisation and exerting authority).

The *processes* translate into decisions concerning both venues. In participation the focus is on processes originating from strategic control, but the most common and varied implications regard processes assigned to hierarchical control, which can be of two types: organisational decision-making processes (involving the achievement of the firm's objectives and the use of its resources – first of all human resources – in view of efficiency) and distributive decision-making processes (which make available to the firm's actors assets not included in the contract which may extend to non-immediate material benefits) (Chapter 8).

A comparison of current participatory perspectives with such venues and processes enables us to put forward three *theses* developing the concept of participation illustrated earlier.

1 Participation involves hierarchical control but also strategic control

The first instance is more acceptable and simpler because hierarchical control concerns the use and enhancement of subordinate employment.

Though far more difficult and complex, the second instance is relevant because – as we observed about the "firm market" and its crises or reorganisations – strategic decisions often affect workers' conditions and prospects too dramatically to be considered not amenable to correction, mediation or negotiation. This sphere of participation should be assessed without undermining the legitimate responsibility of those exerting strategic control based on ownership rights, over the reduction of risk in capital inflow and expenditure in view of arrangements capable of consolidating the firm. Here lie the difficulties and problems.

On the other hand, decisions by those holding such control are not always due to objective factors and conditions; they may be due, instead, to the behaviour of employers and managers who do not "love" their firms but buy them and sell them as real estate, and do not aim at profitability or consolidation on the market.

As the current debate tends to confirm that the firm is chiefly but not merely an economic unit, this fact should be carefully considered when decisions and alterations are introduced that concern the prospects of its actors, without necessarily forfeiting efficiency and competitiveness.

2 Participation does not apply directly to organisational decision-making processes

Functional needs and the use of authority roles require that the holders of hierarchical control should be free to make organisational decisions and take on the responsibilities attached; decisions that are respected by the other actors and, when needed, can be partly shared by them if they are the result of consensual agreement or considered useful to improve the firm's functioning. This means that the holders of hierarchical control, within the confines of each institutional context and in accordance with the rules fixed and accepted by such actors, may achieve an adequate degree of efficiency if they enjoy a high degree of freedom in the performance of their managerial duties, in the use of authority (though by diverse ways and means) and in the employment of the qualities and skills available in the firm's community.

This freedom has proven necessary also in the cooperative firm, which is able to compete with other firms especially if it can rely on the same managerial authority.

Using the same criterion we believe that within the terms of codetermination, industrial democracy could now be revalued, provided it does not allow for direct intervention by workers' representatives in such decision-making processes but accepts their influence over strategic decisions in the firm's institutional bodies.

3 Participation applies primarily and directly to distributive decision-making processes

Constraints on participation in the case of organisational decision-making processes are offset by the inherent opportunities of distributive processes. These allow compatibility between the firm's needs and benefits available to its staff: economic benefits and professional or citizenship benefits, whether real or potential.

Distributive processes are subjected to decisions shared by the holders of hierarchical control and employees, who are entitled to intervene in such processes; in this sphere the holders of hierarchical control greatly constrain their freedom in organisational decision-making.

The application of participation to distributive rather than organisational processes should not be viewed in exclusive terms: its initiation and outcome practically produce "retroactive" effects on organisational decision-making processes and even on strategic control, whose strength varies in different organisational forms.

In the distributive sphere are entirely included profit sharing and participation by means of access to capital shares; however, the latter may extend to strategic control if the size of stakes and the will to exert control allow it.

Cultural and organisational participation can be placed in the same sphere, especially when non-tangible assets are available, even though this is often introduced as a perspective that should include decision-making processes and organisational structures.

In these pages only brief mention is made of the implications of these theses for the features of each participatory form. The point will be taken up again in further detail at the end of the last chapter.

10

In this research, as in others before it, great attention is devoted to an important and interesting modern phenomenon whereby innovative and constructive experiences are possible in labour relations and employment, with a positive consequence for business.

Having introduced the main features of the progress and problems of participation, it seems fitting to add a few observations on the order and position of its *overall extension*.

Without making any prediction on the prospects of each form, it may be said that participation is not destined to occur in a generalised way; it does not seem likely that it will try to become a standard and constant means of regulation in relations between the firm and its employees.

Its applications – at least in the medium term – will not be equal to those due so far to collective bargaining, and not only because the two may coexist. On the other hand, in times of decline or loss of efficacy, collective bargaining will only partly be replaced by participatory events.

Because of its factual and potential qualities, participation should not spread in a generalised manner, as it seems more apt to be promoted and implemented in certain economic and productive settings associated with special conditions in single firms. The political and institutional context may surely favour certain participatory forms but its influence is weaker than in the past. Consolidated instances of participation, especially those involving firms of great productive and symbolic importance, may generate imitational processes but it is hard to say where and when they will occur.

In spite of its long history and the motives that currently legitimate it, participation will not become a very widespread means or regulation because, as we mentioned earlier, it is not a strictly necessary or exhaustive arrangement.

This is true for the productive world, which can rely on other criteria for employing labour, ranging from intensely regulated negotiation to highly restricted negotiation. Many firms have organisational arrangements and a working population that make participatory institutes and practices hardly attractive or practicable. Even firms that consider participation an advantage are not always able to measure its positive effects; thus it is rightly claimed that participation should be judged on the merits of its indirect contribution, which as such is deeper and subtler than results observed in terms of mere "accountancy".

Participation offers an arrangement which is functional to the competitive requirements of the economic system, provided it respects the constraint of compatibility with the firm's efficiency objectives and is not too expensive. Other useful features include the containment of conflict and industrial relations marked by a fair degree of certainty and predictability. However, it appears inadequate to these needs, since it does not allow for generalised and binding applications as in collaborative regulation by concertation.

By definition participation tends to favour employees. Normally – that is disregarding the variety or positions and duties – it is judged by employees according to the benefits offered by or attributed to its action rather than its formal and procedural traits, as in the striking instance of German codetermination (Chapter 4). Its application is not necessarily accepted as an alternative to legal provisions, contractual protection and representative structures, because – apart from other considerations – the present forms of participation have a limited and incomplete range as they envisage no protection in many areas of employment.

In a wider outlook, participation reveals a crucial limitation: it embodies little solidarity, involves only interested workers, is not easily extendable to others, and hardly ever takes into consideration the fate of those without a job or in the process of losing it. Though unwanted and worsened by many external factors (starting from the decentralisation of industrial relations), this obstacle is clearly insurmountable.

These remarks do not wish to lessen the prospects of participation or restrict them to a narrow area; indeed it will preserve its rich variety of themes and meanings, but only within certain limits, with no prospect of permeating the whole sphere of labour relationships and conditions.

1 The nature and domain of participation

1 What is meant by participation?

As we mentioned earlier, participation consists of opportunities and experiences aimed at altering or improving workers' relations and working conditions and very often also their socioeconomic standing in society. Reference is made to three major domains: subjects, context and venues.

The subjects, now as in the past, are employees, that is the community of manual workers and office workers.

Context is provided by industrialised capitalist countries with political systems of representative democracy because of the close ties often invoked between political democracy and participatory processes, and consequently to the cultural and political conditions provided by these countries to the proposals and experiences of participation. However, participatory forms have also developed in countries with no representative democracy, as in the case of Yugoslav self management.[1]

Venues are a key feature for defining participation.[2] In its long history, the prevailing level has been the firm itself, but other wider venues occur, especially at the national level,which involve almost invariably direct or indirect implications for relations between the firm's actors.

At the national level, the directions and hopes of participation may often acquire a marked political significance: in the past this involved changes in actual social relations and institutions suited to this aim; during the last few decades its purpose has been more simply to favour specific interests of workers through political and institutional processes.

At the level of the firm, the political element has gradually waned, as participation tends to consists primarily of a number of remedial measures making the functioning of production units more equitable and/or efficient.

These brief notes are enough to show that participation can act in two spheres: political rationale and economic conditions. The former concerns mostly benefits available through the consolidation and implementation of democratic systems; the latter challenges the asymmetry inherent in the subordinate employment relationship.

Participatory perspectives and proposals, or rather a part of them, focus on connections between the political and the economic system,[3] in order to expose the influence of the economic system on the functioning of political democracy and often to alter or improve employees' working conditions, either because they are unsatisfactory or because they form the structural basis of social and political settings where inequality is widespread.

In its first phase – if a common feature exists – participation concerns the opportunity of changing actual social relations, starting from the transformation or gradual improvement of the employment relationship, sometimes in view of improving the basic working of formally democratic systems, and often aiming to apply the method and means of democracy to productive relations.

In later phases and especially during the last few decades, the link has weakened between the working of democratic systems and the improvement of employees' conditions and status; this depends chiefly on the fact that democratic systems have carried out a significant redistribution of resources and in the meantime workers' collective initiatives have gained ground thanks to trade union action. This link is no longer present in recent participatory initiatives sponsored by entrepreneurs and managers.

2 Participation and economic democracy

The impact of participation in the sphere of political rationale and economic conditions is clearly witnessed by the terms "economic democracy" and "industrial democracy", which subsume most participatory proposals and events. The term economic democracy refers – often indistinctly – to a type of economic system capable of achieving a fair or fairer distribution of work, income and wealth.[4]

Different notions of economic democracy may be envisaged, focusing on the distinction between economic democracy mediated by the market, by economic policy, or by participatory institutes.[5]

The first notion – typical of the liberal tradition – is interpreted through market behaviour and rests on the assumption that citizens are free to choose as to occupation, consumption, use of savings, investment, and entrepreneurial enterprises; thus individual gains and collective benefits are reconciled.

The actual working of the market places strong and well-known constraints on economic democracy: apart from recurring flaws in performance, compared with conditions of optimum competition, authors have always highlighted and discussed the inequality (not only in economic terms) among actors and social groups.

The second notion, which is realised through economic policy, contemplates both in theory and in practice the intervention of public actors (representing the democratic system) in economic and social processes. Economic policy serves to steer, correct and integrate market behaviour and acts as a supplier of public commodities, distributes tangible and non-tangible resources, stabilises the market and fosters economic development.[6]

Public intervention in such processes is constant and diversified but it may also vary in extension, effectiveness and efficiency – especially as concerns redistributive intentions and results – owing to a number of factors, such a the influence exerted over democratic institutions by holders of economic power.

The third notion – which is realised through participatory forms and institutes – embodies intentions and hopes that aim to raise the degree of correction to market behaviour and widen the domain of economic democracy due to economic policy. It is typically: initiated usually outside the political-institutional sphere, though at times favoured and supported by it; due to the initiative of social groups and their organisations rather than the public actor (seldom to a combination of the two); placed at different levels but mostly just under the level of production units.

The implementation of these three notions is complementary in the experience of capitalist countries.

As for the first notion, it must be admitted that market behaviour fosters and ensures the basic structural and procedural conditions of economic democracy and at the same time places factual constraints on it that are hardly avoidable. The political-social (and economic) need to control and correct this behaviour cannot replace the "laws" of market economy without damaging its degree of efficiency and development.

As for the second notion, it is notable that the chief domain of economic democracy is economic or economic-social policy. This ensures full legitimation to intervention in economic processes – whether in general terms (mostly through the fiscal burden) or in more specific terms – in view of greater equity and for the common good; when this is not the case, the institutional conditions for a change in direction are provided.

The nature of the third notion is thus harder to define and has in fact been the object of different interpretations. As for its nature, two facts are worth noting: its domain is not as necessary as that of the first two notions. The contexts discussed here can exist, function or achieve a marked degree of equity even without implementing this part of economic democracy, which displays a great number of forms – some linked to specific ideological and political conditions and thus not destined to last in time – while economic policy (though varied in direction and outcome) appears to ensure continuity in the performance of the tasks listed above.

There are two main interpretations to mention: one is more idealised while the other is more pragmatic.

The former – often invoked in cultural and political circles seeking to alter the capitalist setting – views this part of economic democracy in a perspective that extends beyond the firm's confines (towards the macroeconomic level),[7] or it envisages the need for its experience in the firm to influence the appearance of the political system.[8]

The latter interpretation – shared by actors and groups seeking to introduce negotial and collaborative corrections to these settings – recognises that this part of economic democracy can be simply implemented at the level of the firm, as in fact has often happened, and yet it also provides for participatory forms at the national level (such as agreement by concertation).

The first interpretation tends to stress only employees' expectations and interests, disregarding or underestimating the importance of their counterpart's attitude and compatibility with the market's economic behaviour; therefore it is selective in its actual or potential proposals and experiences.

The second interpretation seeks to correct the employment contract typical of the capitalist firm – which affirms that workers' are subjected to the employer's authority, payment of fixed wages is due, and cancellation is possible at short notice[9] – taking into account that such corrections may appear acceptable to both sides and take place through exchange processes; in this view there are no inflexible, predetermined attitudes to the extension of participation or to the assessment of its forms.

It should also be noted that the operational instances stemming from the first interpretation are very limited and at present almost nil, while the second interpretation has been widely tested. It also appears more suited to follow recent trends in the capitalist economy and is free of obsolete ideological traits.

Using a literary metaphor, the more idealised interpretation may be compared to the "poetic" element and the more pragmatic interpretation to the "prosaic" element in participatory economic democracy.

The author, as readers may have noticed, has opted for the "prosaic" interpretation.

The use of the term "participatory economic democracy" enables us to explain a couple of points.

The first of these, which is merely procedural, is the decision to use the above term or "economic democracy" from now on to mean the part of economic democracy associated with the third of the notions listed above.

The other point is more problematic as it concerns the relationship between this part of economic democracy and participation which – as we claimed at the beginning of this paragraph – includes a host of participatory proposals and instances.

As for the lexical associations of these terms, "participation" refers to the range of opportunities and forms that allow changes and improvements in employees' conditions to take place, while "economic democracy" refers to the motives and objectives pursued through specific forms.

As an example let us take the cooperative: this is one of the many possible forms of participation whose reason and purpose is to replace one of the inherent aspects of labour in the capitalist firm (namely its separation of those contributing labour from those contributing capital).

As for domain, the question is whether participation and economic democracy share the same domain; in other terms, whether they refer to the same type of event.

As regards our interpretation of economic democracy, the answer is essentially affirmative. Economic democracy and participation, though distinct in the features mentioned above, refer mainly to the same event.

This interpretation allows a wide extension of economic democracy and, as we shall see below, it also includes all the forms of industrial democracy.

Indeed, most of the proposals and instances of economic democracy – especially those implemented or implementable – are found at the level of the firm or depart from the firm, which is the most natural and direct level of workers' participation.

This answer poses the problem of whether recent participatory forms and proposals – those largely due to the initiative of employers and managers – should be included in the sphere of economic democracy.

At this stage it may suffice to observe that even if they are not inspired by the explicit intention to offset the asymmetry inherent in the employment contract, these forms tend to improve both relations inside the firm and workers' conditions, and they have often initiated in fact during negotial confrontation with workers' representatives.

Our perspective favours an extensive application of economic democracy, with reference to its domain. The presence of different and heterogenous participatory forms does not mean they can be considered equivalent. The pragmatic approach does not represent a neutral position, which in fact would hardly be sustainable in this area.

In fact our research purposes to be at the same time expository and evaluative. Having defined the relationship between participation and participatory economic democracy, we shall examine the features and evolution of the latter.

Intervention in and correction of market processes arising from economic policy and participatory forms are normally classified as political allocation of resources.

Market processes are the result of spontaneous relations among actors with equal civil rights – the kind of equality discussed by Tocqueville [10] – in accordance with existing social conditions; such relations are normally of little amplitude, fragmented and governed by the rules of contractual practices.

21

Political allocation as defined by Easton[11] is typified by the imperative destination of resources, its amplitude is greater, it is related directly or indirectly to the whole of society[12] and it includes different classes of resources although economic resources are the most prominent.

Political allocation of resources is carried out chiefly and by definition by the public actor through economic and social policy.

Economic democracy implemented by participatory forms and institutes – the object of this research – differs from economic policy insofar as: it is promoted by social groups and their organisations, even if the political-institutional sphere may be involved; it normally acts on processes of resource distribution without compulsory measures but by means of exchange between social actors or by the dominant initiative of a single social actor, and is therefore hardly extendible to the whole of society.

Compared with the political allocation of resources, the nature and peculiarity of participatory economic democracy places it in a progressive scale of rights at stake in capitalist societies with representative democracy; a similar progression is found in the civil, political and social rights considered by T.H. Marshall,[13] which may be integrated by rights arising from the economic democracy of participatory forms.[14]

The constant demand for this part of economic democracy is due to the fact that political scenarios do not necessarily foster greater welfare and equity. In its progress, representative democracy has ultimately moved in this direction, but with different results, regressive phases, and constraints either structural or due to the expectations and will of the majority of voters. Although economic and social policy remain the key area of economic democracy, this may completed by the part of economic democracy sponsored by social actors. And indeed while economic policy may move in the direction of increasing the implementation of rights, the part of economic democracy due to participatory forms is warranted only if it broadens and strengthens such rights.

The perspective of participatory economic democracy, associated with the above duties, raises *two fundamental issues*: its relation to political democracy, and its relation to the working of the economy and primarily of the firm; these issues underlie or are present in many points of our account and will be addressed directly in the closing chapters.

They have become more visible as a result of the development of democratic capitalistic systems and more urgent because of recent events affecting them.

Greater attention has been devoted to the second issue by observers (including the author) who view improvements in social and working conditions in a "detached" and realistic manner.

But it is known that many supporters of economic democracy have not shared or accepted this approach, especially in the past.

Economic democracy and the search for justice and equity in the economic-social sphere were often perceived in European countries – referred to in these pages – as part of the plans and programmes of Marxist-inspired culture, whose objectives were antagonistic to productive relations.

With time another approach has arisen, especially in the social-democratic beliefs and organisations of central and northern Europe. Within the institutional setting of representative democracy this approach advocated a number of changes – sometimes major ones – to the capitalist economy, alongside its confidence in the potential achievements of pluralistic interaction between organised collective interests.

The major difference between these approaches – apart from the one mentioned – is that the former developed mostly at the level of ideology and militant pedagogy, while the latter has produced a wealth of actual experiences, either by its advocates involved in government duties or through the action of labour organisations.

Among the ideas and experiences of the second approach should be included those sponsored by Christian-oriented political and trade union movements, which differed at first from social-democratic movements but gradually became more similar in later decades.

Economic developments in capitalist countries, during the 1970s and later, in conjunction with other political and sociocultural factors, have deeply affected the first as well as the second approach. We have in mind the declining will and hope of changing the key features of capitalist settings; the utter failure – not only in economic events – of the alternative model provided by the countries of "realised socialism"; the long prevalence of redistributive policies which achieved considerable results and yet produced an excess in demand that posed great problems to economic policy;[15] and at present the prospect of a single European market, which is bound to increase the constraints on domestic economic policies with results that have so far been problematic for social policies.[16]

These developments combined with political and sociocultural factors have strongly marked the antagonistic approach, making it totally obsolete and limited to to the debate within limited or marginal political groups.

The same events and the preservation of previous achievements have caused difficulties in terms of programmes and consensus to the social democratic approach and consequently the reappearance of genuine reformist objectives, with greater obstacles to redistributive policies.

A significant example of this is the situation of Scandinavian countries in recent years.[17]

Without attempting to trace the progress of intentions and experiences in the field of participatory economic democracy, it may be useful to consider three significant phases in its development, which in certain settings tend to overlap.

The first phase – associated with the development and crisis of capitalism up to the Second World War – witnessed a strengthening of the antagonistic approach and of the more radical varieties of the social democratic approach. The prevailing concern was to alter workers' conditions by introducing deep changes to the capitalist productive structure, applying solutions and means that involved the entire economic system and, in certain instances, even the institutional traits of society.

This objective was a priority in the agenda of left-wing movements throughout North Mediterranean countries but was also found, for example, in German revisionism until the 1950s.[18]

The second phase coincides with the decades following the Second World War, a long period which redefined the balance between capital and labour in industrial relations and developed welfare systems. This phase reached its peak in the 1970s when in the face of persistent conflict in relations between social partners, collaborative intentions and objectives were developed in other contexts through the institutes of industrial democracy and concertation practices.

The third phase, more recently, has marked a comeback – or at times a mere mention – of economic democracy and more widely of participation. Compared with the previous phase, greater prominence is taken by two aspects among others: arrangements planned or implemented involve above all the social actors; and the "climate" in industrial relations has shed its antagonistic or traditionally conflictful themes and references, giving way to more collaborative arguments and forms between subjects and their representatives in productive venues; and most notably compatibility between workers' demands and economic requirements supported by firms and governments has become a standard constraint.

3 Participation, collective bargaining and industrial democracy

The range of proposals and experiences of participation makes it difficult to define its recurring (if not unifying) features. The claim that such features consist of a tendency to enhance the value of labour and its providers, though maintainable, appears too general and extensive.

It is too general and therefore scarcely significant because of the different motives and objectives which determine it.

It is, above all, too extensive because labour enhancement has been carried out by other means, i.e. collective bargaining and legal provisions whereby employment criteria have been constantly and cyclically corrected.

Even if legislation has sponsored, especially in recent times, participatory forms and institutes, our attention will focus mostly on the relationship between collective bargaining and participation.

The former instrument is inherently different from the latter. In a deliberate simplification, collective bargaining may be said to: pursue the achievement of specific economic and prescriptive conditions safeguarding workers, while they preserve the distinction of functions and interests between the sides concerned and reach a degree of equity in employment relationships, but do not openly envisage to overcome the asymmetry inherent in the position of those offering and those employing subordinate labour.

Instead participation assumes that negotiated conditions for the protection of workers are not sufficient, as it is necessary to remove or reduce the distinction between functions and interests (in favour of workers or by reconciling the parties involved) and to achieve greater equity in employment relationships, especially through formal and recognised measures correcting the above asymmetry.

Where they are observed, differences are not so sharp in reality, especially if the events of the last ten to fifteen years are considered. The negotial processes and objectives that have appeared in this period, integrate bargaining and participation [19] as the two appear hardly incompatible with each other. This trend has not affected all the forms and institutes of participation but mostly those where the participatory perspective has made no progress because of the lack of collective bargaining and has concerned matters connected to the firm's need for innovation and competitiveness.[20]

The concurrence of bargaining and specific forms of participation allows a reinterpretation of Clegg's famous thesis [21] that when bargaining is sufficiently deep (i.e. carried out at firm level, with the contribution of workers' representatives as negotial actors) a fair degree of participation is truly achieved; thus pure forms of participatory activity are not needed in countries such as Britain or the United States because of their traditional contractual depth, while they are needed in some European continental countries where bargaining occurs in a wider context or there is less negotial activity in production units.

This thesis – which has already shown notable exceptions due to the complementary nature of various bargaining levels and participatory forms [22] – should be revised in our day to accommodate the innovation of participatory proposals sponsored by the entrepreneurial-managerial world and not oriented exclusively to the improvement of workers' conditions. By no chance these proposals have arisen and gained ground also in Britain and in the United States.[23]

Turning back to the question of labour enhancement, it should be emphasised that it has been pursued and maintained not only by legal means but chiefly by collective bargaining. Participatory experiences and proposals, which often follow these means, have also integrated and enriched them. Only in recent years have both been at times in a position to replace bargaining and avoid even trade union mediation.

In many other instances, however, participation and bargaining are mutually complementary, and not only in the present day. The presence of both participatory and bargaining processes was indeed observed during the decades following the Second World War in certain important European nations, notably Germany and Sweden.

This presence has given rise to institutes and practices of industrial democracy that are definable in the following terms: through representatives normally nominated or influenced by the unions, workers participate with their counterpart in formal bodies which in varying degrees are responsible for fixing working conditions or deciding how such conditions should relate to the firm's decisions, with procedures and themes that may surpass the traditional domain and outcome of collective bargaining.

Industrial democracy can be interpreted historically as an extension and enrichment of the negotial-bargaining rationale. At the same time it differs considerably from bargaining for the above-mentioned qualities concerning the nature of bargaining as compared to the participatory rationale.

More precisely, the instances of industrial democracy differ from bargaining practices on the following points: the lower incidence of power-based relations between the sides, the establishment of joint and mixed institutes safeguarding both labour and the firm's policies, and its lasting and natural implementation in the firm. Though these points stress the separation of industrial democracy from collective bargaining, it must be remembered that the bargaining method has long developed collaborative practices and results, not only in settings with a solid industrial democracy background; thus it is not always possible in practice to find a clear border between the two events and generally the former does not replace the latter.[24]

What are the relations of industrial democracy to participatory economic democracy?

In our interpretation, economic democracy subsumes industrial democracy.[25] The latter replicates the general features of economic democracy (such as its initiation outside the political-institutional sphere and the fact it does not appear to be necessary) and yet displays its own peculiarities.

Unlike other instances of economic democracy, its origins and the conditions for its success lie within industrial relations systems. This participatory direction perfects and enlarges the range of such systems, rather than adding to them or offering alternative arrangements.

Industrial democracy includes institutes and experiences which by full mutual recognition of the entrepreneur's functions and of workers' collective representation enable these to participate formally in decisions (or rather, in certain decisions) concerning the firm's existence.

Industrial democracy is one of the few arrangements that alter employees' conditions in qualitative terms, without setting objectives that are inherently unacceptable to employers.

The notion of industrial democracy brings us back to the basic difference between our interpretation of participatory economic democracy and the interpretation referred to as more idealised. While we tend to view economic democracy and industrial democracy on the same plane (though the former is in a wider sphere which includes the latter), the advocates of the second interpretation place them on separate qualitative planes: the former on a "higher" plane and the latter on a "lower" plane. They tend to stress the limits of industrial democracy and its low-key position compared with economic democracy, by means of the following arguments: it concerns the conditions of employment without a properly "democratised" public policy;[26] it shows little concern for distributive processes, as it reserves the firm's surplus of profit exclusively to its members; and it acts only in single firms of the manufacturing sector.[27]

These arguments essentially reintroduce the main theme of the idealised interpretation, which views economic democracy in a perspective that has to surpass the firm's confines, although some of its advocates – such as Macpherson [28] – accept that industrial democracy probably acts as a powerful drive behind the "higher" plane of economic democracy.

Reaching closer to the heart of the matter, we shall now add a few observations.

The institutes and practices of industrial democracy produce direct, negotiated, formalised participation in the most problematic area of social relations in capitalist society, that of subordinate employment; conversely the domain and opportunities of participatory economic democracy at the level of society are more limited, as we shall see.

Industrial democracy certainly implies a limited and fixed degree of solidarity, which excludes even from its most successful contexts the involvement of a considerable part of the working population. However this limit is functional to almost all participatory forms, which permits us to confirm the assumption that in capitalist and democratic settings economic policy is the main and foremost domain of economic democracy.

The scarce concern of industrial democracy for redistributive processes is offset by the fact that it does not stand as an alternative to contractual protection, which in its traditionally successful contexts (as in the case of Germany) normally displays a high degree of coordination and (national and regional) extension, and thus ensures generalised protection to employment.

The restriction of industrial democracy to the manufacturing sector is a historical fact due to its long dominating position in industrial relations systems; today, however, openings (and sometimes actual instances) are also found in other sectors.

4 Past and present

Participation has notably produced a great range of proposals and events. This prominent and constant trait stands out clearly if past and present are compared.

The present shows two relevant features among others: it includes a number of institutes and practices that highlight common themes and areas of interest among actors in industrial relations; and a great part of participatory experiences are marked by the employer's will to innovate human resource management and industrial relations,[29] while the use of conflict as a normal resource in trade union action is being redefined.[30]

Current participatory prospects differ sharply from those prevailing in the past, which may be summarised into two types.

The first scenario, which emerged between the end of the last century and the 1930s, consists of theories and programmes that – uneasy of social relations under capitalist liberal societies and eager to outline and alternative to class war and to the use of conflict itself – looked to the opportunity and need for a stable harmonisation of workers' and employers' interests; chiefly (but not exclusively) through the implementation of a corporatist arrangement, as envisaged by many authors of Christian-oriented beliefs[31] but also by a great rationalist thinker like Durkheim.[32]

The traits of this scenario are no longer found in present participation, save for the scarce practicability or inevitability of conflict which they both share. Current participation is indeed modelled on a consolidated and advanced variety of capitalism; it does not aspire to replicate the nature of employment relationships in the political-institutional sphere; it is no longer (since long before recent events in Eastern Europe) under the pressure of competition by revolutionary or antagonistic proposals.

Another major difference is the fact that the perspective of stable harmonisation of interests is essentially – with a few exceptions and the degenerate corporatist model exploited by fascist and authoritarian regimes – nothing more than a series of intellectual contributions (however distinguished) and programmes; instead current participation – despite its cultural basis and solid substantiation (as in the case of Japan) – has developed at the operational level in a wealth of actual experiences.

In spite of these deep differences, it is easy to wonder if current participation is not really a revenge of the advocates of stable harmonisation.

Its great weakness, related to its good intentions, was to envisage potentially equitable social relations in contexts where social relations were decisively unfavourable to workers, and it found no practical or ideological agreement from the entrepreneurial side.[33]

Current participation, on the other hand, has arisen after decades of pluralistic regulation of interests, after repeated employment regulations due to collective representatives and legal provisions, with the recognition and (not necessarily marked) use of conflict, and after dramatic socioeconomic and institutional changes to capitalist settings.

The second scenario is more consistent than the first one as for theories, programmes, and actual experiences. It appeared during the last century but, unlike the former, it lasted far longer and reached into recent times.

To this scenario belong Marxist-inspired schemes and programmes, social-democratic thought and initiatives, and Christian-oriented political and trade union movements.

The common factor behind this varied array is its ability to interpret and support employees' interest, rights and hopes. In general it can be said that the common inspiration is primarily a desire to alter and/or improve the conditions of subordinate employment as related to social relations typical of the capitalist firm.

Its fundamental difference to current participation is far-reaching: the scenario was, of course, never accepted by employers as it opposed in different degrees either them or their employment criteria; it sought to represent above all the interests of workers, who were the centre and symbol of subordinate employment; it often planned to reject the method of collective bargaining in favour of more advanced or radical qualitative gains.

With time, this source of inspiration has deeply changed or adjusted its objectives and forms. Its overall evolution points in the direction of a gradually weaker radicalism in its demands for change in the capitalist productive and social setting. This trend has not been consistent or simultaneous throughout industrial nations (not even in Europe) and has at times reversed its direction.

In the reduction of radicalism, three tendencies are briefly observable.

1   The gradual decline of explicitly or actually antagonistic perspectives, which by definition aim to alter employment relationships by introducing substantial changes to the capitalist system (in ownership, for example) through arrangements centred in the political-institutional sphere (nationalisation) or reflecting advanced goals of the trade union movement (as in the Swedish proposal on workers' investment funds,[34] which remains the most emblematic instance of reversal).

2   The continuity of the perspective based on conflictful relationships between employers and workers, which tends to maximise union power and achievements in the firm and/or in a wider sphere. Collective bargaining is often regarded as the most frequent instrument in this perspective but bargaining is known to take on other functions as well.[35] The same perspective – traditionally associated, for example, with the Italian trade union experience[36] – has produced, especially in the last

ten years, a weakening of conflictful relations and has practically (rather than explicitly) accepted or proposed more collaborative practices and institutes.

3   The appearance of a perspective that provides for collaborative intentions and experiences by the sides involved (employer and workers' representatives), with joint-responsibility and full recognition of their legitimacy and needs. This perspective usually implies an institutionalisation of venues and matters involving real or potential common interests and a limited use of conflict.

Thus, apart from employers' aims and needs, current participatory proposals and experiences stem from forms and experiences due to the scenario of change and improvement in employees' working conditions. Less evident is the legacy of the stable harmonisation scenario, though there is a new lease of life to its assumption that the protection of labour interests and dignity does not necessarily imply an extension of the sharp distinction between employer and employees.

The most interesting point is that in many current situations the different forms and institutes of participation co-exist and are interlaced. This fact has its structural basis in the increasing constraints of compatibility and flexibility and is favoured by the actors' behaviour; especially by the variety and compliance of managerial styles in the use of workforce[37] and, not least, by the adaptability of union representatives in the face of innovations previously attributed to the perspective of conflictful-negotial relations.

5 The complexity and plurality of elements

The doubtless complexity of the phenomenon of participation[38] calls for adequate analytic clarity[39] – a quality often lacking in the literature and debates – especially as its past and recent forms must be taken into account and if comparative remarks are to be made.[40]

This requirement calls for two (rather intuitive) clarifications.

Our research refers to participation in its collective dimension[41] and does not consider individual participation, such as the worker's contribution to technical-productive solutions. Within this dimension, instances of "indirect participation" (through representatives and shop stewards)[42] prevail over those of "direct participation" (first-hand involvement of workers).

The participatory potential of bargaining practices is kept distinct in this research from explicit forms of participation. Of course we shall focus on the latter and will not consider the participatory implication of collective bargaining, unless they display elements of explicit participation.

Participatory events are approached with reference to various elements, which need to be listed in this chapter.

First of all, their *domains*, which are essentially three: *context* consists of capitalist countries with representative democracies; the *subjects* are employees, taken as individuals or social groups, who interact with other actors (essentially employers, the state and political parties); the *venues* are levels of which the firm is the prevailing instance.

The great variety of participatory events is due in substance to the evolutionary progress of capitalist democracies and to special factors involved in single events and individual countries: for example ideological traditions in the area of capital/labour relations, the state's position and type of intervention, and the atittude of employers and managers to organised labour. In the development of this variety stand out the intentions and aims of actors, especially of workers or those representing their rights and interests. All these changing intentions and aims revolve around *models* whereby the phenomenon of participation becomes visible now as in the past; they enable the researcher to understand the rationale and fundamental reasons of its development and to notice the main differences and possible intersections within its proposed or implemented instances.

Several *directions* may be observed in each model: these mark more specific paths associated with the model, which reflect the intentions and objectives that actors intend to pursue: they help to understand the meaning, significance and implications of the motives of participation.[43]

In turn, within each direction are found the *forms* of participation (a term often used elsewhere) which refer to: the theoretical and factual features of the phenomenon; the matters or areas in which the sides express their common interests, or the will of one side to alter or improve its position as related to the positions and prerogatives of others; the institutes, processes, negotial practices and customs of participation.

The next paragraph and following chapters will centre on these elements and chiefly on the gradual sequence of models, directions and forms. Finally a mention is due to another element, namely the *intensity* of participation. For some authors [44] participatory forms may be sequenced along a scale of intensity, according to the greater or lesser degree of workers' participation in the firm's decision-making processes. A similar method seems adequate for many major forms (particularly if associated with industrial democracy) but is not equally applicable to other forms, such as those making participation dependent on the firm's economic results or striving to enhance the value of human skills, commitment and creativity. It is therefore well evident that intensity cannot suitably be assessed by common, uniform criteria.

6 Models, directions and forms of participation

This paragraph provides a first overview of participatory models and of the directions associated with each model, as well as a description of historically observed forms. References are made both to the past and the present, in line with the approach taken. As for the models, their rationale and nature are discussed mostly as they appeared in their first stages; at present they appear clearly distinct from each other. However, as actors' intentions and practical applications in particular evolved, these models have embodied changes that eventually altered their original appearance. The process tends at times to reduce distinctions between models, as may be seen in the culture and practice of participatory directions and their respective forms, which can move closer in later phases and allow actual "contamination".

This research indicates that participatory models are essentially three: the antagonistic, the collaborative, and the integrative.

1   *Antagonistic participation*, or participation with antagonistic components, includes proposals and arrangements that tend to the *effectively alter* the asymmetry inherent in employment relationships and often even the condition of employees in society.

2   *Collaborative participation* includes proposals and instances that envisage *improvement* in workers' socioeconomic standing and the *correction* of asymmetry, without altering the capitalist institutional setting or the firm's corporate name.

3   *Integrative participation* includes a body of proposals and practices that aim to involve workers (not necessarily through their representatives) in the firm's working and/or to *commit* them to its activities and fate.

Within the models suggests above, the following directions may be seen. The antagonistic model comprises two directions:
a   workers' influence and control over economic life and
b   the explicit extension of the political democracy method to productive relations.

The first of these directions displays intentions or programmes with antagonistic intentions and objectives, as found in numerous forms of worker control in the Italian experience of managing councils (*Consigli di gestione*), and in the Scandinavian experience of investment funds.

The second direction, although lacking (especially at present) the will to actually alter the capitalist setting, offers an alternative to the use of subordinate employment by means of arrangements such as the cooperative and self-management.

The collaborative model comprises the following directions:

a   political participation implemented through concertation agreements and practices; it is observed in pluralistic and neo-corporatist political exchange;

b   participation of workers' representatives in public institutions dealing with economic-political problems and policies, general interests and/or workers' special interests, and workers' socio-professional conditions (welfare, job training, labour market);

c   participation seeking to encourage and enhance saving by workers. It may be termed "financial participation" and normally translates into the form of social insurance funds;

d   participation of varying intensity concerning the firm's decisions; it notably involves the domain of industrial democracy. Its forms are information and consultation rights, codecision, codetermination and co-management.

The integrative model displays two main directions, namely:

a   economic participation, which aims to involve workers in the firm's functioning by allowing them to participate in its results, chiefly through forms of profit sharing (that is a variable portion of wages linked to the firm's functioning according to preset parameters) and employee ownership (meaning special concessions for the purchase of shares by employees);

b   cultural and organisational participation, founded on workers' commitment to the firm's mission, values and constant need for adjustment. Despite earlier instances, its present relevance is apparent in the themes and programmes of "total quality".

If these models are referred to the present situation, it may be observed that:

i   the antagonistic model is today essentially obsolete both in theory and in practice. It survives in the cooperative arrangement, although its actors have intentions and contexts far different from the past;

ii   the collaborative model, after yielding considerable results in the decades following the Second World War, remains useful for spreading collaborative needs and intentions, even if these are no longer due to this model alone. Moreover, its most challenging directions and forms either come up against greater difficulties (as in the case of concertation) or fail to produce any major new experiences (as in codetermination);

iii the integrative model shows a marked relevance to the culture of productive settings and its present applications, as well as a capacity to alter its original basis by negotiation of objectives and trade union mediation.

As for the venues of participatory processes, it is notable that they occur chiefly at the level of the firm. Indeed, participatory events have shown an increasing concern for employees in their productive settings moving from past to recent times.

These models, directions and forms are briefly summarised in Table 1.

Table 1
The models, directions and forms of participation

Models	Directions	Forms
Antagonistic participation	Workers' influence over economic life	Workers' control Managing councils Investment funds
	Explicit extension of the political democracy method to productive relations	Cooperative Self-management
Collaborative participation	Political participation (concertation)	Pluralistic exchange Neo-corporatist political exchange
	Presence of workers' representatives in public institutions	Advisory bodies Bodies with executive and monitoring duties Managing bodies
	Financial participation	Supplementary social insurance funds
	Participation in the firm's decisions (industrial democracy)	Information and consultation Codecision Codetermination and co-management
Integrative participation	Economic participation	Profit sharing Employee ownership
	Cultural and organisational participation	"Total quality" schemes

Another important point should be added to this picture.

Both in the antagonistic model and the collaborative model (less often now than in the past for the latter) there appears to be a common theme that regards the debate on concentration of economic power as such and above all in its damaging effects on the political and social level. It is not included in the integrative model often sponsored by large firms, on the grounds that such firms are more suitable for achieving and preserving competitiveness in a competitive international market.

This is a recurrent theme in the programmes of left-wing political and trade union movements, such as the work plan of the Cgil in Italy [45] and the new Bad Godesberg manifesto (1959) of German social democracy.[46]

However heterogeneous, the objectives that these movements aim at are strikingly similar because they relate directly to the working of the economy, to the protection of employees' interests, and to constraints placed by concertation and economic powers on democratic life itself.

This context reintroduces the theme mentioned at the beginning of this chapter, namely that of economic participation as a phenomenon that unfolds at the economic level but also at the level of democratic method.

In particular, the implications of such constraints reflect the main concern of a vast amount of literature and debate on the "limits" of political democracy; according to Eisfeld,[47] for instance, this has not yet given rise to a genuine, substantial democracy, primarily because of the power wielded by large firms.

This thesis is shared by many other authors – such as Lindblom,[48] who analyses market power as a form of political power – and Dahl,[49] who looks at large firms as creators of inequality not only in economic terms.

It may be useful to close the chapter by simply recalling the meaning of a few key terms used in this research (apart from those included in the glossary), namely participation, participatory economic democracy, and industrial democracy.

Participation concerns the body of proposals and experiences tending to alter or improve employment relationships and employees' socioeconomic conditions. It appears in many forms that extend to all the three models.

Participatory economic democracy consists of a series of actions and institutions capable of altering processes governing the allocation of resources (tangible and non-tangible) arising from the market and from the typical events of capitalist economies. It shares this function with economic policy but differs from it in the following points : it is promoted by social groups and their organisations, although the political-institutional sphere may contribute or be involved as well; it acts on processes of resource distribution, normally avoiding compulsory measures through exchanges between social actors or by the dominant initiative of a single actor; and it is unlikely to extend to the whole of society.

35

Economic democracy, embodied in different motives and objectives, is a phenomenon that mirrors the different forms within antagonistic and collaborative models. The inclusion of the integrative model and its forms within the same domain is however controversial. Being an explicit derivation of the collaborative model, industrial democracy belongs to the domain of participatory economic democracy, chiefly because it replicates and heightens the features mentioned above. Nevertheless it exhibits unique traits like the fact that its instances arise from and owe their success to industrial relations systems, unlike other participatory forms of economic democracy.

Notes

1   Cf. ILO, *Workers' Participation in Decisions within Undertakings*, Geneva 1981.
2   Cf. L. Gallino, *Dizionario di sociologia*, UTET: Turin 1978, pp. 498-9.
3   Cf. G. Ruffolo, *La qualità sociale. Le vie dello sviluppo*, Laterza: Bari 1985, Part 1.
4   C.B. Macpherson, *The Rise and Fall of Economic Justice and other Essays*, Oxford University Press: Oxford 1985, Chapter 3.
5   Cf. M. Nuti, 'Democrazia economica: mercato, politica e partecipazione', in M. Carrieri et al., *Il progetto 'Democrazia Economica'*, CESPE papers, No. 3, Rome 1991.
6   Cf. D. Fano, 'La politica economica', in V. Castronovo and L. Gallino (eds), *La società contemporanea*, UTET: Turin 1987, Vol. 1.
7   See, for example, M. Nuti et al., *Prospettive di democrazia economica e democrazia integrativa in Italia*, CESPE papers, Rome (undated).
8   R.A. Dahl, *A Preface to Economic Democracy*, University of California Press: Berkeley 1985.
9   Cf. M. Nuti, 'Codeterminazione, partecipazione agli utili e cooperazione', in B. Jossa (ed.), *Autogestione, cooperazione e partecipazione agli utili*, Bologna: Il Mulino 1988; and G. Seravalli, *Il cervo e la lepre. Una ricerca sul 'sistema' delle imprese cooperative*, Angeli: Milan 1991, Chapter 1.
10   Cf. R. Aron, *Les étapes de la pensée sociologique*, Gallimard: Paris 1967.
11   D. Easton, *The Political System*, Knopf: New York 1965.
12   G. Poggi, *The Development of the Modern State*, Hutchinson: London 1978.
13   Cf. G.P. Cella, *La solidarietà possibile*, Edizioni Lavoro: Roma 1989.
14   W. Korpi, *The Working Class in Welfare Capitalism. Work Unions and Politics in Sweden*, Routledge 1978, Chapters 4 and 11.
15   Cf. L. Bordogna and G. Provasi, *Politica, economia e rappresentanza degli interessi. Uno studio sulle recenti difficoltà delle democrazie occidentali*, Il Mulino: Bologna 1984.

16   W. Streeck, 'La dimensione sociale del mercato unico europeo: verso una economia non regolata?', *Stato e mercato*, No. 26, 1990.

17   Cf. B. Amoroso, 'Development and Crisis of the Scandinavian Model of Labour Relations in Denmark', and G. Rehn and B. Viklung, 'Changes in the Swedish Model', in G. Baglioni and C. Crouch (eds), *European Industrial Relations. The Challenge of Flexibility*, Sage Publications: London 1990.

18   Cf. W. Abendroth, *Aufstieg und Kreise der deutschen Sozialdemokratie*, Pahl-Rugenstein Verlag, 1974, 3rd ed.; and G.E. Rusconi, 'La socialdemocrazia tedesca oggi', *Prospettiva sindacale*, No. 36, 1980.

19   Cf. G.P. Cella, 'Contrattazione, partecipazione, gestione sui luoghi di lavoro', *Prospettiva sindacale*, No. 67, 1988.

20   Cf. G. Della Rocca and L. Prosperetti (eds), *Salari e produttività. Esperienze internazionali ed italiane*, Angeli: Milan 1991.

21   H.A. Clegg, *Trade Unionism under Collective Bargaining. A Theory Based on Comparisons of Six Countries*, Basil Blackwell: Oxford 1976.

22   Cf. R.B. Peterson, 'Swedish Collective Bargaining. A Changing Scene', *British Journal of Industrial Relations*, No. 1, 1987.

23   Cf. G. Della Rocca and L. Prosperetti (eds), *Salari e produttività. Esperienze internazionali ed italiane*, op. cit., Chapters 2 and 7; and M. Ambrosini et al., *Transforming U.S. Industrial Relations*, Angeli: Milan 1990.

24   T. Treu, 'Cogestione e partecipazione', *Giornale di diritto del lavoro e di relazioni industriali*, No. 4, 1989.

25   G. Sartori, *Democrazia. Cosa è*, Rizzoli: Milan 1993, Chapter 1.

26   M. Nuti, *Democrazia economica: mercato, politica e partecipazione*, op. cit.

27   M. Carrieri, *Non solo produttori. Percorsi di democrazia economica*, Angeli: Milan 1992, p. 29.

28   C.B. Macpherson, *The Rise and Fall of Economic Justice and other Essays*, op. cit.

29   Cf. G. Baglioni and C. Crouch (eds), *European Industrial Relations. The Challenge of Flexibility*, op. cit.

30   A. Accornero, 'La terziarizzazione del conflitto e i suoi effetti', in G.P. Cella and M. Regini (eds), *Il conflitto industriale in Italia. Stato della ricerca e ipotesi sulle tendenze future*, Il Mulino: Bologna 1985.

31   G. Baglioni and B. Manghi, *Il problema del lavoro operaio. Teorie del conflitto industriale e dell'esperienza sindacale*, Angeli: Milan 1967, Chapter 3.

32   Cf. R. Aron, *Les étapes de la pensée sociologique*, op. cit.

33   Cf. R. Bendix, *Work and Authority in Industry*, Harper & Row: New York 1963; and G. Baglioni, *L'ideologia della borghesia industriale nell'Italia liberale*, Einaudi: Turin 1974.

34   Cf., among others, G. Rehn and B. Viklung, 'Per un riformismo più avanzato senza compromesso di classe', in CESOS (ed.), *L'Europa sindacale nel 1982*, Il Mulino: Bologna 1984.

35   R. Bean, *Comparative Industrial Relations. An Introduction in Cross-national Perspectives*, Croom Helm: London 1985, Chapter 4.

36   G. Giugni, 'Appunti per un dibattito sulla democrazia economica', in G. Baglioni et al., *Democrazia industriale e sindacato in Italia*, Quaderni di Mondoperaio, No. 5, Rome 1977.

37   See, among others, S. Negrelli, *La società dentro l'impresa. L'evoluzione dal modello normativo al modello partecipativo nelle relazioni industriali delle imprese italiane*, Angeli: Milan 1991, Chapter 9 and elsewhere.

38   J. Vanek, 'La partecipazione operaia: storia ed esperienze concrete', in P. Bellasi, M. La Rosa and G. Pellicciari (eds), *Fabbrica e società. Autogestione operaia in Europa*, Il Mulino: Bologna 1972.

39   See ILO, *Workers' Participation in Decisions within Undertakings*, op. cit.; and G. Seravalli, *Il cervo e la lepre*, op. cit.

40   Cf. R. Blanpain, 'Analisi comparativa del diritto del lavoro e delle relazioni industriali', in R. Blanpain and T. Treu (eds), *Diritto del lavoro e relazioni industriali comparate*, Edizioni Lavoro: Rome 1980; and G. Baglioni, 'La comparazione nelle relazioni industriali: problemi di metodo', *Giornale di diritto del lavoro e di relazioni industriali*, No. 37, 1988.

41   T. Hanami, 'La partecipazione dei lavoratori nella fabbrica e nell'impresa', in R. Blainpain and T. Treu (eds), *Diritto del lavoro e relazioni industriali comparate*, op. cit., p. 333.

42   Cf. IDE, *Industrial Democracy in Europe*, Clarendon Press: Oxford 1981, Part 1.

43   Cf. M. Colasanto, *La questione della democrazia industriale*, Vita e Pensiero: Milan 1982, Chapter 1.

44   Such as T. Treu, *Cogestione e partecipazione*, op. cit., pp. 600ff.

45   Cf. G. Amato, M. Magno and B.Trentin, *Il piano d'impresa*, De Donato: Bari 1980.

46   Cf. W. Abendroth, *Aufstieg und Kreise der deutschen Sozialdemokratie*, op. cit.

47   R. Eisfeld, *Pluralismus zwischen Liberalismus und Sozialismus*, Verlag W. Kohlhammer: Stuttgart 1972.

48   C.E. Lindblom, 'Il potere di mercato come potere politico', in A. Baldassarre (ed.), *I limiti della democrazia*, Laterza: Bari 1985.

49   R.A. Dahl, *A Preface to Economic Democracy*, op. cit., Chapter 2.

2 The decline of antagonistic participation

1 The rationale of antagonistic participation

This model comprises proposals and solutions that seek to alter the asymmetry inherent in the employment relationship and often also in the employees' social conditions.

Antagonistic participation can be traced back to the more radical trends in the scenario aimed at altering the above conditions and, to a certain extent, it is not alien to the perspective which relies chiefly on the balance of strength of each side and resorts to conflict as its ultimate resource (Chapter 1).

The rationale of this model depends on the conflict of interests between workers and employers, which it considers inevitable; workers' representatives do not appear too willing to share the responsibility of running the firm, unless major changes in business or in the economic system are introduced; accordingly, the mutual recognition of legitimation can only be forceful or uncertain.

In itself, antagonistic participation cannot escape contradiction, because of the inherent incompatibility between the noun and its qualifying adjective. Despite the ambiguity and uncertainty observed so far, contradiction can be overcome if this type of participation is implemented in view of deep changes to the capitalist system of production and ownership. Its applications are indeed often viewed as a change or means leading to wider objectives of economic democracy. Even if such objectives concern the employment relationship and workers' conditions in the firm, their framework and outcome lie on a different plane, which depends on macroeconomic and politico-institutional changes.

It is a well known fact that the directions and forms of this type of participation were conceived mainly in past, prior to and immediately after World War I; some lasted into the post-war years with distinctive innovations. Most of them belong to the long, tortuous attempt of socialist culture and organisations to "exit" the capitalist system so as to overcome the shortcomings of trade union claims in the workplace and of social relations in general.

Within this model, the more antagonistic forms were only roughly outlined and remained an aspiration, or were implemented only at special times (as, for instance, during the political and social unrest following the war) and were activated in limited albeit evocative cases. The less openly antagonistic forms were applied more widely and revealed an adaptive capacity to different conditions which gradually reduced their antagonistic intentions and objectives.

The model unfolds essentially in two directions, which may be defined as: workers' influence and control over economic life; and an explicit extension of the political democracy method to production relations.

Both directions share the above rationale although their historical development was considerably different.

The first direction is more directly antagonistic and either states its reasons (when defining a programme) or at times leaves them implicit (when setting its objectives for labour protection and liberation); it tends to alter and overcome the capitalist economic set-up or the functioning of firms by influencing and controlling workers by democratic means in order to introduce structural changes or amplify workers' interests (not only their claims).

The second direction is typified by its attempt to apply openly the democratic method to the management of productive processes and the selection of employment criteria. Democratic methods and means are known to be present also in many other participatory proposals and instances, but in this direction they reveal an eminently institutional character. The direction is in fact only indirectly and partly antagonistic, as it provides for types of business which are alternative to the capitalist firm proper, with which it can co-exist. Accordingly, this direction produced experiences that were gradually incorporated into market economy.

2 Workers' influence and control over economic life

Our discussion of the forms that may be attributed to this direction of participation will centre on the more important or meaningful forms, without attempting to be exhaustive.

It is perhaps unnecessary to point out that the plans and programmes developed in this direction originated from Marxist-inspired culture. Among the great variety of approaches we shall focus on those who acknowledge the key importance of actions and instruments involved in production relations, viewed both *per se* and as significant contributions to the overall transformation of social relations. However, the context of this direction does not concern exclusively such plans and programmes. In fact it also includes re-

40

formist traditions, which renew the links with its original inspiration, as well as trade union tendencies and experiences that seek to impose criteria for the concession of labour openly in conflict with those of capitalist economy. This means that the context regards intentions and experiences that are not always related to broad antagonistic aims (economic and institutional systems as a whole) and are not necessarily linked to objectives whose nature is ultimately political.

In the area of antagonistic participation, great importance is given to the perspective generally known as *workers' control*. This form of worker intervention in the economy (present from the late nineteenth century until after the Second World War) comprises motives and solutions that differ greatly at times and yet its equilibrium point rests on theories and policies that tend to change the capitalist economy, especially by introducing a new industrial order where firms are controlled entirely or partly by workers' representatives.[1]

In the United States, according to Daniel De Leon,[2] the workers' struggle is justified if it becomes a political struggle and thus trade union action itself should prepare workers to wage an open, explicit war for the control and management of firms; this implies a change from union representation to council-type institutions.

In the same country and period (at the turn of the century), Eugene Debs pursued a balance between political organisation and the organisation of workers' demands: he acknowledged trade union freedom in monetary protection but stressed that by abandoning the political perspective, day-to-day achievements would eventually be lost.

In Britain, George Douglas Howard Cole's proposals were highly influential during the early decades of this century. The author's Fabian background influenced his position in favour of a peaceful transition to democratic socialism by political organisation and electoral competition, relying on a broad policy of business socialisation closely connected to trade union organisations. He was the at the centre of the debate on "guild socialism", an opinion movement advocating workers' control over industry and a reorganisation of the state and the economy based on the professions.

In Germany, after the First World War, the manifesto and intentions of social democracy,[3] especially in its 1925 Heidelberg version, propounded a struggle against capitalism aimed not only at wider state control over the economy but also at developing a council movement capable of implementing the workers' right to participate in economic organisation alongside the trade unions.

Just after the Second World War, German social democracy upheld its anticapitalistic stance; it propounded far-reaching changes to capitalist structures by democratic parliamentary action and – in line with the Weimar tradition – workers' control of the economy and workers' participation through the socialisation of key industries and banks.[4]

41

In Italy, Antonio Gramsci viewed the firm as a producer of conflict and new institutions, and as a point where society is shaped. In this perspective, the alternative to traditional political parties and to the unions' bargaining rationale depends on the establishment of councils; these bodies aimed to found a brand of socialism well-rooted in workers' actual conditions, as experienced after the First World War in the Turin area.[5]

In Italy again, an interesting early form of workers' control were the managing councils (*consigli di gestione*) that first appeared during the struggle for liberation and took hold in the factories of Northern Italy soon after the Second World War; they were conceived as an instrument for democratic control of capitalist development and were expected to enable workers to participate in the management of firms.[6]

After the exclusion of left-wing parties from government in 1947, the councils gradually declined; they should not be interpreted as a revival of the 1920s struggle for workers' control and labour councils, i.e. as a means for seizing power.[7] Among their original motives and actions there appeared, alongside the aim of solidarity in view of national reconstruction, both production-oriented goals and bureaucratic tendencies showing a readiness to collaborate with employers.

In effect, the experience was ultimately non-collaborative and appears plausible only within the framework of an advanced state-controlled economy, supported by ideological and political components antagonising the capitalist system and pursuing a high degree of economic democracy.

Goals and experiences due to inherently antagonistic motives have been present for a long time in actual trade union initiatives – and not only in connection with radical policies for the "liberation" of workers.

The strongest convergence of such initiatives is observed in the collective will of workers to preserve or regain power and rights connected with the provision of their performance, professional conditions and the quality of work, and the intention to obtain new rights on performance and protection.

In either case, workers and their organisations signal a need for control [8] that involves the curtailment of employers' duties and contemplates a change in the firm's functioning at the level of labour organisation.

The chief difference between this type of control and explicitly antagonistic control lies in the fact that it does not normally allow for the creation of bodies suitable for institutional changes inside the firm and for relations between the parties involved; its demands and achievements are committed to defensive practices, bitter confrontation, bargaining actions and legal provisions.

By these means, trade unions have displayed for years their opposition and support in view of better environmental and professional conditions (e.g. work-pace regulations, tasks-position-wages ratios, control on the access of new employees) [9] and have pursued a formal regulation of employment whose features and significance do not always differ greatly in practice from the perspective of workers' control.

All trade union initiatives have, to a different extent and in various ways, propounded formal regulation. This characterised the development of North American trade unions despite their well-known pragmatic and economy-oriented outlook; thus Selig Perlman – their most prominent spokesman – claimed that workers are encouraged to join forces to assert their *ownership* as a group of the whole range of labour opportunities available, and to exert control over the distribution of such opportunities.[10] On the European scene, formal regulation embodies a well-established tradition emerging either as a continuum (e.g. on the question of working hours) or at special times, when unrest is strongest.

Formal regulation requires union action even after a period of success for the workers' control perspective; in particular, the 1968-73 cycle of disputes opened a phase characterised by an egalitarian wage policy and by the search for a new type of labour organisation.[11]

Over the last twenty years, instead, its action has been considerably reduced as a consequence of far-reaching reorganisation processes and of the firms' intense demand for flexibility. This has led to deregulatory employment policies but has also weakened the more rigid institutes and practices by collective bargaining or forms of codecision between unions and management.[12]

Since the appearance of more urgent objectives (protection of real-term wages and of employment) and greater constraints on compatibility, the claims and recent results of formal regulation have addressed the needs of individual workers rather than the direct relationship between labour organisation and performance. Hence the trade unions' stance on working hours (now the chief object of negotiation), in-plant social services, and the treatment of certain disadvantaged subjects (such as disabled workers).[13]

This position differs sharply from the objective of workers' control and from practices that placed increasing restrictions on the firm's functioning and on the use of labour. In point of fact, the unions often abandoned (if they had not done so previously) their criticism of organisational arrangements in productive environments and their attempt to introduce deep changes, thus revealing a clearly adaptive and innovative capacity that interacted with the participatory forms and themes. The retreat should also be viewed in connection with structural data such as changes in workforce composition, in the number and tasks of shop-floor and manual workers, in the spread of unconventional employment relationships (especially part-time).

On the other hand, this retreat may be interpreted as a serious defeat of organised labour, as a rapid decline in its functions and aims. Such feelings may be found in left-wing political and trade union circles and are memorably expressed by a leading figure like Alain Touraine.

In a 1984 book,[14] he argues that "classical" trade-unionism is dead because its action is centred no longer on production relations but on union policy; this is founded on ties with the political parties and on the trade unions' tendency to become political actors themselves, thus participating in the decision-making system which originates economic and social policies.

According to Touraine, trade-unionism is such when it embodies the labour movement, i.e. when it pursues organised conflictful action in view of changes in the social means of managing the industrial economy.

This type of trade-unionism, which leaves out non-shopfloor or non-industrial workers, did not evolve demands and negotiations governed by collective bargaining but developed chiefly in terms of *control*, implying a change in the type of social subordination present in industry. It rejected any involvement in participation in management; its aim was not to negotiate but rather to impose restrictions on the employers' power.

The labour movement comprises only workers' initiatives engaged in the primary conflict within industrial society, which takes place inside production and therefore in the factory.

But during the late 1970s and early 1980s, the workers' movement was serious weakened. Trade union organisations – well aware of this process, which ran parallel to the slow de-industrialisation of Western countries – pursued internal unity through political action and collective bargaining, while preserving a minimum commitment to claims (improved salaries and opposition to dismissals). This role has not ended, and yet the history of the labour movement is nearing its end.

Touraine's book contains clear overstatements of trade union experience and development, such as the lack of consideration for initiatives safeguarding non-shopfloor and non-industrial workers, or the scarce importance given to claims.

On the other hand, the book is commendable for its emphasis on the importance and significance of problems concerning the formal and professional regulation of employment and for its recognition of the autonomous nature of organised labour, which reflects the natural tensions in subordinate labour and the protection of workers' personality, not only compliance with contractual terms.

Touraine's mistake, however, involves three important aspects: deciding *a priori* that control over the manner of production and over business organisation is the highest form of trade union action; arguing that when this form interacts with other forms of collective protection it declines and is adulterated; underestimating the significance and meaning of the other forms, namely negotial or participatory practices and trade union political action.

Touraine was able to link the rise of the labour movement to the pursuit of control, but in his picture the other two aspects are allowed very little empirical and interpretative evidence.

The history of trade union action and of the "labour movement" extends almost continuously to the political sphere, which invariably strengthens or limits its degree of independence; bargaining is not the sole device regulating wages (a constant object of workers' initiatives and expectations) but also a practice that has produced a host of rules governing the use of labour; the success of trade union experience is measured by the accumulation of such rules and therefore by results, but very seldom by uncompromising confrontation between the sides involved; trade union policies for the defence of employment against restructuring processes or trends in the economic cycle do not reflect the minimum role of organised labour but regard directly the social problems and costs of a capitalist economy.

The proposal and experience of *workers' investment funds* belong to a period and context far removed from those of workers' control.

The proposal, first made by the Swedish trade union movement in the 1970s, offered a new and unprecedented antagonistic perspective applied to a country with solid industrial relations and a long-lasting experience of concertation practices.

This perspective has taken on a broader historical meaning, i.e. the possibility of assessing and predicting the potential and confines of reformist programmes in a capitalist market economy.

The proposal and experience of investment funds have not been successful. Had the outcome been positive, they would have produced new ownership arrangements of the socialist type, or at least a strengthening of the centralised neo-corporatism[15] already present in Sweden for several decades. But owing (at least primarily) to these two factors, and especially to the first one, the ambitious project failed to take off.

The investment funds affair appears as a culturally and politically coherent whole but in fact it comprises two parts: an initial project, known as Meidner Plan (1975), and the law enforcing it (1983).

At heart, the plan resembles a strong programme for economic democracy, which responding to the initiative of a collective social actor, informs relations between workers' and employers' representatives in firms and reaches to the macroeconomic level in view of gradually altering the nature of capital ownership. Its objectives were as follows: to pursue a more centralised and solidaristic pay policy (thus reducing the firms' margin of decision by differential wage increases),[16] to counter the concentration of wealth due to self-financing, to increase workers' influence on economic processes;[17] at certain preliminary conditions such as full employment and a high level of capital formation supported by investment funds.[18]

At the same time, workers were to be guaranteed an increasing portion of the firm's earnings by gradually dislocating profit into a fund system owned by the workers and managed by their representatives. The plan concerned any firm with more than 50 or 100 employees; the proportion of net profit involved was either 10 or 20 per cent; many factories were to become workers' property in 20-30 years, but their control over certain major industries would be felt in only 3-5 years.[19]

The initial plan was a focus of trade union and political debate and action, and it underwent a number of changes, due (not solely) to the bitter opposition of employers and of moderate political parties.

Altogether, the changes weakened the aim of ownership and investment socialisation in view of workers' participation in the establishment and employment of capital; they are apparent in the law, which prescribes: a 6 year trial period; the use of 20 per cent profit exceeding a certain sum, allowing for inflation; that none of the established funds could hold more than 8 per cent of a firm's shares, that workers should contribute 0.2 per cent of gross wages to the funds as an additional payment by employers into their state pension scheme.[20]

Compared to the Swedish labour movement, the investment-fund proposal undoubtedly represents a more advanced and radical stage. Its advocates, who could no longer accept the dominance of capital in the economic and productive sphere, tended to overcome the entrenched compromise of the mid 1930s, in favour of a redistribution of economic power and its democratic control.[21] The proposal affects the running of firms and managerial prerogatives, outlines a new arrangement for managing the economy and tends to a gradual collective takeover of firms by workers and their organisations.

Unlike our presentation, the author views this proposal as a reformist approach and emphasises its gradualness.[22] However, despite its gradual development, the objectives are extremely radical. This becomes clear if we compare it with the current Swedish law on codetermination (Chapter 4), which is considered part and parcel of the new economic democracy programme.[23]

To explain the form of this proposal and the reiterated intention to implement it, the following factors should be taken into account: the very strong position of trade unions, alongside the governing socialdemocratic party supported by an absolute majority of votes; the interest in an advanced stage of economic democracy shown at the time by the three Scandinavian countries;[24] the programmes chosen have a common theme which may be expressed in a metaphor: welfare capitalism has converted workers into adult citizens in the political and social arena, and yet the institute of private ownership still regards them as children in the economic arena.[25]

Other more specific factors identified include: the workers' desire to avoid the constraints of a centralised wage policy;[26] the attempt to favour collective saving and investment in conjunction with highly dynamic taxation and social spending;[27] the fact that in terms of mixed economy Sweden appeared more backward than other European countries.[28]

Taken as a whole, the choice of funds was essentially politico-ideological, as it rested on the belief that reformism could move on to further stages and that advanced capitalist systems would ultimately withstand an unprecedented coalition of so-called pluralism and truly antagonistic projects.

This unlimited reformist programme was unattainable, even at the height of trade union power and support by a "friendly" party; therefore, from its first appearance onwards the plan was repeatedly reshaped and presented as a trial. Indeed the life of investment funds came to an end in 1990, when they were included among supplementary pension funds.

Besides the considerable difficulties involved in its goals, the plan was destined to confront other major problems; among these a long transitional phase, which was extremely likely to witness uncertainty and change in economic decisions, managerial prerogatives and relations between management and control.

Another highly sensitive problem was due to the trade union origin of the plan and to trade union control on firms and investments. This inevitably touched the problem of the plan's compatibility with political democracy itself, since a consolidated and widespread fund system can produce a political economy actor parallel or not to the political set-up chosen by the people.

Finally, the original plan contained a flaw that would sooner or later become apparent. It was conceived for a single country and underestimated the growing internationalisation of the capitalist economy, as well as the economic and institutional requirements necessary to integrate into the market a national system characterised by the presence of large concerns. An advanced capitalist country can maintain a high degree of freedom (compared to other countries) in its political-institutional set-up, but far less in its economic system and laws.

The investment-fund adventure attracted a great deal of interest in many European political and trade union circles, but it was not re-launched in other countries because they lacked the potentially favourable conditions of Sweden. Furthermore, the venture appeared unfamiliar to countries with collaborative experiences and too challenging for countries with a prevalence of trade union and left-wing traditions, combined with vaguely antagonistic cultures and strongly conflictful attitudes.

However, the proposal and experience of investment funds remains the only coherent, tested form of economic democracy with an antagonistic slant in the last few decades.

Clear confirmation of this is provided by the Italian *fondi di solidarietà* (solidarity funds), whose origin was influenced by the approach and mechanism outlined by the Meidner Plan and yet differed considerably from the latter in its objectives and implications.

Supported by the CISL union at the start of the 1980s, the fund envisaged a loan by workers equal to 0.50 per cent of wages; it was never implemented, mainly because of the opposition and ambiguity widespread among left-wing political and trade union organisations.[29]

This initiative was among the attempts made at the time to coordinate wage policies and establish concertation practices capable of curbing inflation; it also originated an animated debate on the shortcomings of the claim-based rationale and its possible corrections.[30]

The Italian proposal resembles the Swedish plan insofar as it aims at the collective intervention of workers in the process of accumulation. It differs greatly, however, in two significant features: it tends to restrain workers' consumption and encourage saving; it tries to pursue such objectives by relying on workers' resources; and it slowly abandons its ambition to gradually or partly acquire capital ownership of firms.

The proposal is in effect far less radical than its Swedish counterpart. It remains outside the antagonistic model, which is clearly declining rapidly.

The recent development and diffusion of institutes which reserve capital shares to workers does not prescribe the compulsory distribution of firm ownership; instead, it aims to capitalise on their savings, increase integration with the firm's activities and implement supplementary security benefits (Chapters 3 and 5).

3 Explicit extension of the political democracy method in production relations

This direction of the antagonistic model refers to the cooperative firm, especially cooperatives producing goods and services, and to another form – namely self-management – which is established differently but may in fact function in the same way. The inherent nature of these two forms can be appreciated by following Vanek's division between:

a   firms where earned income is not distinct from investment income because members contribute both labour and capital and are therefore also owners (worker managed firms);

b   firms where investment and labour are remunerated separately, capital is borrowed, all decisions concerning production are taken by the workers or their delegates, and workers take the firm's earnings after production costs have been paid (labour managed firms).[31]

Clearly, the first case refers to cooperative firms and the second to self-management. These two forms constitute an institutional alternative to the capitalist firm although the first one in particular was generally and increasingly meant to function within a capitalist system. In effect they are not identical with the proposals (outlined in the previous paragraph) that tend to establish a new industrial and economic order.

The crucial common feature of these alternatives lies in the fact that workers participate in the firm's life, because they are neither subordinated to nor dependent on others for its ownership and/or management. In principle, they hold the legal ownership of the firm and/or are responsible for its functioning, and exert such rights by applying the political democracy method. The standard procedure for a cooperative meeting, for instance, allows each member one vote regardless of his capital share.

The political democracy method also prescribes the establishment (by different procedures) of representative bodies charged with running the firm and formally responsible for it. Forms of delegation that attenuate direct democracy are also observed in self-managed firms.

Workers thus avoid in principle the typical condition of subordinate labour; in practice, however, the criteria for employment and workforce remuneration are often problematic and – combined with two other points, namely the use of entrepreneurial authority and the degree of efficiency – they become a testing ground where both participatory forms can prove their potential for implementation and survival.

In capitalist countries, the cooperative firm is undoubtedly the more significant, widespread and long-lived of the two.

The cooperative movement arose, gained ground and was first regulated in various European countries – e.g. Britain, France, Italy, Belgium and Austria – during the last decades of the 19th century.[32]

Although the movement has not admittedly developed with the same gradualness and continuity of overall economic growth, it is now widespread and plays quite a considerable role, especially in the primary sector and (with greater national differences) in construction, manufacturing and credit-insurance.[33]

This claim calls for a major distinction. A great part of the movement consisted of firms that were cooperatives in formal terms but differed inherently from the cooperative illustrated above. Particularly in certain sectors – such as the agricultural and food industry – firms were usually established by producers seeking to improve distribution and strengthen their market position. The outcome differs greatly from the cooperative among workers, devised to escape their wage-earning condition.

The functioning of workers' cooperatives themselves is rather diversified in its compliance with the spirit of cooperative rules. Compliance can be positively affected by specific socio-cultural traditions present in the environment; conversely, it may be pursued with less determination as the firm expands and produces highly-competitive goods and services (if the cooperative cannot rely on special markets or products).

The degree of compliance is therefore more likely to be stricter among small construction cooperatives and looser among large cooperatives in the credit sector. In Italy, for instance, many firms in this sector have only the institutional structure of a cooperative and banks operating as real cooperatives are a significant exception.[34]

The above observations reintroduce the theme of the connection between cooperatives and political democracy, which has not been univocal and has also acquired (not only in recent times) further motives and aims.

The phenomenon first resulted from the search for a type of firm based on a democratic institutional framework, viewed as one of the most effective means for protecting workers against exploitation, liberating labour and securing equal conditions in labour performance and valuation.

Subsequently, as literature focused on the harmful political and social consequences of the power wielded by large corporations, the cooperative solution was viewed as a bulwark for political democracy, corroded by the social relations established in capitalist firms.

Nowadays the motives are generally less noble and more practical. The most common is surely the desire to experiment the quality and persistence of this unique type of firm on the market in response to the challenge of growing competition. In this light, the democratic requirement is used as a resource to muster consensus, produce identification and raise the commitment needed to experiment the new form.

This fact alone does not cancel the unique qualities inherent in the cooperative firm, which is unfettered by the centralised planning of state companies and public ownership, even though it can be regulated and favoured by state intervention. Its members, as we know, own the firm and contribute both labour and capital, so there is no separation between earned income and investment income; this replaces one of the main features inherent in the capitalist economy, namely the distinction between labour providers and capital providers. Because of this substitution, the cooperative movement has often been the object of conflicting judgements, emphasising its qualities and defects, its potential and limits.

The qualities and potential coincide largely with those attributed to other participatory forms, supplemented by those typical of the cooperative. They include structural and strategic reasons for avoiding conflict, they enhance loyalty and commitment to the firm, favour the growth of entrepreneurial competence and skills and the acceptance of risk by all the subjects involved (wage or income flexibility).[35]

Its defects and limits are less generic and more circumscribed, and call to mind a long-standing debate among economists.

They concern primarily the key role of capital investment, which can include: individual contributions by members to risk capital, individual contributions by members to common capital through appropriation (indivisible property), or the inflow of external capital.[36]

In the first two instances the firm may be defined as a "pure" cooperative, as each member is also a worker in it. The third case is different, because it allows contributions of capital by other subjects, i.e. members who are not employed in the firm.

The problems associated with the first two cases centre on the opportunity to run the cooperative as a profitable venture; those associated with the third case regard its very feasibility, given that outside capital providers are seldom allowed to influence the firm's life by relying only on the criteria that govern cooperative meetings.

Capitalisation is a key issue in all cases and it often confines the cooperative experience to the less capital-intensive sectors and to small-scale firms.

Criticism also focuses on the social implications of cooperation, which is accused of tending to become a closed institution that limits benefits to its membership and is unwilling to admit new members.[37]

Indivisible property – whereby each cooperator is remunerated as a wage-earning worker – was chosen to avoid this danger, but it failed to elicit greater flexibility or commitment. Individual property avoids this problem, although it may enable employee-members to secure most of the net profit, with negative effects especially on self-financing.[38]

The problems mentioned above help to explain why the cooperative has not produced reliable and consistent results. Its profitability and capacity to retain market shares both vary according to the organisational arrangements made and to the presence or absence of favourable external (economic and institutional) conditions.[39] Various adjustments have been studied and proposed to make it less vulnerable than the traditional cooperative. Two such examples are: at the operational level, the Italian 1992 law encouraging the inflow of external capital (from backing members), with the ensuing constraints on reserve funds; and, in its approach, Meade's "differentiation principle", embodying the need to reconcile the cooperative's working continuity and the fair treatment of its actors, which prescribes that when a worker joins a "cooperative company" (*cooperativa per azioni*) he must hold fewer shares than the workers already involved in it, even if he performs the same tasks.[40]

When this direction of the antagonistic model was introduced earlier, we made a distinction between the cooperative firm and the self-managed firm. Part of the literature on the subject seems to ignore this difference; indeed, economic theory has not yet produced an unambiguous definition of either of the two, nor has it clearly outlined the "ideal types" of non-capitalistic firm.[41]

In our view, the lack of distinction is perhaps more understandable when it concerns the "pure" cooperative where all members are employed, because none of the workers feels subordinate to the others – as in self-managed firms.

Diversified features do exist, however, which are also quite important in practical terms.

At "heart" of a cooperative is the replacement of ownership, while at the "heart" of self-management is its type of organisation and management of production processes. This feature is also shared by cooperative firms, but does not appear – at least in principle – as prominently as in the experience of self-managed firms.

The separation between the actors responsible for business management and those responsible for policy and results control – resolved in cooperatives through a mandate delivered by the meeting to administrators and directors, and favoured by the benefits available to worker-members as owners of the firm – is a point that seems more complex and usually less often respected in self-managed firms, which allow less room for delegation and require the constant, direct involvement of workers as a whole.

Self-managed firms appear inherently more vulnerable than cooperative firms – even considering "pure" cooperatives, which are more similar – because they lack the provision of capital from members, which is highly significant in structural terms and capable of strengthening the ties between firms and their worker-members.

The considerable fragility of self-management is due also to its ideal features. If implemented adequately, self-management constitutes the sharpest alternative to the capitalistic firm. It represents the most radical instance of extension of the political democracy method to production relations, with its ensuing difficulties (e.g. applying the majority principle). It embodies the workers' direct interest and involvement in the firm's decisions and thus in managerial functions. Hence workers acquire a managerial role, and external capital providers are remunerated without any responsibility or involvement in the firm. A split is observed between the firm's conduction and these providers that not only badly hinders the raising of capital but results also in excessive risks for those required to provide it and, ultimately, for the workers themselves.

The perspective of self-management appears therefore to be highly controversial in theory and laborious in practice. It has often exerted a strong attraction over certain sections of the European labour and trade union movement, releasing high amounts of hope and expectation, ranging from utopian schemes (a network of self-managed firms extended to the whole of society) to intervention in single firms troubled by financial and employment problems.

The idea of self-management has a long history. Authors spanning from Proudhon to Bakunin, from Fourier to Blanc and Owen, have reasserted and theorised the belief that workers' alienation and class domination can be overcome primarily by increasing their control on working conditions.[42] The self-management perspective is still producing literature where it appears as the key to the full realisation of democratic principles in business management[43] and as a means for achieving an economic set-up more de-

52

sirable for man and society but also more efficient – in many cases – from a strictly economic and technological viewpoint.[44]

In advanced capitalist countries, self-management acquired these connotations only in a few emblematic cases, and has remained altogether a rather limited and often short-lived experience.

The main impediments, outlined earlier in the paragraph, were reduced in practice by the fact that self-managed firms are normally associated with social ownership, as they belong to an entire community or to the state; they submit to regulations governing the state sector or are supported by public money. Unlike other participatory forms, in fact, self-management has also developed in non-capitalist countries [45] (such as Yugoslavia, where the public economic system decentralised the regulation of production at the firm level) or in countries with collectivist-oriented economic and social institutions, like the kibbutzim in Israel.

In capitalist countries, support provided by state legislation and contributions may be decisive to experiences often originated by business crises or by the lack of productive ventures in scarcely industrialised environments.[46] Such experiences usually involve smaller, less capital-intensive firms marked by a common sense of insecurity.

Several exceptions are observed, starting from the famous case of Mondragon in Spain. This, however, cannot be simply classified as self-management because it includes a coordinated pool of manufacturing and service companies (e.g. a bank and several educational institutions) as well as firms resembling (producers' and consumers') cooperatives.[47]

Our doubts about the self-management perspective in capitalist society – especially today – do not imply disregard of its significance nor of its potential for implementation, which can left to political reasons and criteria with prevalently social aims. By relying on economic criteria alone, self-management is highly unlikely to appear as an organisation or, above all, as a firm acting in the marketplace. On the other hand, if social or public ownership became a precondition for implementing the self-management perspective, we would lose one the essential features of participatory economic democracy, that is the lack of a direct or decisive role for the public actor.

Apart from the traditions and politico-social reasons mentioned above, good opportunities are open today for firms established *ex novo* and run by those who work in them. The firms involved usually belong to the service industry (not only the high value-added), are small sized, involve lower starting-up costs than manufacturing firms, are highly adaptable to changing demand. The phenomenon is certainly interesting, but will not be discussed here.

The division between cooperative firms and self-managed firms does not occur in Robert Dahl's authoritative works, which at present propound the extension of political democracy to production relations.

Dahl[48] begins by observing that the notion of democracy has not secured the democratisation process a sweeping victory, given the persistence of bitter inequalities (especially with reference to the United States) in citizens' access to political participation.

Among the chief causes of this unsatisfactory condition are the economic differences due to fact that firm ownership and control produce inequality in income, property and social status, and that their management is hardly democratic both formally and in practice.[49]

He then analyses the possibility of an alternative economic structure capable of strengthening political democracy and equality by reducing inequalities due in particular to the capitalism of large corporations.

The alternative involves the establishment of collectively owned firms governed democratically by all the subjects employed therein, namely of self-governed firms – termed cooperatives, self-managed firms, etc. – characterised chiefly by their compliance with the criterion of equal voting rights (one man one vote).

Reasons underlying this choice are, among others, the following: the economic order should not only be seen as a means for producing goods and services but also for producing a wide range of values, first of all the democratic values; this stems from the view that the economic order is an instrument at the service of consumers, workers and citizens, and that men are not mere producers or consumers of goods and services, as claimed by economic theory; for employees in particular, as for most human beings, work is a basic component of life (it takes up more time than any other activity and deeply affects income, consumption, family life, friendships, leisure).

A system of self-governed firms does not ensure generalised equality, but nevertheless it may favour a fairer regulation and redistribution of resources, reduce antagonistic relations also within society and in politics, and raise the level of consensus in production units.

Among the objections to his proposal, the author focuses on the remark that the average citizen is not adequately trained to run a firm, so that responsibility is inevitably taken up by a minority.

Dahl replies with arguments like the following: even in a capitalist company sovereignty officially belongs to the shareholders but actual decisions are controlled by the managers; in a large self-governed firm, the workers may well delegate most of their authority to an elected council, which will be responsible for selecting and replacing managers; democratically governed firms need not function better than others. Even if they function like the others they are superior for their additional democratic qualities.

This process cannot be secured by trade union protection alone, which does not offer workers democratic control of the firm, even if the unions are admittedly indispensable for reducing the instances of authoritarian management.

Dahl admits that the self-governed firm faces an uphill journey and he stresses that the numerous failures experienced so far could be avoided by an adequate system of internal and external support. As for the external support, he mentions suitable sources of credit, broad training schemes, plans to aid the launch of new products and set up new firms – as observed in the case of Mondragon.

The internal reasons for success are found especially in smaller firms, which for many years have formed a reserve of innovation and employment; they include greater loyalty, wealth and productivity for workers (is in the Japanese model) and the opportunity for workers to take over firms in trouble, although the proposal cannot unfold its entire potential in this area alone.

Robert Dahl's contribution is vindicated by its highly ideal attempt to re-state the extent and implications of political and economic inequalities, but the remedies he suggests appear scarcely convincing or realistic.

The alternative firm governed by democratic criteria deserves a few critical remarks. Dahl does not adequately confront the crucial point of its functioning in economic terms. Its "superiority" as a source of wider democratisation processes may appear artificial if it lacks constant consideration of efficiency requirements. The self-governed firm can be qualitatively different from other firms and remain so, provided it manages to achieve the same economic results.

In his search for an optimal form of firm, Dahl neglects or underestimates the historical significance and practical outcome of other options that do not require difficult institutional arrangements. The progress of industrial democracy in Europe and the high level of employment regulation reached by North American trade unions before the 1970s, both provide a clear example of this. At the same time, he overestimated the political effects of altered social relations within firms, especially those of smaller dimensions.

Like other advocates of the self-managed or self-governed firm, Dahl emphasises the advantages due to the high level of consensus achieved, to the loyalty and involvement of all internal actors, and to the sharp decrease in the sources of conflict.

These claims rest on a solid foundation. Yet the advantages – which are also attributed to other participatory forms (Chapter 6) – do not simply imply fewer problems for the firm's management: a close link between the intensity of participation and declining conflict is inconceivable; the chances and opportunities for conflict do not dissolve when the institutional basis of subordinate labour is altered. Such chances and opportunities regard major aspects, such as the relationship between individual and collective interests, and between wage policies inspired by equality rather than incentives. There is another more sensitive point, i.e. career development, which creates great tension in firms wherever workers are "in charge". It cannot be simply resolved by including the task among those assigned to top management, because this consists of people delegated by those whose behaviour they should measure and appraise and because the latter demand more openness and rewards than is normally required or accepted in other firms. This problem is a real source of contention and resentment, even in cooperatives, which can cause delays and functional complications in decision-making.

Notes

1   Cf. A. Marsh, *Concise Encyclopedia of Industrial Relations*, Gower Press: Portsmouth 1979, p. 347.

2   The information on De Leon and the following authors is taken from G. Baglioni and B. Manghi, *Il problema del lavoro operaio. Teorie del conflitto industriale e dell'esperienza sindacale*, Angeli: Milan 1967, Chapter 3.

3   In W. Abendroth, *Aufstieg und Kreise der deutschen Sozialdemokratie*, Pahl-Rugenstein Verlag: Cologne 1974, 3rd ed. On socialdemocratic strategy and the more radical left-wing thinkers, see G. Vardaro, 'Il diritto del lavoro nel laboratorio Weimar', in F. Fraenkel et al., *Laboratorio Weimar. Conflitti e diritto del lavoro nella Germania prenazista*, Edizioni Lavoro: Rome 1982.

4   Cf. G.E. Rusconi, 'La socialdemocrazia tedesca oggi', *Prospettiva sindacale*, No. 36, 1980; and H.J. Sperling, 'Il caso della Mitbestimmung', in G. Giugni et al., 'Il potere in fabbrica. Esperienze di democrazia industriale in Europa', *Quaderni di Mondoperaio*, No. 11, 1979.

5   Cf. P. Spriano, *Gramsci e L'Ordine Nuovo*, Editori Riuniti: Rome 1965, pp. 72ff. See also G. Romagnoli, *Contro la legge ferrea. Organizzazione e rappresentanza nel sindacato*, Rosenberg & Sellier: Turin 1992, pp. 71ff.

6   Cf. P. Craveri, *Sindacato e istituzioni nel dopoguerra*, Il Mulino: Bologna 1977, Chapter 2.

7   L. Lanzardo, 'I Consigli di gestione nella strategia della collaborazione', in A. Accornero et al., *Problemi del movimento sindacale in Italia 1943-73*, Feltrinelli: Milan 1976, p. 327.

8   C.L. Goodrich, *Le frontiere del controllo. Uno studio sulla politica di fabbrica*, edited by G. Della Rocca, Edizioni Lavoro: Rome 1984, Chapter 19.

9   Cf. A. Accornero, *Il lavoro come ideologia*, Il Mulino: Bologna 1980.

10   S. Perlman, *A Theory of the Labor Movement* (1928), Macmillan: New York 1949.

11   C. Crouch and A. Pizzorno (eds), *Conflitti in Europa. Lotte di classe, sindacati e stato dopo il '68*, Etas Libri: Milan 1977; and A. Accornero, *La parabola del sindacato. Ascesa e declino di una cultura*, Il Mulino: Bologna 1992.

12   Cf. M. Regini and C. Sabel (eds), *Strategie di riaggiustamento industriale*, Il Mulino: Bologna 1989.

13 Cf. A. Accornero, *La parabola del sindacato*, op. cit., Chapter 7.

14 Cf. A. Touraine et al., *Le mouvement ouvrier*, Arthème Fayard: Paris 1984.

15 According to P. Santi, 'Economia della partecipazione e relazioni industriali', *Giornale di diritto del lavoro e di relazioni industriali*, No. 43, 1989, p. 445.

16 Cf. S. Lugaresi, 'Democrazia economica e risorse di potere', in M. Carrieri et al., *Il progetto di "Democrazia economica"*, CESPE Papers: Rome, No. 3, 1991.

17 R. Meidner, *Employee Investment Funds. An Approach to Collective Capital Formation*, Allen & Unwin: London 1978.

18 A. Martin, 'La contrattazione in Svezia: politica dei redditi e coesione organizzativa', *Stato e Mercato*, No. 2, 1981.

19 Cf. B. Gustafsson, 'L'esperienza svedese della cogestione e dei fondi dei lavoratori', in A. Baldassarre (ed.), *I limiti della democrazia*, Laterza: Bari 1985, pp. 133ff.

20 Cf. R.B. Peterson, 'Swedish Collective Bargaining. A Changing Scene', *British Journal of Industrial Relations*, No. 1, 1987.

21 W. Korpi, *The Working Class in Welfare Capitalism. Work Unions and Politics in Sweden*, Routledge & Kegan Paul: London 1978, Chapter 1.

22 R. Meidner, *Employee Investment Funds. An Approach to Collective Capital Formation*, op. cit., Chapter 9.

23 S. Finardi, 'Fondi dei salariati e comando sullo sviluppo: il caso svedese', *Laboratorio Politico*, No. 3, 1981.

24 B. Amoroso, *Rapporto dalla Scandinavia*, Laterza: Bari 1980.

25 B. Gustafsson, *L'esperienza svedese della cogestione e dei fondi dei lavoratori*, op. cit., p. 112.

26 M. Carrieri, *Non solo produttori. Percorsi di democrazia economica*, Angeli: Milan 1992, Chapter 2.

27 D.R. Cameron, 'Spesa pubblica, sviluppo e inflazione: una analisi comparata', *Stato e Mercato*, No. 4, 1982.

28 R. Meidner, *Employee Investment Funds. An Approach to Collective Capital Formation*, op. cit., Chapter 9.

29 Cf. G. Baglioni et al., *Zero cinquanta. Pro e contro il fondo di solidarietà*, Edizioni Lavoro: Rome 1981.

30 See, among others, the compilation 'Afferrare Prometeo. Per misurarsi col capitalismo', *La rivista trimestrale*, No. 62-63, 1980.

31 Cf. B. Jossa, 'Teoria economica e cooperative di produzione', in B. Jossa (ed.), *Autogestione, cooperazione e partecipazione agli utili*, Il Mulino: Bologna 1988, Chapter 3.

32 Cf. E. Lama, 'Cooperazione', in *Enciclopedia Italiana*, Vol. 11, Milan-Rome, 1931.

33 Cf. G. Geroldi and S. Caselli, 'L'economia partecipativa. Idee e pro-

blemi per lo sviluppo di una nuova impresa', *Prospettiva sindacale*, No. 82, 1991.

34   On this point, refer to G. Baglioni, *Osservazioni sui caratteri e sul funzionamento del modello cooperativistico e della Banca Popolare di Milano*, 1992 (typescript).

35   M. Nuti, 'Democrazia economica: mercato, politica e partecipazione', in M. Carrieri et al., *Il progetto "Democrazia Economica"*, CESPE Papers: Rome, No. 3, 1991.

36   G. Seravalli, *Cooperazione e autogestione nel settore industriale*, La Nuova Italia: Rome 1988.

37   Cf. E. Morley-Fletcher, 'Presentazione' to the Italian edition (Feltrinelli: Milan 1989) of J.E. Meade, *Agathotopia. The Economics of Partnership*, Aberdeen University Press: Aberdeen 1989.

38   Cf. L. Zan, *L'economia dell'impresa cooperativa*, UTET: Turin 1990.

39   Cf. G. Seravalli, *Il cervo e la lepre. Una ricerca sul «sistema» delle imprese cooperative*, Angeli: Milan 1991, Chapter 1, pp. 40ff.

40   J.E. Meade, *Agathotopia. The Economics of Partnership*, op. cit.

41   B. Jossa, *Teoria economica e cooperative di produzione*, op. cit., p. 77.

42   L. Gallino, *Dizionario di sociologia*, UTET: Turin 1978, pp. 51-2.

43   See, for example, P. Rosanvallon, 'Autogestione, democrazia industriale e democrazia parlamentare', in G. Giugni et al., *Il potere in fabbrica. Esperienze di democrazia industriale in Europa*, op. cit.

44   J. Vanek, *Imprese senza padrone nelle economie di mercato*, edited by B. Giuliani, Edizioni Lavoro: Rome 1985.

45   Cf. ILO, *Workers' Participation in Decisions within Undertakings*, Geneva 1981, Chapter 5.

46   Cf. M. Baglioni et al., *Oggi l'autogestione. Forme ed esperienze di cooperazione industriale in Italia*, Edizioni Lavoro: Rome 1980.

47   Refer, among others, to A. Gutiérrez Johnson and W. Foot White, 'The Mondragon System of Workers' Production Cooperatives', *Industrial and Labor Relations Review*, October 1977; and H. Thomas and C. Logan, *"Mondragon": An Economic Analysis*, Allen & Unwin: London 1982.

48   R.A. Dahl, *A Preface to Economic Democracy*, University of California Press: Berkeley 1985.

49   R.A. Dahl, *Democracy and its Critics*, Yale University Press: New Haven 1989.

3 The directions of collaborative participation

1 The rationale of the collaborative model

Collaborative participation comprises proposals and experiences that allow for an improvement of workers' socioeconomic standing, thus redressing the asymmetry inherent in the employment relationship, without altering the institutional set-up of capitalism or the corporate nature of the firm.

The essential requirements of this model are as follows: a consideration of matters and problems that can be approached and managed according to interests that the sides involved regard as common and conductive to mutual benefits; full recognition of workers' collective needs and of their representatives' role by the counterpart or by other actors, starting from the State; a parallel recognition by workers and their organisations of the formal and concrete legitimation of the actors with whom they interact; combined initiatives in favour of workers' interests and dignity and of the needs and aims of such actors, by means of exchange; an acceptance of responsibility and respect by workers' representatives for an efficient running of the economic system and/or firm.

When these requirements are met, conflict is unlikely to become an endemic factor in employment relations: at least in theory, collaborative participation and conflict cannot remain unrelated facts, as the former cannot avoid affecting the latter.

In practice, relations between the two are less clear cut, because not every aspect of their relationship is in the realm of participation, because opposition and friction often develop during the selection and implementation of participatory institutes and commitments, and finally because of the contribution by more general factors (such as the political situation) which may influence alternatively the actors' participatory or conflictful tendencies.

All this explains the considerable difficulties encountered by collaborative participatory forms and at times their provisional nature, especially for forms that place higher demands on the sides involved. At any rate, hindered progress can hardly hide an important fact: in the decades following the Second World War, this participatory model produced considerable results and still holds a remarkable potential, it embraces numerous themes and applications not due to the strength of each side, and finally it constitutes a "workshop" where specific interests can agree with broader objectives.

The intentions and realisations of this model have greatly contributed to render obsolete the more clearly antagonistic perspective: unlike the rationale of opposition, their rationale has sought to reconcile workers' interests with their counterparts', in view of mutual benefits. The realisations are due mainly to the initiatives of organised labour and to its expressions aiming to improve the employment relationship and workers' conditions without demanding any radical change and usually turning to the conflict resource with caution.

In this model, workers are explicitly represented by trade unions or by elected bodies generally influenced by them. The emphasis on the role of trade union representation may seem unnecessary, but it is not. It is not always present in antagonistic forms (when these provide for representation and objectives expected to overcome the shortcomings of trade union protection) and is by no means automatic – as we shall see – in the rationale of integrative participation.

The State has also played an important part in promoting this model; its role is evident in legal provisions establishing institutions suited to collaborative practices, supported by resources capable of fostering such practices. State action – which varies across the spectrum of collaborative forms – does not conflict with the traits we observed in economic democracy, as it does not curtail the fundamental role of social groups and their representatives.

It is less easy to define intentions and behaviour on the employer's side. Never or hardly ever does this act on its own initiative, at first. Its degree of acceptance of collaborative participation is by no means uniform and – leaving aside the differences between various nations – it tends to be lower when a form involves the firm directly than when it allows for applications outside the productive environment. Employers have shown more interest, though intermittently, in such forms; they are still suspicious, however, of any form that will affect the firm, and at times exert an outright opposition attempting to restrict the extent of participatory commitments.

A brief overview is needed to explain why such positions are taken.

The entrepreneurial world, even when its is not alien to collaborative institutes and practices, only accepts those that entail moderate costs and, above all, few constraints on its prerogatives.

Entrepreneurs have often claimed (sometimes not without reason) that collaborative proposals and provisions do not ensure concrete mutual benefits and that the consequent exchange processes are unbalanced to the benefit of workers and their representatives.

The entrepreneurial world has repeatedly voiced its suspicion and opposition, especially in the initial stage. Once the measures are taken, however, it is able to adapt and to limit effectively their dreaded consequences. This has happened, for example, in the important case of German codetermination.

Entrepreneurs have often accepted such measures thanks to the decisive contribution of factors beyond the mere estimate of advantage: e.g. political conditions, pro-labour political parties and strong trade unions. Under such conditions, collaborative participation represented before the 1970s only a second-best solution for employers.

Collaborative participation notably developed in the countries of north-central Europe, with contrasting or later examples also in other countries such as Britain and Italy.

Such cases were plentiful and hardly coherent and developed in the following directions (to which this chapter and the next are devoted):

a   participation realised by concertation practices and agreements;
b   participation in consultation, control or management by workers' representatives in public institutions;
c   financial participation by means of supplementary benefits;
d   participation in the firm's decisions by forms of industrial democracy.

2 Concertation practices and agreements

Concertation may be defined as participation by large organisations of interests in economic and social policy decisions, through collaboration practices and agreements with the State, whereby mutual concessions and constraints of various nature are exchanged in different ways.[1]

The venue of concertation practices and agreements is macroeconomic and political, although experiences have also been tried in smaller contexts. The nature of concertation is eminently political, with implications and effects on industrial relations due chiefly to the constraints placed on social partners. Indeed, the long-term key factor are income policies, approached with various devices.[2]

The objectives set by actors are partly due to the specific features of each country, right from the start of such agreements. However, they may be presented overall as an attempt to reconcile the need for economic support and stability (which involves competitiveness, employment, inflation, revenue and public expenditure) with distributive processes, especially those due to claim-oriented and protective initiatives taken by the unions.[3]

For the trade unions, commitments based on the concertation rationale are offset by resources provided by the State and by the recognition that they represent the world of employment. Other conditions in favour of concertation are: the existence of pro-labour governments, the centralising or coordinating skills of social partners' organisations, the legalisation of commitments taken by the actors involved, the collaborative tradition and tendency of organised labour.

This combination of conditions has permitted the most stable experiences to develop, as in Sweden. Whenever one of such conditions was missing, the experiences have been less stable and more vulnerable[4] but, on the other hand, they have reached environments once alien to the collaborative rationale (such as Italy, for instance) as a consequence of economic difficulties and changing economic prospects.

Concertation first acquired a certain prominence during the period of constant economic growth following the Second World War. It became dominant in the 1970s, as growth slowed down and recession set in. In the 1980s, concertation declined sharply. It became harder and more complex in countries with a long-lasting collaborative tradition, owing to the changing orientation of the actors involved (especially entrepreneurs) and to the scarce resources that governments could provide.

Now that the typical phase of concerted agreements is over, the remaining concertation is due to objective needs and a sense of responsibility by the parties involved rather than mere convenience (at least in the short term). Possible landmarks in this field are the Italian "Protocol on income policy" (July 1992), followed by the July 1993 agreement (extended to contractual arrangements and employment policies), the Swedish solidarity agreement (September 1992), the trade unions pay restraint and the social deal proposed by the German government (accepted in March 1993).

The rationale of concertation spread after the Second World War in environments upholding the spirit and instruments of pluralism, but reached well beyond the sphere and confines of pluralistic schemata. In industrial relations, pluralism constitutes a tested means for regulating interests and results by repeated negotial-bargaining practices, with no yardstick to measure interest priorities in view of common goals.

Concertation, on the other hand, tends to merge functions and to restrict the effects of such procedures, channelling the interests at stake in industrial relations into objectives shared by the sides and above all into wider economic and political objectives supported as such by the public actor.

This transition is normally defined as "neo-corporatism",[5] with reference to explicit formal agreements between the State and the actors in industrial relations, whereby the State engages the actors in its decision-making processes, while the latter are granted concessions and have to accept specific constraints.

Pluralism and neo-corporatism can be viewed as alternative ways of regulating interests by socials partners only on the plane of conceptual construction. Both orientations exemplify extreme attempts to define reality, where concrete experiences take place. There are no historical instances of pure pluralism or neo-corporatism. Experiences can only be interpreted according to the prevalence of the former rather than the latter, with reference to the changing nature of their main traits.

However, certain basic differences remain between the two models of regulation. Neo-corporatism is not simply a variant of pluralism. The presence of large interest organisations in the institutional-political arena reflects a widespread condition (less common today than in the past), but the practices ascribable to neo-corporatist arrangements mark qualitatively different types of presence.[6]

The non-alternative nature of pluralism and neo-corporatism and the existence of concrete instances characterised by a variable mixture of their requirements, are the two factors behind our choice of the term "concertation" to indicate those agreements and practices that extend beyond the domain of pluralistic schemata.

These two factors also explain why it is not easy to pinpoint, within the confines of concertation, clearly distinct participatory forms, as with other participatory models or directions. The means of concertation can be compared to a territory in which all differences resemble variants of a single rationale for regulating interests.

In this light a brief mention is needed of the experience of concertation prior to the 1970s and of its implementation in the same decade.

We have observed two variants in this experience, namely pluralistic political exchange and neo-corporatist political exchange.[7]

The first variant is characterised by: a relative separation between trade union action in industrial relations and its political implications, with no direct involvement of trade unions in the politico-institutional arena and with little intervention by the State in such relations; preferential relations of trade unions with a "friendly" political party to which the political functions are delegated, and (vaguely institutionalised) bilateral relations with pro-labour governments; the provision on the State's part of long-term commitments and resources (development, welfare, full employment), provided the trade unions do not exert their full bargaining power and accept an income policy (with coordinated claims).

The second variant is characterised by: the increasingly politicised interests of large organised groups and the decreasing independence of industrial relations, offset by a direct presence of trade unions in the politico-institutional sphere; cooperation between the State (not necessarily in the form of pro-labour governments) and workers' and employers' representatives, established by trilateral relations according to variably formalised procedures; acceptance by the State to negotiate economic policy decisions with the above representatives, in exchange for their agreement to reach and accept an income policy (by centralised claims management) on wider objectives.

Instances ascribable to the pluralistic exchange variant are prominent, though scarcely uniform: most notable is the Swedish experience, starting in the late 1930s, which forms the "Scandinavian model"[8] alongside Denmark and Norway; the German experience of "concerted action" arose from the great 1967 coalition and the socialdemocratic governments from 1969 onwards; the English experience extended from the Second World War to the mid 1960s. All these instances of pluralistic exchange covered a period of constant economic growth, Keynesian policies and successful reformist political parties in office.[9]

The whole range of neo-corporatist exchange is even wider and can be related to three situations.

The first situation defines many European countries at the end of the Second World War, when organised social groups reached a strict agreement on the need for economic reconstruction and reconversion. This was partly a prelude to later neo-corporatist arrangements; it lacked prominent features such as the concession of decision-making power by the State to large interest organisations; it rested on exceptional transitory conditions prior to the political balance that followed. Examples of this are France and Italy, which rapidly reached a high degree of political polarisation.

The second situation refers to Austria – typified by extensive, stable institutions for concertation – Holland and to a lesser degree Belgium. It involves factors far removed from the interests of large organised groups, factors concerning cultural and social divisions and tensions, mostly ethnic and linguistic, but also religious allegiance. Compared to the need for consensus and convergence, which may be threatened by such divisions, monetary and professional interests are to a certain degree incorporated by the aim to preserve national identity.

This aim was attained mainly by coalition governments (between reformist and denominational parties), stable concerted compensation and income policies, and a rapidly expanding welfare system.

The third situation refers mostly to the 1970s and later. This period clearly witnessed a stronger demand for concerted management of interests represented by social partners, which became more complex and difficult to approach, even in environments ascribable to the second situation.

The third situation includes the evolution of countries where pluralistic political exchange prevails (Germany and Sweden), the end of concertation in one of these (Britain) and the atypical introduction to a traditionally alien country (Italy).

In Germany, alongside pluralist practices, neo-corporatist oriented institutes appeared even earlier (e.g. the important role of the State and the law in industrial relations) and were not substantially altered under Mr Kohl's government.[10] In the mid 1970s, a number of problems developed in codetermination (Chapter 4) and especially in economic policy decisions, leading to high tension in the coalitions between the SPD and the Liberal Party, Government and trade unions, the SPD-DGB block and new environmental and pacifist groups.

In Sweden the "Scandinavian model" entered a period of decline, due to excessive public expenditure and to a deteriorating economic structure. Certain innovations (such as provisions on codetermination) seemed to move in the neo-corporatist direction. At the same time, however, social partners redefined their stance on the traditional compromise with the State, as in the case of workers' investment funds (Chapter 2).

Even Italy experienced concertation, despite the fact that before the 1970s it displayed none of the essential requirements (listed at the start of this paragraph). Italy stepped almost directly from pluralist to neo-corporatist practices, with no real phase of pluralist political exchange.

Owing to these two factors, the Italian experience of concertation was marked by strong trade union and political tension, great instability, implicit rather than explicit convergence, and a wide variety of agreements. Such concertation processes were not short-lived, as they depended on urgent economic requirements and above all on the need to curb inflation, and reappeared – as noted above – in the early 1990s.

If we turn back to the European scene, the 1980s were characterised by an overall decline of concertation, by greater difficulties wherever it was relaunched and yet by a widespread tendency to greater public intervention in industrial relations.[11]

This type of situation developed in countries with a traditional neo-corporatist approach, such as Holland and Belgium. In Germany, up to the eve of unification, trade union action in the political market became weaker, while collective bargaining preserved a key role in the regulation of labour conditions (wages and working hours) and trade unions reduced centralisation. Sweden preserved its concertation practices and institutions and on several occasions the government suggested compensatory measures (especially tax relief) to curb wage rises. A series of social agreements was reached also in Spain, with varying results and degrees of trade union support; these have no doubt contributed to strengthen representative democracy and to legitimise the requirements of an expanding capitalist economy, but exposed the weakness inherent in society confronted with the pervasive role of the State. In France, interestingly, neither the socialist majority nor its president introduced concertation processes: after the first two years, economic policy and measures in favour of workers and their representatives were normally set and implemented without allowing the unions to play a leading role.

Neo-corporatist experiences in the 1970s arose after a period of industrial relations generally favourable to labour, after the struggle of 1968-73. These did not undermine the development of industrial relations – even if they occurred in a period of critical economic conditions and new structural problems [12] – but only involved the reduction of labour costs, leaving out other significant aspects of industrial relations. Generally speaking, they achieved greater union rights, employment regulation and forms of industrial democracy.

The situation changed rapidly in the 1980s, when actors changed their behaviour and attitude, as a result of more competitive economic settings, urgent constraints on public budgets and the need to preserve market shares for domestic production.[13]

Governments (apart from anti-union policies in Britain and the United States) aimed to regain authority rather than share it with their social partners. Employers often considered too burdensome the commitments arising from such practices and demanded flexibility above all.

Trade unions experienced a severe loss of quality in their power and "statutes", due to lower representation and problems with its management. Moreover, they had to cope with the effects of higher unemployment, a more varied workforce and range of employment relations, and the challenge of technological and organisational innovations in firms.

Unlike the previous decades, every aspect of industrial relations was involved. A uniform regulation of employment relations became less feasible or justified (due to the range of subjects needing protection). In-plant relations became more important and widespread, with the presence of managerial strategies hostile to or in competition with the unions; these found it much harder to secure new gains, especially if they relied on their organisational strength. Much of their action appears in fact defensive, except for the issue of working hours which was reintroduced in order to preserve employment.

In the development of concertation, from its first appearance to the latest experiences, the benefits attainable by have labour undoubtedly tended to decrease, although it has been presented and implemented mostly in settings with strong (or stronger) trade unions and consequently a focus on labour needs (as well as the economy) in the political arena.

These facts call for a brief mention of two special aspects of concertation in literature, namely the motives of the actors involved and the relative stability of concertation experiences.

As for the first aspect, the emphasis is placed either on the actors' convenience (i.e. the costs-benefits ratio) or on necessity (i.e. the economic conditions that induce the activation of concertation practices).[14] The difference between the two raises two points: the emphasis on convenience tends to represent actors who accept concertation practices for their benefits or reject them when a cheaper alternative is available; the emphasis on necessity tends to represent actors who negotiate the best conditions by such practices, knowing there is no better alternative.

This dualism between convenience and necessity is applied primarily to the trade union actor, who can be strongly affected by another element, owing to its strategic approach: that is whether necessity is more or less consistent with the rationale and commitments of concertation.

The respective weight of convenience and necessity also depends on the concertation variable; clearly, with pluralistic exchange the opportunities of meeting actors' demands and needs are much higher than with neo-corporatist exchange. But concertation is such especially when it succeeds in combining the specific needs of interest organisations with broader interests and aims – in particular when the economic situation is unfavourable. In such cases it is possible to assess the collaborative attitude of social partners and their ability to overcome strategic resistance or personal convenience (often presumed rather than real, and always short-term).

The second aspect concerns the degree of stability. Many observers remark that, with the exception of contexts that meet all the essential requirements (listed above), concertation practices tend to be unstable, provisional and high-tension.

This view seeks to demonstrate that such practices are feasible only in suitable periods and places, and cannot therefore function in less adequate periods times and places. However, if concertation is viewed as a political means of collaborative regulation of the economy and distributive processes (required especially under unfavourable objective conditions), then instability becomes a "consubstantial" aspect. Concertation is by its very nature highly likely to arise from variably successful attempts, and frequently renegotiated agreements with no long-term solutions.

To a certain degree, it bends the actors' natural functions; it engages the public actor, who in a way interacts on a par with other actors despite its far higher political and institutional legitimacy; it involves measures in the sphere of industrial relations and yet directly and explicitly connected to economic policy; it normally originates from economic conditions but these often vary rapidly, especially as regards the domestic effects of international events; at times it is activated by a low degree of formalisation and legal support.

These instances of concertation practices – indicative of their inherent complexity – enable us to raise two questions: their position in the realm of participatory economic democracy and their relation to political democracy. The two questions are hardly identical and yet reveal significant connections.

The first question can be addressed by placing concertation next to the features attributed earlier to participatory economic democracy (Chapter 1). In comparison, concertation exhibits several unique traits: it does not simply issue from initiatives by social groups and their organisations, because the public actor's contribution is essential; it unfolds in processes for the allocation of resources based on compulsory measures, even if such measures are taken agreed with social partners; unlike other participatory forms, it extends to the whole of society and entails consequences for subjects and groups not involved in concertation agreements; finally, it takes place at the national level and regards the firm level only in the course of implementation (chiefly as a result of income policies).

The second question can be addressed in the same manner and is more significant as it concerns the quality and extent of economic democracy arising from concertation.

This allows a high degree of solidarity in employment and escapes the restrictions of almost all other participatory forms which, although positive and significant in terms of objectives pursued, exhibit a limited degree of solidarity.

Concertation supports actors representing interest groups before the proper institutional actor charged with economic policy. Economic policy measures are often influenced by social groups or by classes of economic operators; in the case of concertation, however, agreements are evident and declared, with greater recognition of employees' and of employers' representatives.

Concertation consists of operations related to the sphere of political decisions; its outcome falls mostly within the domain of economic policy but is characterised by a proportion of supplementary consensus due to the coinciding goodwill of the social partners involved; these, in turn, ensure the attainment of such results.

Concertation has achieved variably successful results as a means for running the economy by agreement and for meeting the needs of social partners. So far, it remains the only truly tested "invention" of participatory economic democracy at the macro level, unlike antagonistic proposals for workers' control over the economy.

The advantages secured by workers and their representatives have not always been substantial, nor have all the agreements been in their favour. In countries with concertation experience, wage levels are not normally any higher than elsewhere, but distributive measures and social services are more advanced.[15] By no mere chance, in fact, concertation practices are altogether accepted less willingly and consistently by employers than by trade unions (among those with collaborative traditions and cultures).

This holds true for the past. What about the future? Can such practices be realistically re-introduced in the near future, after the difficulties of the 1980s and the rare attempts of the early nineties?

As we know, concertation agreements can be activated and function only at certain conditions, which are not easy to predict. It can be claimed, however, that income policies based on inflation control, competitiveness and interest rate action represent a problem at present,[16] especially for countries where trade unions are strong and enjoy political "status".

If concertation agreements are introduced, these will probably be characterised by two facts: they will originate from objective needs (even more so than in the past decade) and, at the same time, they will produce no immediate or short-term benefits for employed workers.

These two aspects should be related both to the difficult challenges imposed by international competition on domestic economies and to the state of the labour market; the latter comprises a vast number of unemployed workers and will retain a "fossilised" proportion of indifference even during economic recovery, as workplace security is gradually eroded in large companies and in areas where employment was traditionally safe (as in Japan).

More than ever, possible concertation measures will not centre on employed workers; or more precisely, the compensative benefits due to income policy constraints will not advantage the employed. Such measures will tend to concentrate on employment policies (which now play a central part even in countries prone to concertation) and any public resources available are likely to be used to limit social costs to the employed or to support the productive system. In this perspective, concertation practices will increase solidarity, meaning more political significance and fairness but also a harder way forward.

The second question concerns the relationship between concertation and political democracy, and in particular its neo-corporatist variant.[17]

More simply, we believe that concertation has good qualities in practice but bad ones in principle: it can be understood and appreciated for its contribution to the economic-social balance, but it hardly provides a basis for the proper functioning of political democracy.

Let us start with some of the bad qualities.

Political democracy evolves in the institutions of representative democracy, where power is retained by the people who can transfer it to subjects or parties delegated to exert it and take the relevant decisions.[18] Concertation introduces other actors, who take part in decision making without being designated or delegated by the electorate.

With concertation, the State surrenders part of its decision-making authority and opts for distributive intervention in favour of specific organised interest groups – however widespread and prominent – without granting equal opportunities to other groups.

The public actor that normally activates and leads concertation processes is the Government, which in so doing takes on (economic and social policy) commitments that extend beyond its institutional counterparts (Parliament and the presidency), and by negotiation with the other actors involved in such processes it pursues and achieves consensus – unlike the trust expressed by such counterparts, which it cannot rely on.

Admittedly, the executive power exerts a degree of independence due to the functional position of authority granted by Parliament.[19] The recognition of such independence, however, depends on the manifestos subscribed by governing political parties (only before their voters and Parliament) and the legitimation of these manifestos should not depend on their acceptance or rejection by other actors.

Concertation agreements contribute to alter the fundamental principle of representative democracy, whereby the majority is responsible for government. By such agreements, government decisions can be extended also to those citizens who have not elected the majority; this is possible and often happens in political-institutional venues (coalition governments, associate arrangements, etc.) but is not the case of concertation; moreover, citizens represented by organised interest groups have two means of voicing their political will and safeguarding such interests, namely the ballot-box and organised groups active in the area of concertation.

These bad qualities tend to expose a considerable degree of incompatibility between concertation and representative political democracy.

If this is true, why was concertation introduced in so many European countries, even those with deep democratic roots? The answers available touch different levels, each connected to the others.

It is probably unnecessary to recall that employees have been widely viewed as the underprivileged side in social relations shaped by the capitalist economy and, as such, deserving protection and capable of expressing their needs and interests collectively. Normally, concertation practices also engage employers' representatives, but at their root is often the intention by the public actor to recognise, albeit within wider aims, the above needs and interests.

These practices were often introduced in view of objectives and needs in the economic and social sphere. In this light, concertation can be regarded as a fair and at times more effective option than its alternatives, such as a prevailing anti-union orientation of the executive and political parties (in Britain and the United States during the 1980s) or unilateral intervention by public authorities in industrial relations (as in Belgium and Denmark in the same period).

In the countries that applied it most widely, concertation was followed by collaborative institutes and experiences in other venues, with local tripartite agreements and forms of institutional participation in the firm (industrial democracy). In general, countries with concertation traditions have shown greater economic stability and higher social cohesion,[20] with wider redistribution processes and a higher amount of public property.

In fact, concertation engages in economic policy the two most important social groups, which alongside concessions in their favour also accept constraints and limits to their action in compliance with common interests (including, in the best cases, those of social groups excluded by concertation processes). This represents a major remedy to source of incompatibility between such processes and the correct functioning of political democracy.

Furthermore, the above constraints and commitments offer a certainty to all economic operators and as regards the position of the domestic economy

70

on the world market because they affect wages and labour costs, which are key indicators of economic trends.

In the end, concertation practices force social partners to surrender part of their bargaining freedom; this avoids to a certain reliance on spontaneous behaviour measured mostly in terms of power, whose consequences can undermine economic policy orientations or lead open conflict.

3 Representation in public institutions

The crucial feature of this participatory direction lies in the presence of employees' representatives in institutions and bodies either public or sponsored by public authorities.

Its aims, which are multiple and often interrelated, may require the contribution of labour to general economic-social policies, the participation of its representatives in the action and legitimation of public structures and institutions, and finally the protection of workers' professional and existential interests and needs.

This direction of participation follows the rationale of the collaborative model as regards the position and roles taken by the actors involved, the function of the State and its representatives, the frequent presence of employers' alongside employees' representatives, and the matters dealt with by the said bodies and institutions. However, it may differ from the other directions in the same model in a relevant aspect, as social partners are not necessarily vehicles of collaborative intentions and awareness. Indeed, the institutional and formal nature of this participation allows social partners to be present in their "official capacity", which is recognised, predictable and therefore not necessarily conductive to precise decisions and revisions or to the acceptance of concrete responsibilities.

The degree of collaborative, responsible awareness varies as a result of many factors and, to a certain extent, according to the way of appointing social partners' representatives, which may be by co-option (on the public actor's initiative), designation (by workers' unions and employers' organisations), or ballot (direct appointment by workers). In theory, awareness should rise from the first to the third of such means, but in practice things can be different.

Among public institutions, participation is very widespread in all European countries and activated far more often than other collaborative directions. It is found in countries (such as Sweden and Germany) with strong trade unions and collaborative traditions, in countries where trade unions have grown since the last war but lack these traditions (such as Italy),[21] and in countries with weak trade unions and with antagonistic elements (such as France).[22]

This participation first appeared at the start of the century and developed rapidly in the following decades, leading to a significant degree of agreement among European countries.[23] Compared with other participatory forms, it is highly stable and scarcely affected by the changes in industrial relations systems and in connections between industrial relations and the politico-institutional sphere. It is sufficient to recall the condition of Britain during the eighties.[24]

This participation appears less problematical than the others, although in recent times it has encountered certain difficulties. In fact the following points need to be considered: it is a means of involving the representatives of organised groups reserved at times not only for workers and their counterpart, because other economic groups (farmers, merchants, etc.).also sit in certain public bodies; it occurs outside the firm and therefore does not touch industrial relations directly nor does it affect the use of entrepreneurial prerogatives; and finally it assigns mainly advisory duties to social partners.

Special attention should be given to two aspects of this participation regarding its extent and levels of application.

The first aspect is the wide range of venues and functions it covers in many countries. The extreme case is probably Italy, where representatives of the trade unions and employers sit in countless bodies within public administration or public law.[25]

The second aspect is the fact that this form of participation acts at different levels. Besides the national level, it is decentralised into local bodies and agencies set up by the central public actor or supported by local authorities. A clear example of this is the Belgian situation after the constitutional reforms of 1970 and 1988.[26]

Both of these aspects indicate that it is by no means easy to distinguish separate forms of participation in public institutions.

Without claiming to have exhausted the whole array of national situations, we believe that most participatory instances can be classed broadly under the three forms defined below.

The first form concerns institutions where workers' representatives, generally alongside those of other social and productive groups, contribute to define the direction of political-social policies against the background of general interests and needs. Such institutions are obviously activated centrally, have primarily advisory powers and are present in countries both with and without a tradition of collaboration and concertation.

Under this form we can list: the National Economic and Labour Council in Italy; the National Council of Workers' Associations and other bodies for economic-social partnership in Austria;[27] the Economic and Social Council and the recent Labour Foundation in Holland;[28] the Central Economic Council and the National Labour Council in Belgium;[29] the Planning Committee and the Economic-social Council in France.[30]

The second form involves public administration institutions or specific public agencies either with executive duties or responsible for proposal or control. Here workers' representatives are called to assist in the good running of such institutions or agencies, to promote dialogue between State authorities and society, and to voice the needs of civil servants (who still suffer restrictions to the negotial-bargaining method in several countries).[31]

This form can appear in two variants whose purpose and practice cannot always be clearly separated.

The first of these includes all situations where representatives bring the workers' "voice" into venues that are alien to their interests and need for protection or are unrelated to the workers they employ.

The other variant includes situations where representation concerns workers employed in the venue of participation and as such acts to protect and value their needs.

This distinction can be noticed by looking at Austria and Italy. The Austrian experience illustrates the first case, with representatives sitting – among others – in the commissions for family policy, land planning, pricing and export policy.[32] The Italian experience covers the first case and also the second, with representatives on the boards of governors of ministries and public authorities such as state railways, among others.[33]

The third form regards the participation of trade union representatives in institutions that in terms of resources managed and aims pursued relate directly to workers' interests and affect their economic, professional and social conditions. This form – which often incudes decision-making implications and management sharing – concerns primarily social security institutions, labour market agencies and vocational training bodies.

It allows both central and peripheral participation, is compatible with bilateral solutions (due to agreements between trade unions and employers) and is widespread in Europe, where it incorporates different traditions and methods with very little uniformity.

It is almost impossible to make a comprehensive assessment of this participatory direction, because of its many expressions, varying environments and different periods of activation.

Certain factors undoubtedly affect its functioning and results. The positive ones that deserve mention are the solidity and efficiency of public administration, the innovative capacity and legitimation of the political system, and the managerial traditions and skills of trade union organisations. Among the negative factors, is the scarce willingness of employers to participate seriously in collaborative bodies and the plurality and competitiveness of such organisations. This brings us back to the Italian experience, which has favoured conditions of false "codecision" at the expense of efficiency in public structures; the weak practical effects of this participatory direction are reported also in the case of Sweden.[34]

At first this direction concerned cases in which the recognition of workers' rights and needs in the political-institutional sphere was limited to specific bodies (generally those active in the labour market). Later, it embraced cases of wider recognition, sometimes without the conditions necessary to the development and successful working of collaborative institutions and practices.

Participation in public institutions over the last few decades has accompanied concerted collaboration, though not always: in fact it lacks the requirements of concertation, and primarily a set of constraints on behaviour accepted by all the social partners involved.

This type of participation remains equally distinct from industrial democracy, especially in the case of codetermination (Chapter 4): its influence on the action of participatory bodies is not subject to efficiency checks or market control and, moreover, workers' representatives have fewer duties and a less direct obligation to answer and be accountable to those whom they represent.

What about the future prospects of this participation? The question may be addressed in the light of the three forms illustrated earlier.

The first form – that is the presence of social partners' representatives in central advisory bodies – will remain significant and viable if some kind of agreement arises at the national and community level between the public actor and social partners as regards the conduction of the economy and the respective implications of competitiveness and the social sphere (above all in terms of employment).

As for the second form – which concerns the presence of such representatives in specific public institutions and bodies – no significant potential can be envisaged in our view. This opinion may be unduly conditioned by the disappointing Italian experience. Nevertheless, various considerations can be brought to bear in this direction. Compared to the first steps in the establishment of bodies included in this form, the present offers far more opportunities to debate and criticise the decisions and functioning of such bodies, and organised labour can make its contribution without the "privilege" of institutional participation; today these bodies require standards and levels of efficiency far higher than ever before, because of the complexity of their duties and the close relationship between the action of public authorities and the progress of economic competitiveness; representation itself has become equally complex as a result of diversification in the labour market and among job descriptions, ruling out any straightforward interpretation of the social and extra-contractual needs of a workforce that is no longer as homogenous as it was at first.

The third form is another matter, as it regards the management of bodies and institutions where workers' resources and economic, social or professional conditions are at stake. Here the labour market, social security and vocational training are of great importance to domestic and Community economic and political relations, while at the same time they significantly affect the conditions and prospects of a high proportion of the working population; both current and expected changes are bound to increase their importance. This sphere is therefore a critical area of collaborative participation outside the firm and a testing ground for the propensity and capacity of organised labour to manage social processes in a responsible way.

4 Financial participation

This direction of collaborative participation is visible above all in the use of supplementary pension funds that integrate compulsory national insurance.

It comprises experiences and institutes that tend to improve the socio-economic conditions of workers: it assists them at the end of their working career; it has strong repercussions, both tangible and non-tangible, in the last stage of their lives; but it requires their commitment and economic contribution in the previous stages.

Without going through all the technical details,[35] the phenomenon of supplementary pension schemes can be approached by focusing on its main aspects, which point to a host of complex and varied backgrounds.

This is evident if we look at the very nature of funds, which are formally a financial instrument and as such cannot be evaluated without reference to the criteria of profitability and efficiency.[36] At the same time, funds are of great social significance because: they involve a variety of actors and subjects seldom equalled by other financial products; they are directly related to national welfare systems but extend also beyond their traditional confines; they affect distributive processes and at the same time can influence mechanisms for the production of wealth.

Notably, the phenomenon originated from the demographic, cultural and occupational changes of recent decades, and in particular: from the imbalance due to a falling proportion of active workers against a large and growing number of elderly people; from changes in the pattern of employment (e.g. the increase in atypical employment relations); and from the recognition that the elderly are active subjects who play a special role in social relations, with growing needs and demands.

These changes have driven the search for diversified additional arrangements in the area of welfare and social security.

In many European countries, in fact, social security systems rest on three "pillars": compulsory national insurance, supplementary pension funds (by firm, profession or sector), and individual insurance.

Such changes have made it increasingly difficult for compulsory national insurance to balance revenue and payments; consequently there has been an upward trend in the "equilibrium rate" that measures the percentage of gross wages of the working population needed to ensure a given average payment to all those entitled to a pension, without running into debt. Because of this trend, the amount levied on wages to balance payments is destined to grow excessively, thus undermining the "cross-generational solidarity pact" that lies at the foundation of national insurance and its functioning.

These problems have certainly contributed to the success and growth of supplementary pensions schemes, which address needs different to state insurance and, at the same time, aim to avoid the risk of investing workers' savings in individual insurance.[37]

A fundamental difference observed between the first and the second "pillar" is that while the former is based on the "distributive" method, the latter relies primarily on "capitalisation" – although the two methods are not always completely distinct. In the first case, regular contributions are not set aside as financial reserves but go to pensioners; in the second case, instead, contributions are treated as financial reserves, to be employed by holders at the end of their working lives.

Another fundamental difference is that between reasons and functions. National insurance aims to guarantee an acceptable safe income to workers until the end of their lives; this income has fluctuated in time and still varies significantly throughout Europe.[38]

With supplementary pensions, income security is expanded to enable retired workers to maintain their standard of living essentially unaltered. This type of scheme extends their economic and social "citizenship" and increases their opportunities in everyday life. By making the most of their savings, it can provide benefits and advantages equal to those usually offered by real estate to other social and professional groups. It is also important to stress that the supplementary pension is a major factor of social stability and cohesion, as it adds a financial dimension to the status of employees by accumulating their savings. Moreover, it can influence the financial markets,[39] is profitably employed by institutional investors and can contribute to the quality of economic growth – especially when the resources available are oriented to the innovation of production and long-term commitments.[40]

At this point, without attempting an exhaustive description of the phenomenon, an outline of certain features is necessary.

Supplementary pension schemes are by nature collective and can be divided into two main forms,[41] with the former prevalent over the latter. The first form involves obligatory funds additional to relatively low national pensions and based on the mixed principle of capitalisation and distribution, as in France and Britain. The second form includes funds based on capitalisation to integrate reasonably high national pensions and is not always compulsory, as in the Danish system and in the recent law decree by the Italian government (April 1993).

76

Funds are financed by both employees and employers, generally in a proportion of one third to two thirds respectively. At any rate, the employee's share is never higher than the employer's and in Germany the most common are "internal funds", which are entered in the firm's balance sheet and explicitly exclude contributions on the worker's part.

With supplementary pension schemes, funding affects the social partners in every country. Yet, the role of the public actor is equally important in terms of supervision and support.

State control is present in all the countries examined, with several differences between bodies in charge and methods employed. It is normally exerted within the legal and institutional framework that regulates the management of savings and financial products, plus special provisions to ensure this is consistent with its social security purposes. For this reason the main share of the portfolio generally consists of state bonds (as in France), with the notable exception of Britain (where shareholdings are the norm) and Germany (where portfolio composition reflects that of the banking and insurance sector).

State support is provided mostly by tax concessions. All observers recognise their key importance to the success of the phenomenon. For the beneficiaries of funds, this means an opportunity to obtain preferential tax conditions for setting aside personal savings.[42]

The means of implementation of state support, connected to its supervising action, are influenced of course by the different national fiscal systems. The prevailing tendency, however, is apparently: to make contributions totally exempt (only for the proportion of income necessary to social security); to allow concessions on income deriving from the use of reserves; and to tax the work performance using the normal rates levied on personal income.

The last important feature is fund management, which regards in particular the agencies and subjects responsible for it.

As for the organisations, the arrangement prevalent in most countries is management by insurance companies.

In some countries, especially Germany, an important part in the management of investment is played by banking companies. The third arrangement, adopted by France, assigns this role to a state insurance institution. Other countries have mixed or option-based systems, as established by the Italian decree mentioned earlier.

A distinction regarding the responsible bodies must be made between funds established and supported by employers and funds financed jointly by employers and employees.

The first case – limited to the German experience where a multitude of company insurance schemes is available – allows for representation of workers on a supervisory board either by the designation of half of its directors or by the election of the whole board of directors by all beneficiaries.

In the second case, equal bilateral representation subject to a public supervisory body is the most common solution. It applies in Belgium, France, Holland and Denmark. Other arrangements, however, are also found: in Britain, for instance, the law does not rule out equal representation, even if it emphasises the professional skills of subjects entitled to manage funds; in Sweden, instead, workers' representatives appointed by trade unions can be the majority.

Supplementary pension schemes are widespread in Europe. They are firmly rooted in several EC countries, such as Germany, Britain, France and Holland, and especially in Sweden.

Other countries (Italy, Spain and Portugal) are now discussing measures and proposals to switch from specific, limited experiences (as in the Italian banking sector) to new regulations in favour of further development.

The range of instances of this participatory direction is very wide, as witnessed by the major aspects highlighted above. This is also demonstrated by important features of the phenomenon in other countries.[43]

In Sweden, under the ATP system, supplementary pension schemes lie between national insurance and security activated by collective bargaining (for single categories of employees) and covers about 90 per cent of the working population. Under the recent approach of the LO[44] trade union confederation, the system is further extended to increase the formation of collective capital and to encourage savings and the diffusion of wealth, with the contribution of different actors (pension funds, the State, municipalities) which require special financial structures to offset an excessive concentration of wealth.

This approach appears on one hand far removed from the antagonistic nature of the Meidner Plan (Chapter 2), while on the other hand it preserves non minor aspects of Swedish reformism, namely: its intention to produce a diffusion of economic power, the prominent role of public savings, the extra-firm nature of pension funds (at national and local level), and the intention to give funds a role in welfare investment (in housing, energy, and the environment).

In Britain supplementary pension funds – which affect 60 per cent of full-time employees and are closely connected to the firm – act as major financial intermediaries since they hold over 30 per cent of the share capital of British companies, and are managed with little trade union control.

The German situation is similar to the British for the considerable importance of supplementary pension schemes and their position in the firm. The specific features are that: firms (medium-sized to large) often promote a range of insurance schemes; these include pension funds, with a preference for direct disbursement, based on the employer's "pledge" to grant employees the agreed conditions; this initiative and others fall under the rationale of industrial democracy typical of the country (in particular as regards supervision by workers' representatives).

In France supplementary pensions have a lower profile, compared with the countries considered above, as they form part of a very diversified system; they have little influence on the action of institutional investors and do not seek to alter the distribution of economic power (quite the opposite of the Swedish situation).

The variety of supplementary pension schemes and their growth potential throughout EC countries are a real problem for current integration processes. Both elements are an impediment to the introduction of Community regulations; these address the need to encourage the free movement of people and in particular (unlike the past) highly qualified subjects and the protection of their respective rights.[45]

Community competence in the area of social security, though very limited at first, was extended under the Maastricht Treaty to cover its complex issues. However, the treaty upholds the principle that in this field Community decisions should be unanimous and not simply by majority vote (as happens instead for other labour law matters). The caution of community authorities is due to the considerable direct incidence of social security on labour costs.

EC regulations are inspired either by the principle of harmonisation or by the principle of recognition. The former is consistent with the socially balanced constitution of a united Europe but requires adequate political decisions by each national system prior to EC decision; the latter, which is already applied in the insurance sector, requires that in supplementary pension schemes the funds authorised by a member state should be free to move to any Community country.

At present EC authorities, in agreement with the public and social partners involved, believe that the conditions are lacking to attempt a harmonisation of the systems in force in different countries, whether state-run or supplementary.

The EC commission has therefore suggested a strategy that aims to reconcile the objectives and policies of social protection. In the case of social security, it is centred on contributive pensions, for which two directives have been drafted: one relates such pensions to the free circulation of workers and the other concerns the functioning of pension funds viewed as financial institutions on the internal market.[46]

The participatory direction referred to here we have termed *financial participation*, in consideration of the instruments employed and of their functioning. This definition should not be interpreted narrowly

In fact supplementary pensions directly concern the improvement of workers' socioeconomic position in relationships and in the opportunities offered by society. Like many other instances of participation, their prevalent plane of activation is the firm; however, it is necessarily limited to this plane (some countries have funds reserved to specific categories of employees) and affects not only the occupational and professional position of workers. Supplementary pension schemes are not directly aimed at correcting the asymmetry inherent in the employment relationship and yet they contribute significantly to alter (for a lifetime) the impact of employees' socio-economic conditions.

In our view, this participatory direction belongs fully to the domain of economic democracy because it seeks to integrate and expand the duties and benefits provided by socio-economic policy and because, among its actors, social partners and their representatives have a prominent position. Equally important is the public actor's role, although it is worth noting that also other directions of the participatory model have been activated with political and/or economic support from the public actor.

Supplementary pension schemes offer remarkable collaborative opportunities, though partly latent:

i   the interests involved form a favourable ground for negotial relations between social partners and representatives;

ii   besides the needs of the workers involved, this form of security also takes into account more general needs (such as contributions to the share of wealth reserved for accumulation and productive development);

iii   though only implicitly, they embody the exchange rationale, as workers directly contribute a share of economic resources which they then use alongside the contributions of others in ventures which involve an element of risk that can be offset by their supervisory rights;

iv   finally, they make workers both beneficiaries and participants in economico-financial institutes which the position of wage-earners had traditionally kept them away from.

Some mention is also due of the arguments in favour of a less reassuring and narrower interpretation.

A significant example at the level of concrete experience is the United States, where the immense resources of private pension schemes have often been used for rash speculations or targeted (in the 1980s) by unscrupulous financial operators.[47] An easy objection is that the nature and traits of supplementary pensions in Europe belong on the whole to a picture well removed from the prevailing North American version.

In principle, the advocates of a narrow interpretation claim that they: do not meet the requirements of participation, foster individual expectations and benefits, eventually favour wealthier workers (those with higher savings), and are not a "political" option (unlike other participatory forms) because they are mostly due to demographic factors and to the problems of national insurance.

These remarks are partly justified or, rather, concern real aspects and risks of the supplementary pension scheme. However, they do not appear sufficient to cancel its qualities.

Participation by employees, also by virtue of the definition proposed at the start of this book, can extend to include the modification or improvement of their socio-economic conditions. In our case, this is fully confirmed. The fact that subjects are not given a direct active role is related to the institutional and operational nature of funds and is never a shortcoming or an exclusive requirement of this participatory direction.

The individual link between this type of security and its users is not necessarily alien to the participatory rationale. The recognition of individual rights can guarantee consensus and solidity to the initiative. Funds, however, have a collective dimension and can be interpreted as an updated and sophisticated type of mutuality. On the other hand, even important collective initiatives by workers – including collective bargaining – have always entailed the problem of balancing the advantages to all those involved with individual benefits. An example of this is the recurring difficulty of choosing between wage policies that are tendentially egalitarian or widely diversified.

The hazards of the supplementary pension scheme seem both avoidable and comfortably manageable. The fact that it ultimately favours greatly the wealthier workers has been countered by balanced fiscal support which limits tax-exemption and preferential rates so as to free only the amount of resources needed to achieve given social security objectives.

As for the criticism that supplementary schemes have no "political" status because they are due to structural factors, it is important to note that even in other cases participatory experiences and paths rest on factors that lie outside the employment relation – as, for example, with concertation practices and agreements. The origin of such experiences did not prevent them from acquiring considerable political and social significance and the same can be true for pension funds.

In response to the narrow interpretation of supplementary pensions, an opposite one can be supplied to emphasise their economic democracy potential – especially as regards their role in orienting the economy and distributing economic power – which is subject to various conditions, such as: a tight link between the first and the second "pillar" in social security systems, the presence of funds outside the firm, and the provision of real means of social and trade union control.

If we carry this interpretation to the plane of concrete experiences, two types of supplementary pensions can be distinguished: a solution with greater economic democracy, observed in the approach of Swedish trade unions, that rely on special investment in the social sphere; and a solution with less economic democracy, as practised in major European countries, where funds are established and managed almost like normal financial institutions.

Admittedly, the two solutions – if implemented consistently – can imply different outcomes, because the criterion of optimal profit can prevail in the latter but not in the former.

The first case requires an explicit acceptance by those involved, while by choosing the second this can normally be taken for granted.

Compatibility between the above solutions cannot be ruled out *a priori*. Yet it appears viable only in certain situations, combined with special favourable conditions. In any other situation, instead, the Continental solution will eventually prevail over the Swedish one.

When and if this happens, there will be no subversion of the supplementary pension scheme. This lies in and pertains to the domain of economic democracy, even if it exerts no visible, specific influence on the directions of economic life. In fact it is important to remember: that these effects are additional to the functions typical of the supplementary pension scheme; that it cannot avoid favouring the convenience and advantages of the groups and subjects concerned; and that it preserves its positive features even without broader political and economic implications or results.

The structural and cultural changes which have greatly assisted in the progress of this phenomenon hardly seem to be contigent: it is therefore easy to predict that it will develop and spread even further in the future.

Notes

1   This definition stems from some of A. Pizzorno's contributions, such as those in C. Crouch and A. Pizzorno (eds), *The Resurgence of Class Conflict in Western Europe since 1968,* Macmillan: London 1978, Vol. 2.

2   Cf. 'Introduzione', in M. Maraffi (ed.), *La società corporativa*, Il Mulino: Bologna 1981.

3   See, among others, G. Baglioni, *La politica sindacale nel capitalismo che cambia,* Laterza: Bari 1986.

4   Cf. G. Lehmbruch, 'Liberal Corporatism and Party Government', *Comparative Political Studies,* Vol. 10, 1977.

5   Cf., for example, P. Schmitter, 'Modalità di mediazione degli interessi e mutamenti sociali in Europa occidentale', *Il Mulino,* No. 248, 1976.

6   Cf. M. Regini, *Uncertain Boundaries,* Cambridge University Press: Cambridge 1995.

7   Refer to 'Costanti e varianti in tema di scambio politico', in G. Baglioni, *La politica sindacale nel capitalismo che cambia,* op. cit., Chapter 3.

8   See, among others, B. Amoroso, *Rapporto dalla Scandinavia,* Laterza: Bari 1980.

9   Cf. W. Streeck, 'Le relazioni industriali nell'Europa che cambia', *Industria e Sindacato*, No. 1-2, 1992.

10   Cf. W. Streeck, 'Industrial Relations in West Germany, 1970-1987', *Labour*, No. 3, 1988.

11   Cf. G. Baglioni and C. Crouch (eds), *European Industrial Relations. The Challenge of Flexibility*, Sage Publications: London 1990, Chapter 1 and elsewhere.

12   Refer to 'Stato, politica economica e relazioni industriali nell'Europa degli anni '80', in G. Baglioni, *La politica sindacale nel capitalismo che cambia*, op. cit., Chapter 5.

13   Cf. T. Treu (ed.), *Participation in Public Policy-Making. The Role of Trade Unions and Employers' Associations*, de Gruyter: Berlin-New York 1992.

14   Convergence is emphasised strongly by M. Regini (*Uncertain Boundaries*, op. cit.), while needs are assigned a prominent role by W. Streeck (*Le relazioni industriali nell'Europa che cambia*, op. cit.) and by the author (in his above-mentioned contributions).

15   Cf. J-H. Lee and A. Przeworski, 'Cui bono? Una stima del benessere nei sistemi corporatisti e in quelli di mercato', *Stato e Mercato*, No. 36, 1992.

16   Cf. R. Dore, 'Incomes Policy: Why Now?', in R. Dore, R. Boyer and Z. Mars (eds), *The Return to Income Policy*, Pinter: London 1994.

17   The question first arose in Germany at the end of the First World War, as explained in G. Vardaro, 'Il diritto del lavoro nel «Laboratorio Weimar»', introduction to F. Fraenkel et al. (eds), *Laboratorio Weimar. Conflitti e diritto del lavoro nella Germania prenazista*, Edizioni Lavoro: Rome 1982. On the position of Austria after the Second World War, see F. Klenner, 'La partnership economico-sociale in Austria', in G. Giugni et al., *Il potere in fabbrica. Esperienze di democrazia industriale in Europa*, Quaderni di Mondoperaio: Rome 1979, No. 11, pp. 98-101.

18   See the latest volume by G. Sartori, *Democrazia. Cosa è*, Rizzoli: Milan 1993, pp. 144-146 and elsewhere.

19   G.E. Rusconi, 'Asimmetria delle rappresentanze e decisioni politiche', *Giornale di diritto del lavoro e di relazioni industriali*, No. 30, 1986.

20   Cf. M. Albert, *Capitalisme contre capitalisme*, Editions du Seuil: Paris 1991.

21   Cf. I. Regalia and M. Regini, 'Sindacati, istituzioni, sistema politico', in G.P. Cella and T.Treu (eds), *Relazioni industriali. Manuale per l'analisi dell'esperienza italiana*, Il Mulino: Bologna 1989, Chapter 11.

22   Cf. G. Caire's study of France in the ongoing research supported by the ILO on concertation and participation.

23   T. Treu, 'L'intervento del sindacato nella politica economica', *Giornale di diritto del lavoro e di relazioni industriali*, No. 17, 1983.

24   C. Crouch, 'United Kingdom. The Rejection of Compromise', in G. Baglioni and C. Crouch (eds), *European Industrial Relations*, op. cit.

25 T. Treu et al., *Sindacalisti nelle istituzioni*, Edizioni lavoro: Rome 1979.

26 Refer to T. Beaupain's contribution on Belgium in the ILO research.

27 Cf. F. Klenner, 'La partnership economico-sociale in Austria', in G. Giugni et al., *Il potere in fabbrica*, op. cit., pp. 79ff.

28 Refer to W. Albeda's contribution on Holland in the ILO research.

29 Refer to T. Beaupain's contribution in the ILO research

30 Refer to G. Caire's contribution in the ILO research.

31 Cf. L. Bordogna, 'Retribuzione e livelli contrattuali nel settore pubblico. Italia, Francia e Germania a confronto', in CNEL (ed.), *Retribuzione, costo del lavoro, livelli di contrattazione*, Rome 1991.

32 Cf. F. Klenner, *La partnership economico-sociale in Austria*, op. cit.

33 Cf. M. Roccella, 'Sindacato e poteri pubblici: il quadro istituzionale', in T. Treu et al., *Sindacalisti nelle istituzioni*, op. cit.

34 See Adlercreutz's study on Sweden in R. Blanpain (ed.), *International Encyclopedia for Labour Law and Industrial Relations*, Kluwer, Deventer, 1982.

35 These features are studied carefully in G. Geroldi and T. Treu's research, *Crisi e riforma dei sistemi pensionistici in Europa*, Angeli: Milan 1993, on which our presentation of the nature of the phenomenon is based.

36 Cf. M. Geri, 'Fondi pensione, fondi di accumulazione e previdenza integrativa in Europa e in Italia', in M. Carrieri et al., *Il progetto "Democrazia economica"*, CESPE Papers: Rome 1991.

37 Cf. T. Treu, 'Sindacato, risparmio, accumulazione', *Prospettiva sindacale*, No. 67, 1988, pp. 46-47.

38 See, among others, B. Aldrich, 'The Earnings Replacement Rate of Old-Age Benefits in 12 Countries 1969-1980', *Social Security Bulletin*, November 1982.

39 Cf. A. Porta's contribution in Università Bocconi (ed.), *Verso lo sviluppo dei fondi pensione in Italia. Gli effetti sui mercati finanziari e l'inquadramento istituzionale*, Milan 1991.

40 G. Imperatori, *Fondi pensione e mercati finanziari*, Il Sole-24 Ore Libri: Milan 1991.

41 R. Bruni and G. Geroldi, 'Problemi economici della previdenza in Europa e sviluppo dei fondi complementri', in G. Geroldi and T. Treu (eds), *Crisi e riforma dei sistemi pensionistici in Europa*, op. cit., pp. 188-189.

42 See R. Artoni's contribution in AAVv, *Verso lo sviluppo dei fondi pensione in Italia*, op. cit.

43 On this point we have consulted mainly M. Geri's research, *Fondi di pensione, fondi di accumulazione e previdenza integrativa in Europa e in Italia*, op. cit.

44 See the ambitious document 'Lo stato sociale e il risparmio', published in Italy in *Nuova rassegna sindacale*, No. 33, 1989.

45   Cf. R. Pezzi and P. Sandulli, 'Prospettive comunitarie in materia di previdenza integrativa', in G. Geroldi and T. Treu (eds), *Crisi e riforma dei sistemi pensionistici in Europa*, op. cit., pp. 211ff.

46   Ibid., pp. 61ff.

47   A brief reference to the North American experience appears in M. Calamandrei, 'L'America invecchia sul vulcano dei fondi pensione', *Il Sole-24 Ore*, 4 December 1991.

4 Collaborative participation and the development of industrial democracy

1 The collaborative model inside the firm

Inside the firm, the collaborative model lies in the opportunity to *correct* the asymmetry inherent in the criteria governing the use of employed labour, without changing the corporate nature of the firm itself.

These opportunities include a wide range of different situations and experiences with collaborative outcomes or aims arising from legal measures, collective bargaining, and informal customs and practices.

However, the collaborative direction in the firm is evident in situations and experiences attributed to industrial democracy (Chapter 1) and, above all, in participatory forms extended to include the firm's decisions.

As we shall see, these forms have not occurred in many advanced capitalist countries: they have produced initiatives only in certain parts of Central-Northern Europe, mostly during the post-war decades of constant economic growth (up to the 1960s).

The reasons for the limited spread of such forms – which may be termed "strong industrial democracy" – concern: the nature of this participatory direction; the presence of absence of favourable conditions outside the arena of industrial relations; and the suspicion and tension arising in principle or in practice among the actors involved.

The nature of this direction appears tangibly in the fact that its aims and implications transcend the domain and confines of pluralistic schemata (Chapter 3), and that it involves institutes that seek to integrate bargaining practices through workers' representatives with collaborative intentions and duties inside the firm.

This perspective concerns trade union experiences that view conflict as a viable and legitimate (but not endemic) event in industrial relations [1] and have contributed to the establishment of concertation arrangements.[2] It involves in particular Germany, the Scandinavian countries, Austria and Hol-

86

land. This represents an endogenous condition – that is internal to the arena of industrial relations – for industrial democracy to succeed. However it is largely a result of the influence of exogenous conditions, and primarily of the role of the State.

After the Second World War, the State played a major part in rebalancing the relations between capital and labour, often pressed by the political initiatives and influence of trade union organisations. It intervened directly not only in social legislation but also in support of bargaining and of a regulation of participatory processes.

Intervention in support of bargaining has generally involved countries with scarcely consolidated industrial relations, as in the case of the Italian charter of workers' rights (1970) on union-firm relations[3] and the French Auroux laws (1982) on the application of bargaining rights.[4]

The most interesting actions in participatory processes occurred in those countries where industrial relations were most stable and formalised: in practice, the activation of participatory forms belonging to the collaborative direction was subject to legal regulation, with the decisive contribution of initiatives taken or accepted in the political-institutional sphere.

This was due to the opportunity to regulate such participatory forms by law and equally to fact that the social partners alone were not very likely to establish them.

The integration between pluralistic arrangements and the explicit collaborative rationale constitutes a leap forward: it involves a set of constraints much higher than those due to bargaining agreements; it uncovers the important problem of mutual convenience and thus of acceptability to employers, workers and their representatives.

Among the concrete experiences of strong industrial democracy, political-institutional initiatives have played a decisive part, since only the trade union side envisaged ideal and practical benefits in the activation of collaborative forms and institutes. These experiences have often functioned, though with very little agreement or acceptance – not only at first – on the employers' side. The German case is emblematic in this respect.

The opposition was due to matters of principle (the loss of full independence in managerial prerogatives); to the fact that collaborative relations and commitments add to the legal and contractual regulation of the employment relationship; and to the meaning attached (at least initially) by certain trade unions to this participatory perspective, viewed as a passage to advanced objectives of economic democracy.

In situations of active industrial democracy, it was in fact accepted by employers, eager to gain concrete or potential benefits from the involvement of workers' representatives; at the same time, employers often sought to hinder its spread, limit its functions, and communicate with workers rather than representatives appointed or controlled by the unions. Such situations have caused criticism and doubts even among trade unions, with a prevailing will to protect and strengthen an important institutional achievement whose significance is not yet entirely clear and accompanies the strategy of (socialdemocratic) political parties with a reformist approach.

This orientation is different from that of trade union organisations with no true experience of industrial democracy. In the Anglo-Saxon tradition, business unionism and competitive unionism are dominated by a concern not to harm the independence or domain of protection. Among trade unions associated with the traditional parties of the Left in North Mediterranean countries, collaborative participation seems to foreshadow an uncanny integration of workers' representatives within the business rationale.[5]

The intentions and positions recalled above started to become less relevant and evident at the end of the 1970s. Ongoing changes have made industrial relations systems more uncertain and problematical.[6] The perspective of collaborative participation has been judged mostly *per se*, with little concern for principles; it first appeared under less ambitious forms than those of the previous decades and had to face the challenge of integrative participation.

The comparison between collaborative participation in the firm and pluralistic frameworks – present openly or inherently in political and trade union positions – is mirrored by theoretical contributions. We shall focus on three of these, taken from very different periods: namely the German authors Ralf Dahrendorf, Rainer Eisfeld and Wolfang Streeck.

In his most prominent work,[7] Dahrendorf emphasises the development of industrial conflict regulation through "institutionalisation" and argues that the most efficient and correct forms of development are those that do not alter the division of roles and responsibilities between partners; i.e. the forms that remain within pluralistic schemata and bargaining practices. Dahrendorf's thesis echoes the thesis discussed by Clegg,[8] with a major difference: while for the latter specific forms of participation are pointless if bargaining reaches an adequate depth, for Dahrendorf such forms are essentially incongruous.

Despite their different perspectives, the other two authors argue instead for the need to reach beyond the pluralistic method: Eisfeld views pluralism as an intermediate stage following the demise of liberalism and supplanted in turn by socialism; Streeck emphasises the crisis that affects pluralism due to the moral indifference of social partners for institutions with common interests – as in the attitude of organised labour towards the firm's objectives. Referring to the inside of the firm, the former proposes a prescriptive theory that aims to secure more power for workers; the latter depicts a recent scenario that persuades workers to increase their degree of responsibility.

On the eve of the 1960s, Ralf Dahrendorf, in his innovative class theory, viewed the (manufacturing) firm as an authoritative structure coordinated by imperative norms, with a formal organisation resting on the "functional" aspect in the division of labour and on the "hierarchical" aspect of command roles and subordinate roles – both of which are necessary.

The conflict between those that hold command roles (who seek to conserve the existing authority system) and those holding subordinate roles (who aim to overturn the same system) tends to become less intense and violent as a result of various transformations in industrial societies, and in particular thanks to its "institutionalisation" and to the growth of "industrial democracy". Conflict decreases, essentially, because it is perceived as a natural feature of industrial life and is therefore acknowledged and regulated accordingly.

Three components of this "industrial democracy" – namely trade union organisations, collective bargaining and agreements, and mediation and arbitration institutes – form a coherent framework, based chiefly on the autonomous regulation of conflict and apparent especially in Britain and the United States.

Two other components – workers' representatives in the firm (*Betriebsräte* or works councils) and workers' participation in firm management, observed mainly in Germany – appear quite different to the previous, being based on the principle that seeks to institutionalise conflict by altering the firm's authority structure. These two components, and especially participation in management, lie in an unclear position as they provide for opposition as well as supplementary guidance. They can help to regulate conflict provisionally , but any attempt to eliminate it entirely is bound to fail. As this participation rests on the belief that conflict is an evil, it is a misguided solution, which opposes rather than assist the tendency to reduce conflict.

Without ignoring the great merit of Dahrendorf's general class theory – namely to have analysed the phenomenon passing over the ideological assumptions of most European literature of his time and taking a separate line from the popular North-American authors who predicted an inevitable decline in labour conflict[9] – it must be said that his opinion on works councils and participation, as well as on relations between the two components and collective bargaining, appear hardly sustainable in the face of concrete experience (from the Sixties onwards).

The acceptance of constraints by workers through their representatives – attributed to works councils – is not absent even in the practices and institutes of bargaining, especially when contracts are signed at the level of the firm (a level which Dahrendorf seems to ignore).

Participation in management (as in the case of Germany) does not provide an alternative to the first three components but is additional to them, as it increases the guarantees in favour of workers' conditions. If it functions, the belief that it contradicts the overall tendency to reduce conflict becomes hard to prove.

Instead, great attention should be given to Dahrendorf's critical argument on participation in management, i.e. the opportunity to modify the firm's authority structure, whose functional and hierarchical aspects he considers necessary to the firm's functioning.[10] This is a vital and unavoidable issue, which in a market economy concerns the possibility of introducing collaborative processes and institutes through workers' representation, without undermining the firm's need for efficiency. Dahrendorf does not believe in this possibility and warns of the (far from unfounded) danger of a separation between the duties of representatives and the expectations of workers. When this does not happen – as has often been the case – there remains a difficulty to reconcile the functioning of a competitive firm with the procedures of participation extended to its management.

Since Dahrendorf first defined it, the issue has acquired even greater urgency (Chapter 8) and can be overlooked only by participatory perspectives that seek to alter the status and conditions of subordinate labour in the firm, without accepting its implications for the firm's functioning.

This is the case of the second author listed above. At the start of the 1970s, while analysing the shortcomings of political institutions in capitalist societies, Eisfeld[11] argues that, without a social foundation, political participation remains an impossible delusion. Its achievement hinges on the socialisation of the means of production, which should aim to bring the firm under social control from below rather than establish collective ownership.

Eisfeld has in mind above all the concentration of power in the hands of large concerns, which should neither be abolished nor transferred to the State but governed by in-plant meetings and associations of all those involved, whether directly or indirectly (workers, owners, managers and consumers), avoiding the use of hierarchical decision-making structures. This arrangement implies a set of favourable conditions and especially of government support in terms of legislation, education-information and action against oligopolistic practices. Mention of this author is due because he expresses political and trade union suspicion for the experience of industrial democracy, which in the antagonistic perspective of workers' control (Chapter 2) could only be acceptable if it paved the way to more advanced objectives of institutional change in the firm.

Eisfeld's proposal appears overdue and sustained only by a determined ideological effort. It is clear that he underestimates the difficulties of its implementation and ignores how improbable are the conditions underpinning its realisation. Moreover, he provides very few arguments to substantiate his view that in a market economy productive firms can function even without a proper prevalence of entrepreneurial rationale, technical rationality and efficiency.[12]

Streeck[13] – the third author in our list – wrote thirty years after Dahrendorf and was well aware both of the problems encountered by the competitive firm and of its organisational requirements. Accordingly, he shows a clear vision of the long-term dangers and costs arising from the constant split between command roles and subordinate roles and notes that the exclusive remedial use of bargaining can damage a firm's economic soundness and ultimately the full use of entrepreneurial authority. With collective contracts, the inequality between actors is offset by equal rights for the sides involved, and trade unions are allowed to establish rights of "status" that would not be available to workers as individuals.

However, as the system rests on a sharp division between managerial and trade union responsibilities in the rationale of pluralism, it leads somehow to a de-economicalisation of industrial relations, and distances workers' rights of "status" from economic and productive fluctuations, thus rendering workers morally indifferent to the firm's objectives.

These implications were weakened over the previous decades, when relations were stabler, by the use of concertation and by the institutes of industrial democracy. Today the new features of the economy and of production, combined with a growing need for flexibility, have made "status" standardisation and its estrangement from the firm's economic potential a real obstacle to competitiveness, so that the regulation of employment – viewed as an area for separate action – tends to become increasingly weaker.

In this situation, a polarisation due to two opposite forms has arisen: one involves "free" employment contracts (as in the United States); the other involves internal labour markets with high employment security and high flexibility (in the wake of the Japanese model).

The latter form differs from the results of industrial democracy as to individual ownership of "status" levels and the lack of collective or public rights. It brought Streeck to question the feasibility of the attempt to revitalise competitive capitalism, thus raising the question of whether flexibility can be attained without justice or civil rights.

Still greatly relevant today, this question is less concerned with the form that favours once again the "contract" (which threatens even the pluralistic framework) than with the form that enhances rights of "status": alternatively, there is a need to reconcile collective rights of "status" with the double aim of re-revitalise in industrial relations and of workers' joint-responsibility for the firm.

In conclusion, it is necessary to verify whether there is a new or renewed potential to implement instances of industrial democracy, knowing that economic constraints are now becoming even more urgent and that the political and organisational conditions which favoured such experiences in the postwar decades cannot easily be repeated.

2 The forms of industrial democracy

Instances of industrial democracy comprise a range of forms, which in turn are applied differently and often exhibit provisional features. Viewed in broad terms, the phenomenon embraces the following forms: the rights of consultation and information, codecision, codetermination and its variant co-management. These forms are introduced in certain cases as alternatives; in other cases (the majority so far) they are set up and employed simultaneously; it is notable that in such cases lower-intensity forms normally fall within higher-intensity forms. These forms can in fact be ordered according to their degree of intensity (Chapter 1), which reflects the presence or lack of participatory processes in the firm's decisions and – when they *do* occur – the greater or lesser degree of participation.

We have termed "strong industrial democracy" those forms that allow for a higher degree of participation and include both codetermination and co-management. Consequently, we shall consider all the other forms listed above as cases of "non-strong industrial democracy".

The forms of industrial democracy and collective bargaining are typified, as we known, by inherent differences and also by the fact that their border is not always clear; indeed the latter has been attributed entirely to the sphere of participation.[14] Collective bargaining seems compatible with every form of industrial democracy, yet with very diversified relations due to this variety. It agrees fully with the rights of information and consultation, as one of the main functions allotted to these is the furtherance of negotial practices. It can be placed reasonably close to codecision, especially since the latter embodies a low degree of participation in the decision-making sphere. Both can fulfil very similar functions, in particular when bargaining is at the level of the firm or workplace.

Codetermination has at times coexisted with collective bargaining, especially whenever the latter is negotiated at a wider level than the firm.

Of course, codetermination is not compatible with every instance of bargaining; the benefits and constraints of the former inevitably tend to condition the applicative lines and means of the latter. However, the two phenomena remain distinct as to both actors and institutes, as well as their functions and objectives.

2.1 Rights of information and consultation

By providing information, the employer allows workers or their representatives access to data and explanations on problems and situations that regard working conditions and the firm, after which the two sides exchange views on such data and explanations. With consultation procedures, the employer informs and consults workers or their representatives in order to learn about their needs and opinions before a decision is taken and he preserves the right to apply them, with the only exception of cases requiring the approval of workers or their representatives.

The two types of rights are external and previous to decision-making processes and as such do not imply any responsibility or direct influence of workers over them.[15] These rights are nevertheless significant because among different negotial means they focus on the achievement of orientations and practices that overcome the mere strength of each side involved and increase the opportunities of providing an objective and certified basis for their demands, whereby partners can confront their needs and respective constraints.

The presence of these rights constitutes a precondition for the realisation of industrial relations shaped by mutual recognition and, above all, by the abolition of prejudicial distrust of the other side. Their implementation, at least in the long run, is bound to favour negotial processes, with greater rationalisation and opportunities for dialogue rather than conflict, by the introduction of more specific participatory procedures.

Access to information was upheld, as mentioned earlier, with the purpose of favouring the development of collective bargaining, though it has not always issued from collaborative intentions. The provision of information to workers' representatives has always been defined chiefly in legal terms, as illustrated by the duty to bargain in good faith under the 1935 National Labor Relations Act in the United States, by the duty to disclose the firm's conditions under the 1975 Employment Protection Act in Britain, and by the 1976 Swedish law on management and production processes in the firm. In other contexts, such as Italy, access was introduced as a genuine bargaining institute by the clauses of national sector-contracts.

Access to information is often coupled with the right of consultation in relations between employers and works councils and other similar bodies. In countries like Germany, Austria, Belgium and Holland, the employer has a legal obligation to provide information to councils in view of greater collaboration. In other countries – such as Italy – the last twenty years have witnessed a shift from the recognition of information rights to the development of consultation rights,[16] by the "joint administration" of contracts (at the national level) and the exchange of information on business performance (by means of national agreements).[17]

The nature and range of topics implied in such rights show how diversified their implementation can in different environments. Information may concern salary, working hours and terms of employment and can also extend to labour organisation and economic or financial decisions. The object of consultation may include collective dismissals, plant closures, structural changes in production, and thus the introduction of new technology, alterations in socio-technical systems, personnel training and re-qualification, personnel policies.

The above rights have also played a major part in the stance of national and supranational bodies. In such venues they have provided stimuli and proposals, without entering the realm of specific negotial forms or institutes. After the Second World War, the ILO and OECD produced a host of statements and suggestions in this direction, while the EEC issued directive proposals, especially for Europe.

EEC intervention in this field concerns two types of directives joined by mutual links and similarities.[18]

The first type concerns trans-national firms in particular. Since the "Vredeling" directive proposal in 1980, two others have followed quite recently: one in 1991, for the establishment of European firm committees in EC-wide groups; the other in 1993, for the same purpose but with an important novelty which bars directives from introducing arrangements already in force in individual countries.

The second type concerns draft directives that seek to coordinate national legislation on joint-stock companies. The best-know of these, referred to as "Fifth Directive" provides for participation, including the rights of information and consultation.

These directives have not reached beyond the draft stage, since their submission to the Commission, owing to the lack of agreement among social partners, the resistance of employers and the opposition of certain governments.[19] The failure of the Fifth Directive, in particular, was largely due to its provision of participatory paths and options.

Outside Community venues, however, the rights of information and consultation became a significant component of industrial relations systems in many European countries during the 1980s and later. They remain consubstantial with the institutes of participation in decision-making. Moreover and above all, they have benefited in different ways from the tendencies of collective bargaining (closer adherence to shifting economic variables, decentralisation, regulation of flexibility), from the escalation of negotial or consultive agreements at the firm level,[20] from a more "procedural" interaction between social partners,[21] as well as from the experience of economic participation (Chapter 5).

2.2 Codecision

This form is not simply participatory and collaborative, as it includes institutes and practices that pertain largely to widespread processes of employment regulation. In this sense, the term *codecision*[22] sounds as an exaggeration of the concrete experiences it refers to.

On the other hand, the institutes and practices attributed to this form represent a lasting, broad arena for shared views and cohabitation, agreement and friction between industrial relations actors; also, they precede and surpass the two categories of rights mentioned earlier and cannot be assimilated, formally or practically, with codetermination.

With these points in mind, codecision can be referred to situations where workers' (institutionalised and/or recognised) representatives in the firm are explicitly appointed to safeguard the interests of workers and at the same time to collaborate with the employer and managers; in practice, they ensure the conduction of relations between the two sides, taking into account workers' needs and rights without hindering the normal operation of the firm's structures and production.

This type of representation is generally referred to firm councils, plant councils or other similar bodies (works councils). These issue from all the workers of a firm, but do not appear as trade union organisations, even though representatives can be appointed by the unions or under strong trade union control. It occurs alongside the so-called "dual" representation structure, which makes a distinction between the will of union members and that of workers as a whole.

Relations between the sides involve the firm and councils in particular; however, in several cases joint bodies are envisaged, especially for matters of common interest (such as vocational training) or also for the direct management of certain activities (mainly in the social sphere) by workers' representatives.

The functions of councils are numerous and constantly increasing but not all equally present in concrete experiences. The following may be listed: rights of information and consultation; codecision practices on matters concerning the use of labour, with the preliminary agreement or veto power of workers' representatives; social and insurance problems; supervision over the application of social and collective bargaining laws and dealing with complaints and controversies. In several countries, over the last twenty years, such functions have embraced other aspects attaining to business policy (market prospects, technical innovation, staff turnover and employment), primarily in the field of information.[23]

As for the nature of councils, three features deserve mention: they are set up by legal regulation or by agreement between the sides (normally at the national or sector level); in several situations they hold no proper bargaining functions (even if they produce negotial results) and in certain cases (as in Germany) they lack the right to promote strikes; they reflect a participatory solution that rules out formal participation and responsibility of workers' representatives in the firm's decision-making bodies.

This participatory solution is surely the most common and can be found even outside Western countries.[24] In many European countries, in particular, its roots reach far back in time and it has withstood a great number of changes. These facts help to explain why codecision institutes and practices do not produce a stable and clearly-defined form. They express customs and outcomes that are prevalently participatory, but on the other hand they cover a spectrum of situations where everyday relations between the employer and workers lack any participatory precedents or tendencies.

In the codecisional perspective, the problem of dualism between "optimal" participation and "minimum" cohabitation regulated by the sides may be partly due to the nature of councils (their ambiguity, in Dahrendorf's terms) and more significantly, perhaps, to the action of direct factors: for instance the ideological and organisational traditions of trade unions and their actual degree of recognition by the other side.

Evidence of the participatory difficulties of codecision may lie in the fact that – when firm councils are missing – everyday relations between employers and workers are at times regulated by bodies with different features, that normally show a lack of clear collaborative intentions and yet exercise functions similar in many respects to those assigned to councils.

Such situations involve a small number of countries, with two prominent exceptions, namely the United States and Britain. Here workers' representation depends on delegates (shop stewards) who generally differ from firm councils: because of the minor role of legal and negotial specifications; because they are appointed or seconded by the unions; because they safeguard workers mainly by bargaining production at the workplace (plant or department). This kind of representation shapes the so-called "monistic" structure, whereby the interests of workers are expected to coincide with those of trade union representatives.

Our account of works councils and (as an alternative in participatory terms) shop stewards will focus briefly on two representative cases: Germany and Britain, with a passing reference to the Italian experience.

In Germany (apart from the early cases following the First World War) [25] works councils were regulated by law in 1953 and again in 1972. [26] They sanctioned the general representation of workers, though representatives were overwhelmingly trade union members.

Under a rationale of confident cooperation with the hierarchy, the council participates in joint decisions on working hours, remuneration criteria and job descriptions. Decisions on working conditions and the work environment are taken by management after consulting the council. In matters that concern personnel management (such as training, promotions and transfers, selection and dismissals) the council's approval is binding.

In matters involving the firm's policies (technological and organisational innovation and strategies), the council has a right to be informed. [27]

Two points should be underlined: the functions and rights of this institute are broader that those enjoyed by workers' representatives in many other European countries; moreover, its significance has increased over the last twenty years and in large concerns it often acts well beyond its institutional functions. [28]

In Britain, shop stewards – whose appearance dates from the Second World War – have often seemed free from outside trade union structures, with a degree of independence related to the size of the firm.[29] Their bargaining action has often been informal, highly fragmented and independent of the unions' wider negotial guidelines.[30] This has multiplied the points of trade union strength, also owing to the presence of different craft unions within the same production unit.

Altogether this experience has produced very little collaboration and a muddled industrial relations system. The implementation of informal negotial practices did produce a few collaborative decisions and outcomes, but these are hardly ever dominant; while the prevailing features are a rooted conflict tradition, the accumulation of rights and the inflexibility of regulations governing the use of labour.

Scarce participation and negotial disorder have been the object of repeated corrective attempts. Alongside those tending to implement income policy and the advice of the Donovan Commission (1965-68) on the regulation of bargaining processes and actors, special mention is due of the Bullock Report (1977), which contains the findings of a commission appointed by Government to draft a law bill upholding the goal of full industrial democracy for company control and the recognition of the unions' vital role.[31]

However, the approach and implications of the shop-steward experience were strongly challenged in the Eighties by the anti-concertation policy of the Conservative government, by legal measures that ended an age-long voluntaristic tradition and by the employers' pressing demand for flexibility – though this did not always entail a serious loss of negotial power.[32]

Compared with Germany and Britain, the Italian experience appears less straightforward. In its first long phase (up to the 1960s) workers were represented by an "inside commission" similar to a works council, a body representing all workers in general and therefore not explicitly unionised;[33] in the second phase, there arose a movement of delegate councils, viewed as representatives of work groups or of the trade unions.[34]

In both phases, collaborative practices played only a minor role because of the dominant conflictful culture and the employers' lack of initiative; only in recent years has Italy developed a rich experience of adaptive in-plant bargaining[35] with institutes for joint consultation and negotiation.

2.3 Codetermination

In "strong industrial democracy", collaborative participation consists notably of codetermination and especially of its variant co-management, at least in theory.

Codetermination entails participation of workers in the firm's decisions, through their representatives in its bodies. This implies a departure from pluralistic schemata, even if collective bargaining is not replaced. It may produce friction and opposition, but its main condition is consensus among actors.

Accordingly, codetermination can be defined as follows: it covers situations and experiences in which workers collaborate with their employer by taking decisions that concern both labour and the firm. Such decisions, taken jointly within institutional bodies, are due to the recognition of a range of interests shared by the two sides; this implies a potential or concrete departure from the traditional division of roles and duties of each side.

The degree of collaborative participation in codetermination depends to a great extent on two institutional features, which respectively imply two highly different options.

The first feature concerns the size of workers' representation and translates into minority representation or equal representation.

The second feature regards the venue of participation, which involves essentially either a supervisory board (which appoints the board of directors and often also the managing director) (double system) or the board of directors (single system).

The choice between the above options influences not only the degree of participation but equally its degree of difficulty: arguably, the first and second aspect tend to interact, as a higher degree of participation implies a higher degree of difficulty.

This difficulty lies in the consistent implementation of this collaborative form, i.e. the participation of workers' representatives in the firm's decisions without altering its corporate nature. This appears totally different from the difficulty invoked by those whose evaluation of the form rests on antagonistic considerations and leanings.[36]

The difficulty mentioned above differs of course according to the side involves and depends largely on the extent and venue of participation.

The firm needs to safeguard its entrepreneurial prerogatives to attain positive economic results; taking into account its presence on the market, which includes other firms without codetermination; these lack its advantages but also its costs.

For workers' representatives, it is a matter of: reconciling the "imputed" role arising from their mandate with a role of "acquired" responsibility for the firm's existence, knowing that recognised common interests depend on a series of non-neutral specific decisions by the sides; holding the actual information and real involvement in responsibility they are called to acquire; entertaining good and/or bad relations with workers, considering that these may not be fully aware of the quality and long-term potential of codetermination or of the obligations imposed on their representatives.

For the firm, difficulties increase considerably when minority representation changes to equal representation, because it becomes possible for the views of workers' representatives to prevail in decision-making processes.

The difficulty for representatives appears more marked when they are a minority, as they accept responsibilities that are not balanced by the opportunity to shape the above processes. It should be observed, however, that equal representation charges them with excessive responsibilities, reflecting a role that extend far beyond the influence and control of company decisions and – both in theory and in practice – it may eventually require a sacrifice of ownership rights. In this case, a deep contradiction with the collaborative model would arise.

The difficulties of the two sides decrease when the double system is preferred to the single system. In fact the former maintains a distinction between the stage of "political" decisions in the firm and the stage of their implementation: the supervisory board acts as a "clearing house" for tensions and opposing interests between the sides, if they are reconciled without the action of directly managerial bodies or authorities.

At the edge of "strong industrial democracy" lies *co-management*. The term – often employed inappropriately and applied to the German experience – refers to a participatory form that may be seen as a variant of codetermination; ultimately, however, it is far more radical and problematic, though perhaps more consistent.

Our view, in agreement with others,[37] is that co-management reflects the opportunity to participate in the firm's decisions, with an equal number of employees' and employer's representatives on the board of directors (single system) fully involved as such in the firm's strategic decisions.

Clearly, under co-management the observations earlier referred to double-system equal representation become even more relevant.

When it is applied, ownership rights are no longer guaranteed; there is a tendency to cancel the distinction of roles and duties between employers and workers; even when it survives in its formal and remunerative aspects, the employment relationship is no longer officially controlled by the natural counterpart of labour providers. At a closer look, when applied, co-management realises a kind of "semi self-management" reminiscent of the institute of sharecropping in the farming tradition.

It is indicative, however, that this form has not been tested by implementation. It has produced no concrete experiences, unlike codetermination.

The latter regards experiences that include both the double and the single system.[38] In the first instance, experiences are found in Austria, Denmark, Holland and especially Germany. In the second instance, they occur in other European countries: France and Britain (mainly in the public sector or in nationalised companies) and, more notably, in Scandinavian countries. Outside Europe, experimental cases are found in Japan and the United States (e.g. at the Chrysler Corporation).

German codetermination (*Mitbestimmung*) is undoubtedly the most famous, prominent and widely discussed experience. We shall come back to this at the end of the chapter. In this paragraph only its main institutional features and their development after the Second World War will be recalled.

Such features were affected by three consecutive legislative measures,[39] now all in force simultaneously.

The first measure, under the 1951 Act applied to coal and metal industries with at least than 1,000 employees, introduced a supervisory board formed by: 5 representatives of workers and 5 of the employer, plus an 11th neutral member (chosen by common agreement); thus workers gained equal representation.

The second measure rests on the 1952 Act, reviewed in 1972. The latter, which was passed against employers' opposition, concerns coal and metal industries with 500-1,000 employees and firms in other sectors with 500-2,000 employees; it states that a third of members on the supervisory board should be workers' representatives.

The third measure, introduced by the 1976 Act, extended codetermination to firms with more than 2,000 employees; the supervisory board was made to include a number of members proportional to the firm's dimensions. When these are 12, half of the seats are reserved to workers' representatives and divided as follows: 2 appointed by trade unions (and elected by workers among candidates not employed in the firm); 4 chosen directly by workers, including at least one shop-floor worker, a clerical worker and a top manager. The chairman, who under this law is inevitably close to the owner, is allowed a casting vote when the votes are equal.

This composition, which involves a varied and dishomogenous representation of workers, makes equal representation more apparent than tangible. However this point, more than others, led employers' associations to submit the law to the judgement of the Constitutional Court, which in 1979 declared their objections unfounded.

Among other instances of the double system, the Dutch case deserves special attention. After the experimental consultation promoted by large concerns in the Sixties,[40] legislation introduced a number of participatory institutes,[41] such as the establishment of supervisory boards in firms with more than 100 employees in 1971.

The supervisory board holds ample powers, but its composition is not predefined, as it rests on the practice of co-option. After the first appointments, subsequent ones are made choosing among candidates designated separately by shareholders, top management and workers' representatives inside the firm. The board selects candidates who are neither employees nor trade-unionists. Each of the three actors mentioned above has veto power, although this is seldom used, partly because workers' representatives tend to second independent candidates.

Under this arrangement, workers are given a kind of indirect representation through candidates whose features are acceptable to other actors. It can be interpreted as a device for making workers' interests less evident and explicit, for designating candidates free of trade union influence, and for attaining a more homogeneous body with less risk of internal opposition. This allows codetermination a broader "citizenship" and makes the position of workers' representatives less difficult, as they are recognised by other partners and are not expected to behave strictly in accordance with workers' expectations or trade union demands.

The Swedish solution, based on the single system, was introduced by the 1972 Act which provides for two workers' representatives on the board of directors of firms with more than 600 employees. The better-known 1976 Act extended this requirement to firms with more than 25 employees, with right of representation on the boards of subsidiary companies. Ten years later, the law had been applied in 50 per cent of such cases.[42]

Legislation on codetermination met with bitter opposition from the entrepreneurial world [43] and it arose in conjunction with the new orientation of the LO trade union federation that sought to regulate different aspects of labour relations by legislative means,[44] and as part of a "batch" of measures issued between 1973 and 1979.[45]

Most codetermination provisions appeared as outline laws, requiring integration with more specific measures or negotiation between the sides; which resulted in slow, discontinuous negotiations.

In our view, the Swedish solution cannot be interpreted as a clear-cut union decision in favour of codetermination – even though it overcame the spirit of the "Swedish model", whereby trade unions had pursued social and political objectives, leaving the employers in charge of firms.[46] The arrangement is more motivated by a need to redress at production the constraints due to solidaristic wage policies. Inclusion in the board of directors (though quantitatively modest) is an element among others capable of enriching the safeguards, rights and guarantees in favour of workers; all this at a time of great trade union power, whose attention was still strategically focused on the macro level (Chapter 2).

The Bullock Report was highly influential – not on the plane of experience but on that of single-system participatory proposals – as it pursued a degree of intensity in industrial democracy equal to co-management.

The solution accepted by the majority of members (in agreement with the TUC trade union federation) differs considerably from the proposal made by employers' representatives.[47] It is characterised by the following points: its critique of the German and Swedish experiences – based on unequal representation – which do not allocate the same powers to all directors and may encourage a merely defensive stance on the part of workers' representatives; its pursuit of equal representation of shareholders and workers, each side holding one third of seats on the board of directors; the other third, co-opted by shareholders and workers, is formed by expert representatives of interests outside the firm; the proposal – known subsequently under the formula 2x+y – concerns firms with at least 2,000 employees and is optional (subject to approval by no less than one third of the workers involved).

This solution raised a number of objections even among trade unions, strong opposition from employers (unwilling, as elsewhere, to accept trade union interference in shaping corporate policies) and also an embarrassed reaction by the Labour government, which only one year later presented in Parliament a White Paper on industrial democracy; this envisaged a type of industrial democracy based on voluntary accords between social partners rather than on legislation, thus stressing the role of consultation procedures and showing its support for the double system.

The Bullock Report only remained a proposal, as could be expected. This depended not only on the lack of a suitable approach to certain unavoidable, complex matters (above all the relations between collective bargaining and co-management) but especially on its unrealistic projections on the trade-off between a scenario of opposition and conflict and one of cooperation and marked institutionalisation of industrial relations. The road to industrial democracy in the United Kingdom was still full of obstacles but with a highly advanced arrangement including the requirements as ambitious as the single system combined with equal representation.

This section on collaborative participation would not be complete without some reference to Japan.

The *Japanese experience* is considered at heart the most collaborative of those made in advanced capitalist countries and is both an ideal venue and a historical testing-ground for the propounders of integrative participation (Chapter 6); although it cannot simply be placed under this heading, it is not even easily interpreted in the perspective of industrial democracy.

In Japan, participation is not sanctioned or regulated by legal measures or by major agreements among social partners, so it does not follow overall strategies aimed at a uniform industrial relations system; the lack of State intervention, combined with other factors, has greatly decentralised the phenomenon and produced a wide array of applications.[48]

Japan exhibits a variety of widespread situations and many participatory practices supported by weak explicit institutes. There is no codetermination, which would appear excessive given the workers' high degree of loyalty to the firm and the managerial functions performed chiefly by relying on the trust obtained. Codecision on matters that concern the running of the firm and production processes is apparently not very developed in terms of specific accords and institutes. Greater space has been given to forms of access to information and of consultation rights (business organisation, personnel problems, social security, working conditions) based on the presence of works councils and established by agreements between top management and trade unions or directly by the latter.[49]

The functioning of participatory intentions and practices depends factors that are unique to the Japanese environment, namely its "communitarian" approach to the firm [50] and its structure of trade union representation and collective bargaining.

This approach – firmly rooted in the country's socio-cultural tradition – requires an intense involvement of all internal actors in the institutes and customs it implies (above all lifetime employment in the same firm and seniority-related benefits) and also, especially in small to medium-sized production units, exquisitely paternalistic motives.

Trade union representation, which reaches high membership levels only in firms with more than 500 employees, is assigned to company unions – often organised by individual production units – with no significant ties to wider trade union structures.

This has given rise to tens of thousands of trade unions, with different levels of power and varying protection potentials.

Participation is linked to collective bargaining at the firm or plant level by company unions or negotial works councils. This is one of the main reasons for the lack of explicit industrial democracy institutes and, accordingly, the Japanese experience is a significant instance of non-separation between the direct contractual protection of workers and collaborative contents and implications. The latter two can be considered an extension of the typical functions of bargaining, which in this case reaches well beyond the question of working conditions and can affect matters involving the firm's life and policies – even if employers are not usually willing to discuss major decisions in any depth.

This experience cannot possibly be judged without taking into account the constitutive elements of the "Japanese system". However, from a European viewpoint and as far as workers are concerned, two aspects need to be mentioned.

Participation due to industrial democracy produces no far-reaching solidarity on its own; in Japan this restriction is observed in a very marked form. Although the role of trade unions (in large firms) may be prominent, its action hardly agrees with a trade union movement that tends altogether to pursue greater uniformity among participatory processes.

Collaborative forms and practices are largely due to conditions exogenous to industrial relations, and among these the notable lack of adequate guarantees. Despite their deep roots, at times they only produce feeble offshoots. Such guarantees probably appear unnecessary when growth is prolonged and dynamic; but they may be necessary during a downturn in the economy and employment such as the present one, when the very principle of lifetime employment is threatened.

3 Recent national and Community developments

Since the expansion of the 1970s, industrial democracy experiences have not made much progress, especially as regards their most intense forms. Accordingly, such forms have not extended to those countries that lacked them.

During the 1970s and at present, we can observe a varied range of intentions and practices with collaborative and participatory traits (chapters 5 and 6), but these are only partly assignable to the sphere of industrial democracy. The latter is widely employed in its weakest forms: i.e. information rights and consultive bodies.

This scarcely dynamic trend can be explained by referring to four facts:

a   the profile of industrial relations is deeply marked by economic events and by the structure of production processes, and compared with previous periods it is less affected by political and organisational factors (associated with trade union power and conflict);[51]

b   given the difficulties often encountered by collective bargaining used as an acquisitive negotial process, there remains little space for measures or accords providing for the presence of workers' representatives in decision-making venues, despite the tendency to decentralise industrial relations;

c   the need for flexibility in the use of labour (when this is an object of negotiation) multiplies practices and institutes with participatory elements and brings bargaining closer to cooperation between the sides, but is highly unlikely to reach beyond the often unstable balance between direct protection and adaptive concessions, due to objective constraints;

d   the significant innovation introduced by the entrepreneurial and managerial world to involve workers in results is in fact competitive or alternative to strong forms of industrial democracy.

The "stalemate" experienced by these forms is a significant but not surprising event on the road to participation.

During the Eighties, in fact, the conditions that had enabled and favoured such forms came to an end: a prolonged period of economic growth was followed by increasing tension in world markets and by interdependent domestic economies; neo-corporatist arrangements were followed by political scenes with a concern for the competitiveness of firms and willing, if anything, to favour more flexible and functional forms of worker involvement; the traditional opposition of employers to the access of workers' representatives into decision-making venues was strengthened by new reasons for claiming employers' managerial independence, and a wider range of strategic decisions associated with the constant innovation of manufacturing processes and products; the quantitative decline of typical manufacturing-sector workers was matched by a rise in the number and variety of tertiary-sector workers, whose jobs and interests are far more diversified.

As for recent developments in industrial democracy, we shall only add a little information on events at the national and Community level.

In Germany, codetermination achieved no further recognition. Interestingly, in 1980 trade unions and governing Socialdemocratic Party (in office with the liberals) failed to get a bill through parliament to interpret the 1976 Act still in force today.[52]

In Sweden, the body of laws introduced during the Seventies had to confront the employers' will to regain lost power, as witnessed by new strategies pursuing worker involvement (as in the case of Volvo) and by the difficulties raised during negotiations for the implementation of the codetermination law.[53]

In Italy, certain elements appeared which approached the collaborative rationale (i.e. declining conflict and a more procedural approach to bargaining practices) but they never reached beyond the limit of the weaker forms of industrial democracy (devices for the "joint administration" of contracts, information accords, joint codecision bodies).[54]

In Britain the question of industrial democracy is no longer confronted, although worker involvement has never ceased to exist, mostly as a result of employers' initiatives; it has often aimed to overcome the experience of joint consultation, to avoid and restrict trade union intervention, and to strengthen the position of management in firms where trade unions and delegates are present.[55]

The perspective of industrial democracy has not really taken hold in France, with an expansion of company-level bargaining on the one hand, and on the other an extension of forms of participation and economic "involvement" of workers, normally shared and proposed by employers.[56]

In Spain, finally, recent years have witnessed the introduction, more often in state companies than in private ones, of joint commissions dealing with certain aspects of industrial relations, and various agreements on the participation of trade unions or workers' representatives in the firm's bodies.[57]

The "stalemate" reached by national institutes and experiences of industrial democracy at the start of the 1980s, is reflected at EEC level and in the Maastricht Treaty.

As far as workers' participation is concerned, the Community has made significant steps but, overall, with no substantial results. On the other hand, the issue is a very important "piece" of the social dimension in economic integration processes.[58] This dimension is now (and, perhaps, also in perspective) in a critical and uncertain condition, given that the top priority of the

105

European Single Market is to strengthen and render more competitive its economic and financial structures, with implications that inevitably tend to deregulate markets – and first of all the labour market.

As regards workers' protection and recognition, this dimension can be essentially divided into three components: minimum standards of protection and rights (referred to individual conditions), collective bargaining as a fundamental tool for harmonising employment relationships, and participation by means of industrial democracy institutes and regulations. The second and third components (referred to collective conditions) concern the possibility or impossibility of setting up a labour-inclusive European system;[59] this system is visible in the attempt to reconcile a high degree of economic competitiveness with industrial relations inspired by the European post-war tradition, thus reviving institutes and regulations produced by national contexts where the functions of organised labour are recognised and firmly rooted.

This aim also includes the issue of participation, which may serve to enhance the "citizenship" of labour and its representatives, to redress the imbalance due to a project based on the firms' demand for flexibility, and to outline a route capable of reducing the variety of working conditions.

Despite the reasonable note of these considerations and the great relevance of certain participatory solutions, the progress of industrial democracy at EC level has been very slight.

Among the actors involved, only trade unions – or rather their majority and representation at EC level – have shown a true willingness to support the political supremacy of Community institutions in the social area and, in particular, to support industrial democracy proposals. Through its international organisations or national governments, the entrepreneurial world is still proving hostile or reluctant to accept such proposals and greater uniformity in industrial relations.

This variety of positions strongly limits the capacity of Community institutions to make proposals, at least in the short-to-medium term, so it is hard to envisage any support to substantial forms of participation.[60]

The situation outlined above is reflected in the Maastricht Treaty and past or recent Community orientations.

Social policy was notably one of the most controversial issues at Maastricht. Among its most appreciable results was the extension of social decisions (e.g. improving the employment environment, information and consultation) subject to majority vote, thus overcoming the constraint of unanimity. As for its proposals, the Treaty simply incorporated a number of guarantees of individual protection (health, equal treatment for men and women, etc.).

As for the Community, two types of proposal deserve mention. The first and more recent is an action programme drafted by the Commission in pursuance of the "Community Charter of Fundamental Social Rights for Workers" adopted by heads of state and government in the Council of Europe (with the exception of Britain) in December 1989.[61]

In the case of industrial democracy (a term that, by the way, does not appear in this or in other EEC documents) the Treaty recognised the need for greater information, consultation and participation of workers, with the following shortcomings: it contains no indication of participatory forms outside information and consultation rights; the measures envisaged only concern Europe-wide or trans-national firms; on the other hand, the Treaty provides for the introduction of a proposal on employee ownership and financial participation.

The other set of proposals, which represent a more directly operational and challenging testing-ground for the political abilities of Community bodies, involve those directives meant to complete the process of corporate-law harmonisation, with important implications for Community labour law.

In practice this involves two directives, still pending approval after more than twenty years of debate, which define both the coordination of national legislation on joint-stock companies and the nature of limited companies under European law.[62]

Both of these directives embrace the issue of workers' participation, with similar results and an important innovation: they abandon the pursuit of a single form of participation (German-style codetermination, blocked by the objections of employers and many national unions) in favour a variety of forms. Drawing from the experience of different member states, the Commission took into consideration four forms: codetermination in its German variant, codetermination in its Dutch variant, codecision through a "separate" body representing workers, and participation by collective bargaining.

These four forms share two common features: the presence of information and consultation right; and a preference for the double system rather than the single one.

In our view, the novelty referred to is truly viable and sufficiently realistic, since any attempt to harmonise forcefully the participatory perspective is both questionable and unattainable.

It also confirms, however (as argued above) the low degree of political authority wielded by the Community in this area; moreover, it marks a shift away from strong forms of industrial democracy (codetermination) to weaker forms of equal standing; finally, the inclusion of bargained agreements extends the domain of participation to include experiences that can imply collaborative intentions and outcomes but do not *per se* entail adequate institutes or guarantees, apart from the implementation of norms regulating the access to information and the right of consultation.

This does not alter the fact that the directives in question are still pending approval and the likelihood that this will be granted does not seem any greater today than in the past.

4 The special character of codetermination in Germany

At the end of the chapter it may help to concentrate on the experience of codetermination in Germany, for of its clear relevance and because it is a milestone for the possibility of establishing industrial relations that reach beyond the results of collective bargaining.

This experience has functioned and expanded rapidly since the 1950s. If we use the number of workers involved as an indicator, the figures for the first half of the 1980s are as follows: 600,000 in the coal and steel industry (already subject to job reductions); 700,000 in medium-sized firms (500-2,000 employees); and 4.1 million in large concerns (over 2,000 employees).[63]

The implementation of its institutes, according to the findings of specialised studies, was not completely generalised or uniform; not always (as in similar phenomena) was there a full agreement between the guidelines of such institutes and actual facts, with discrepancies among firms as well as industrial sectors.[64]

German codetermination displays important peculiarities, compared with the same participatory form in other countries. Elsewhere the prospect of advancing industrial democracy and/or economic democracy took hold especially during the 1970s. In Germany is appeared much earlier and was closely related to previous and later steps.

Other two relevant aspects deserve mention: in Germany codetermination depends on legal measures, while in other contexts its implementation is optional or delegated to social partners; in Germany it involves workers as such alongside their trade union representatives, while in the Scandinavian countries, for example, it is linked more directly to trade union needs and their desire to enter a venue (the top level of a company) where members can be protected more effectively.[65]

These two aspects are not unrelated to a third feature of great significance. In other countries, including Sweden itself, trade unions or workers have minority representation in the firm's bodies, because agreed provisions and trade union decisions have not pursued a type of control capable of challenging managerial prerogatives or the employer's power within the firm.[66] In Germany, instead, equal representation was introduced by the 1951 Act and formally defined in the 1976 Act and, what is more, it remained a constant objective of the trade union movement and socialdemocratic area. The purpose of this objective is not to disregard the legitimation of entrepreneurial and managerial powers or functions; yet it implies an intention to condition – legally and practically – the decisions that underlie the use of such powers and functions.

This arrangement makes the German experience the most ambitious type of codetermination. In this sense, it not only adds to the instruments of labour protection and enhancement, but also actions an institutional device that – especially in view of equal representation – pursues the opportunity for joint collaborative decision-making, in line with the requirements of the firm and of its employees.

The arrangement has been evaluated in different ways. On the one hand, it may be seen as an "optimal" solution, since it manages to safeguard workers' rights inside the firm's decision-making bodies, without penalising the functions of the entrepreneur or the executive structures; on the other hand it may be considered a "dangerous" solution, because taken separately its legitimacy is doubtful and, if truly applied, its practical implications undermine the independence necessary to those charged with such functions and consequently leads to inefficiency.

Both of the yardsticks briefly outlined above have often resurfaced in the recurring debate on codetermination, especially in the event of legal measures that concern it and have deeply influenced its historical progress.

Codetermination earned wide recognition on the formal plane, but since the 1951 Act the objective of equal representation has been gradually eroded. It has been applied continually, though under rules that fall short of those pursued by the trade union movement. The authors of this operation were notably entrepreneurial circles: in particular, their reluctance to accept equal representation arises from threatened ownership rights and the fear that it would undermine the firm's functioning or even market economy itself.[67]

As for the concrete character of German codetermination, it is important to emphasise that the behaviour of owners and managers is essentially conciliating and respectful of the institute's functions, that the "dangers" attached to equal representation are not real, thanks to the above-mentioned erosion, that the action of workers' and trade union representatives is restricted to the tasks assigned to the supervisory board, with no interference in the duties or decisions of the managerial structure (the board of directors), and that in fact it strongly fosters agreement and conciliation within the supervisory board.

Because of its relevance and peculiarities, the experience of codetermination in Germany raises a number of significant questions on the rationale of collaborative participation inside the firm.

The first question, which concerns its past, can be expressed as follows: why did the most challenging form of industrial democracy take hold in Germany, despite the presence of trade unions sensitive to the economic implications of their action and the constant opposition of employers?

The main reason is found in two points that involve not only industrial relations but also political motives: the need to provide workers with rights compensating their commitment and contribution to overall development;[68] and the need to activate a solution that somehow reflects the criteria of political democracy.[69] These motives are deeply rooted in the past, given that workers' representation on supervisory boards was first allowed by a law was passed under the Weimar Republic.[70] Such bodies satisfy attempts by trade unions and the political Left to introduce institutional devices whereby ownership rights – however legitimate – cannot be exercised without supervision and recognised constraints.

The realisation of these attempts through State intervention and legal provisions contributes significantly to establish a highly legalistic-oriented structure for regulating collective relations between social partners. The introduction of representation in the decision-making sphere and the nature of this regulation offer a guarantee to workers and their organisations, widen the time span for the assessment of their acquisitions, and help above all to curb actual instances of conflict.

Essentially, the collaborative scenario is taking over not because labour has scaled down its aims, but rather because the institutional guarantees and suitable venues are in place for its objectives to be recognised and applied.

The second question concerns the economic effects of codetermination. According to observers suspicious of this participatory form, and considering employers' claims, it is bound to lead to repeated inefficiency – due especially to the constraints placed on the exercise of owners' rights.

This assumption has not so far been fully confirmed by empirical evidence; partly due to the lack of extensive research in the field, which is often focused on formal specifications and their implementation.

Concerning productivity, some observers emphasise the good market position of firms with codetermination; other studies, however, have failed to confirm any significant effect on productivity levels and point out a constant upward trend in wages.

As for accumulation, no clear confirmation is available, although some studies have exposed a tendency to underinvest, due to representatives' reluctance to accept technological innovation and labour-saving options.[71]

Many analysts advise to look at its indirect positive economic effects, because codetermination produces more agreeable – if not less hierarchical – relations, contributes to abate tension and raises the degree of employee satisfaction (especially among highly specialised workers).[72]

The third question regards the relationship between codetermination and workers. It can be approached in two different ways: Has this institute interested and involved workers? How has it influenced their concrete working conditions?

Codetermination has always been welcomed as an institutional and political victory for trade unions. Apart from the unions, it has involved their counterparts and the political system, while workers' intentions and feelings appear less directly involved in its activities. On the other hand, this situation often develops when trade union objectives are neither short-term nor demand-driven. Empirical research in the field tends to show that codetermination is not perceived separately (as for meaning and features) by workers, but alongside other bodies committed to their protection; they appreciate its existence but show no special interest in it.[73]

As regards the influence of codetermination on actual working conditions, it should be remembered that the quality of work cannot be attributed chiefly to this factor, and that other bodies such as works councils are responsible for the same factor.

The issue of better working conditions was addressed more resolutely than before by German trade unions in the 1970s, in order to "humanise work" in the face of technological and organisational change. The issue resurfaced in the 1980s, as part of the programme of the DGB federation, which aimed to extend codetermination to the workplace, together with other objectives such as the introduction of the institute to new manufacturing sectors. Apart from the hesitation shown in this proposal, the objective seemed to undervalue the balance of interests produced by the codetermination rationale. It was never applied and was unlikely to result in more progressive legislation.[74]

In Germany, the formal regulation of codetermination remained as it was in the 1970s, reaching a threshold that it is not likely to breach. Its implementation continued throughout the Eighties, approaching a period subject to factors and situations that could hardly have been predicted.

Finally, the strongest experiences of industrial democracy needs to be addressed as a whole, with the following question: is codetermination a form of collaborative participation "produced" by a certain epoch, or can it arise again today and in the future?

Despite the risks inherent in any attempt to specify the future development of industrial relations, we are confident that in the present and foreseeable future there is little scope or significant space for experiences that explicitly imply the involvement of workers' representatives in the firm's decisions. These experiences develop – as we stressed earlier – only under specific conditions which now appear to be missing, and equally there is no indication of changing conditions to warrant the belief that such experiences could easily be revived. Most probably, they will survive in the (few) contexts that have long known them but can be hardly expected to grow stronger or extend to new contexts.

Strong forms of industrial democracy took hold after the Second World War, in conjunction with concertation practices and accords. However, their fate is not necessarily dependent on concertation. The latter – especially in its neo-corporatist variant – embodies a growing degree of "politicisation" in industrial relations. If this feature is prevalent also today, then it may be possible to envisage a national revival of themes and solutions akin to concertation, in order to favour economic and occupational trends and meet competition requirements. But this fact will not affect firms in the same manner: the growing need for flexibility and innovation... participatory forms such as

111

codetermination, thus inevitably complicating decision-making processes and placing a series of constraints on the use of labour even under the collaborative rationale.

There is no doubt that the future of industrial democracy and all its forms will still be influenced by political-cultural and trade union traditions in different countries. Yet less so that in the past.

Within such traditions, a greater role will be played by structural factors such as supra-national concentration in "key" manufacturing and tertiary sectors; the influence of cautious, controversial Community decisions will also be felt, alongside employers' growing freedom to escape any participatory form they do not entirely approve of.

Notes

1   Cf. G.P. Cella and T. Treu, 'Relazioni industriali', *Giornale di diritto del lavoro e di relazioni industriali*, No. 31, 1986, pp. 482ff.
2   See, among others, our study *La politica sindacale nel capitalismo che cambia*, Laterza: Bari 1986, chapters 3 and 5.
3   Cf. M. Napoli, 'Il quadro giuridico-istituzionale', in G.P. Cella and T. Treu (eds), *Relazioni industriali. Manuale per l'analisi dell'esperienza italiana*, Il Mulino, Bologna 1989, pp. 48ff.
4   Cf. D. Sagrestin, 'Recent Changes in France', in G. Baglioni and C. Crouch (eds), *European Industrial Relations. The Challenge of Flexibility*, Sage Publications: London 1990; and J.D. Reynaud, 'Francia. Una esperienza sindacale con vincoli e potenzialità dovute al quadro politico', in CESOS (ed.), *L'Europa sindacale nel 1982*, Il Mulino: Bologna 1984, pp. 62ff.
5   As stated, for example, by G. Giugni in his foreword to G. Giugni et al., *Il potere in fabbrica. Esperienze di democrazia industriale in Europa*, Quaderni di Mondoperaio: Rome 1979.
6   C. Crouch, 'Afterword', in G. Baglioni and C. Crouch (eds), *European Industrial Relations. The Challenge of Flexibility*, op. cit.
7   R. Dahrendorf, *Class and Conflict in an Industrial Society*, Routledge: London 1959.
8   H.A. Clegg, *Trade Unionism under Collective Bargaining. A Theory Based on Comparisons of Six Countries*, Basil Blackwell: Oxford 1976, Chapter 7.
9   See, among others, A.M. Ross and P.T. Hartman, *Changing Patterns of Industrial Conflict*, J. Wiley: New York 1960.
10 R. Dahrendorf, *Class and Conflict in an Industrial Society*, op. cit.
11 R. Eisfeld, *Pluralismus zwischen Liberalismus und Sozialismus*, Verlag W. Kohlhammer: Stuttgart 1972.

12   As N. Matteucci rightly remarks in his *Presentation* to the Italian edition of Eisfeld's study (Il Mulino: Bologna 1976).

13   W. Streeck, 'Status e contratto nella teoria delle relazioni industriali', *Giornale di diritto del lavoro e di relazioni industriali*, No. 39, 1988.

14   As in ILO, *Workers' Participation in Decision within Undertakings*, Geneva 1981.

15   T. Treu, 'Cogestione e partecipazione', *Giornale di diritto del lavoro e di relazioni economiche*, No. 4, 1989.

16   S. Negrelli, 'Dai diritti di informazione ai diritti di consultazione', *Industria e Sindacato*, No. 37, 1991; and L. Saba, 'Il sindacato e la partecipazione: orientamenti ed esperienze aziendali. Forme, istituti e organismi partecipativi nell'industria italiana', ENI-ISVET Seminar, Rome, April 1991.

17   G. Baglioni and R. Milani (eds), *La contrattazione collettiva nelle aziende industriali in Italia*, Angeli: Milan 1990.

18   Cf. R. Blanpain, *Diritto del lavoro e relazioni industriali nella Comunità europea*, Edizioni Lavoro: Rome 1992, pp. 223f.

19   Cf. G. Arrigo, 'Le proposte comunitarie in materia di informazione, consultazione, partecipazione dei lavoratori', *Industria e Sindacato*, No. 6, 1992.

20   P. Cressey, 'New Technology: An Overview of Regulation', *European Industrial Relations Review*, February 1987.

21   G. Della Rocca, 'Improving Participation: The Negotiation of New Technology in Italy and Europe', in C. Sirianni (ed.), *Worker Participation and the Politics of Reform*, Temple University Press: Philadelphia, 1987.

22   Cf. ILO, *Workers' Participation in Decision within Undertakings*, op. cit., chapters 2 and 7.

23   Cf. T. Hanami, 'La partecipazione dei lavoratori nella fabbrica e nell'impresa', in R. Blanpain and T. Treu (eds), *Diritto del lavoro e relazioni industriali comparate*, Edizioni Lavoro: Rome 1980.

24   Cf. ILO, *Workers' Participation in Decision within Undertakings*, op. cit., Chapter 7.

25   H.G. Nutzinger, 'Codetermination in West Germany: Institutions and Experiences', in H.G. Nutzinger and J. Backhaus (eds), *Codetermination. A Discussion of Different Approaches*, Springer Verlag: Berlin 1989, p. 166.

26   Cf. S. Simitis, 'L'esempio tedesco', in G. Giugni et al., *Il potere in fabbrica. Esperienze di democrazia industriale in Europa*, Quaderni di Mondoperaio, No. 11, Rome 1979.

27   K. Bartölke and E. Kappler, 'Institutional Reform: The Future of Codetermination', in H.G. Nutzinger and J. Backhaus (eds), *Codetermination*, op. cit., pp. 203-204; and S.G. Alf, *Partecipazione dei lavoratori e*

codecisione nella Rft e in Italia: prospettive per una democrazia economica europea, Friedrich-Ebert-Stiftung: Rome 1991.

28 W. Streeck, 'Industrial Relations in West Germany 1970-1987', *Labour*, No. 3, 1988, pp. 24ff.

29 H.A. Clegg, *Trade Unionism under Collective Bargaining. A Theory Based on Comparisons of Six Countries*, op. cit., Chapter 5.

30 J.F.B. Goodman, 'United Kingdom', in A.A. Blum (ed.), *International Handbook of Industrial Relations. Contemporary Developments and Research*, Aldwych Press: London 1981, pp. 599-601.

31 Cf. S. Sciarra, 'Dal rapporto Bullock al Libro bianco', in G. Giugni et al., *Il potere in fabbrica*, op. cit.

32 C. Crouch, 'United Kingdom: the Rejection of Compromise', in G. Baglioni and C. Crouch (eds), *European Industrial Relations. The Challenge of Flexibility*, op. cit.

33 Cf. our study 'L'istituto della Commissione interna e la questione della rappresentanza dei lavoratori nei luoghi di lavoro', in P. Bellasi et al., *Fabbrica e società. Autogestione e partecipazione operaia in Europa*, Il Mulino: Bologna 1972.

34 Cf. G. Romagnoli and G. Della Rocca, 'Il sindacato', in G.P. Cella and T. Treu (eds), *Relazioni industriali*, op. cit., pp. 117ff.

35 Cf. M. Regini and C. Sabel, 'Le strategie di riaggiustamento industriale in Italia; il ruolo degli assetti istituzionali', *Stato e Mercato*, No. 24, 1988.

36 A recent example is provided by W. Eberwein and J. Tholen, 'Participation et contrôle: thèses sur l'évolution des relations professionnelles dans l'enterprise en Allemagne', *Travail et Société*, No. 3, 1991.

37 H.A. Clegg, *Trade Unionism under Collective Bargaining. A Theory Based on Comparisons of Six Countries*, op. cit., Chapter 7.

38 Cf. T. Hanami, *La partecipazione dei lavoratori nella fabbrica e nell'impresa*, op. cit.

39 M. Pedrazzoli, 'Alternative italiane sulla partecipazione nel quadro europeo: la cogestione', *Giornale di diritto del lavoro e di relazioni industriali*, No. 49, 1991, pp. 5ff; H.J. Sperling, 'Il caso della Mitbestimmung', in G. Giugni et al., *Il potere in fabbrica*, op. cit.; Hans Böckler Foundation, Codecisione. Il sistema legale di codecisione nella Repubblica federale di Germania, Düsseldorf, undated.

40 J. Ramondt, 'Netherlands', in A.A. Blum (ed.), *International Handbook of Industrial Relations*, op. cit., pp. 411ff.

41 Cf. B. Veneziani, 'Il progetto olandese', in G. Giugni et al., *Il potere in fabbrica*, op. cit.

42 B. Gustafsson, 'L'esperienza svedese della cogestione e dei fondi dei lavoratori', in A. Baldassarre (ed.), *I limiti della democrazia*, Laterza: Bari 1985.

43 T. Lidbom, 'La via svedese alla partecipazione', in G. Giugni et al., *Il potere in fabbrica*, op. cit.

44 A. Cottino, 'Svezia. L'interruzione dell'esperienza riformista e la ripresa del conflitto', in CESOS, *L'Europa sindacale agli inizi degli anni '80*, Bologna, Il Mulino, 1982, pp. 285ff.

45 Cf. R.B. Peterson, 'Swedish Collective Bargaining. A Changing Scene', *British Journal of Industrial Relations*, No. 1, 1987.

46 G. Rehn and B. Viklung, 'Changes in the Swedish Model', in G. Baglioni and C. Crouch (eds), *European Industrial Relations. The Challenge of Flexibility*, op. cit.

47 Cf. A. Marsh, *Concise Encyclopedia of Industrial Relations*, Gower Press: Portsmouth 1979, pp. 35-36.

48 Cf. R. Bean, *Comparative Industrial Relations. An Introduction to Cross-national Perspectives*, Croom Helm: London 1985, passim.

49 Cf. T. Hanami, *La partecipazione dei lavoratori nella fabbrica e nell'impresa*, op. cit., pp. 343ff.

50 Cf. R. Dore, *Taking Japan Seriously. A Confucian Perspective on Leading Economic Issues*, Athlone Press: London 1987.

51 W. Streeck, 'Le relazioni industriali nell'Europa che cambia', *Industria e Sindacato*, No. 1-2, 1992.

52 Cf. O. Jacobi and W. Müller-Jentsch, 'Germania. Rallentamento economico e potenziale instabilità sociale', in CESOS, *L'Europa sindacale agli inizi degli anni '80*, Il Mulino: Bologna 1982, pp. 148ff.

53 G. Rehn and B. Viklung, 'Changes in the Swedish Model', in G. Baglioni and C. Crouch (eds), *European Industrial Relations. The Challenge of Flexibility*, op. cit.

54 Cf. S. Negrelli, 'Le relazioni industriali nell'impresa', in G.P. Cella and T. Treu (eds), *Relazioni industriali*, op. cit., Chapter 6.

55 C. Crouch, *United Kingdom: the Rejection of Compromise*, op. cit.; and S. Taibly and M. Terry, 'Gli sviluppi delle relazioni industriali nel Regno Unito', *Industria e Sindacato*, No. 17-18, 1992.

56 Cf. A. Lyon-Caen, 'Le relazioni industriali nell'impresa in Francia', *Industria e Sindacato*, No. 12, 1992.

57 Cf. F. Duràn Lopez, 'L'evoluzione delle relazioni industriali in Spagna', *Industria e Sindacato*, No. 16, 1992.

58 See especially W. Streeck, 'La dimensione sociale del mercato unico europeo: verso un'economia non regolata?', *Stato e Mercato*, No. 26, 1990.

59 A concept proposed by W. Streeck, *Le relazioni industriali nell'Europa che cambia*, op. cit.

60 Cf. 'EEC Social Charter: Action Programme Released', *European Industrial Relations Review*, January 1990.

61 The text of the Community Charter was completed in January 1990.

62 See G. Arrigo, *Le proposte comunitarie in materia di informazione e parte-*

cipazione dei lavoratori, op. cit.; and R. Blanpain, *Diritto del lavoro e relazioni industriali nella Comunità europea*, op. cit., pp. 223-38.

63   Cf. G. Geroldi and S. Caselli, 'L'economia partecipativa: idee e problemi per lo sviluppo di una nuova impresa', *Prospettiva sindacale*, No. 82, 1991.

64   D.C. Jones, 'Codetermination in West Germany: Institutions and Experiences', in H.G. Nutzinger and J. Backhaus (eds), *Codetermination*, op. cit.

65   N. Bruun et al., *The Nordic Labour Relations Model*, Aldershot: Dartmouth 1992, pp. 67ff and 79ff.

66   'Sweden: Whatever happened to Swedish Codetermination?', *European Industrial Relations Review*, October 1989.

67   K. Bartölke and E. Kappler, *Institutional Reform: The Future of Codetermination*, op. cit., p. 205.

68   H.G. Nutzinger and J. Backhaus (eds), *Codetermination*, op. cit., 'Introduction'.

69   W.J. Samuels, 'Institutional Reform: The Future of Codetermination', in H.G. Nutzinger and J. Backhaus (eds), *Codetermination*, op. cit.

70   Refer to the historical overview of these institutes in the cited study by K. Bartölke and E. Kappler.

71   Cf. G. Geroldi and S. Caselli, 'L'economia partecipativa: idee e problemi per lo sviluppo di una nuova impresa', op. cit.

72   See, among others, M. Knuth, 'Trade Union Strategy, Codetermination and Quality of Work in West Germany: The Shaping of Work and Technology and its Industrial Relations Implications', contribution to the 12th Conference of the International Working Party on «Labour Market Segmentation», Venice, July 1990.

73   Cf. H.G. Nutzinger, *Codetermination in West Germany: Institutions and Experiences*, op. cit.

74   Cf. K. Bartölke and E. Kappler, *Institutional Reform: The Future of Codetermination*, op. cit.

5 The integrative model and the recent progress of economic participation

1 The rationale of the integrative model

The integrative participation model refers to a variety of proposals and experiences based on the following premises: they provide for ample freedom of initiative by the employer and management; they seek to involve workers – both individually, as specific groups and collectively – in the functioning of the firm and/or to commit them to its life and fate; though not necessarily through their representatives.

Such premises may be linked, as we shall see, to the aims that the entrepreneurial world attributes to integrative participation. But in fact this is not simply guided and supported by the managerial side: in many cases it is applied by means of negotial practices that imply the presence of trade union representatives; some of its forms, moreover, have been favoured in many contexts by support from the public actor.

In spite of these two variants, the integrative model preserves its specific character, as may be seen by comparison with the collaborative model.

The integrative model assumes there is no difference of interests between employer and worker; while in the collaborative model the difference does exist, and can be overcome under certain conditions and institutions.

In the integrative model – as in functionalist sociological theory – conflict is considered an anomaly due to the lack of cultural and organisational conditions that produce "natural" consensus; while in the collaborative model conflict originates from the asymmetry inherent in the wage-earning labour relationship, although it can be prevented and restrained.

In the integrative model, managerial prerogatives are not viewed as on object of participation; the spirit and institutes of industrial democracy, instead, envisage their partial limitation.

The integrative model appears today highly relevant. Its increasing frequency since the 1970s is due to well-known reasons, such as: the decline of highly conflictful ideologies and purely claim-driven trade union orientations; technological and organisational innovations that, in a context of international competition,[1] stimulate an extensive need for flexibility; the difficulty of centralised policies for the determination of remuneration;[2] a preference for participation, in the wake of economic and social results attributed to the Japanese experience.

However relevant, integrative participation does not represent a novelty in the development of perspectives aimed at improving the employment relationship in capitalist firms.

Its distant forerunners can be observed in the spectrum of doctrines and programmes (dating from between the late nineteenth century to the 1930s) sensitive to the need for and possibility of stable harmonisation of workers' and employers' interests (Chapter 1).

This line was taken mainly by Christian-oriented thinkers and is fully reflected in *Quadragesimo Anno*, an encyclical letter of Pope Pius XI (1931),[3] aimed at introducing institutional changes (employee ownership and participation in profit) towards equity and social justice.

A contribution to this line may also be found in the work of the classical economists J.S. Mill and A. Marshall, who aimed to create economic incentives for workers based on business performance, to improve relations with their employer in view of truly cooperative arrangements.[4]

The intentions and programmes of those advocating this line were hardly ever accepted culturally or in practice by employers. Their conversion to workers' economic participation, in particular, has become widespread only in recent decades, although previous cases occurred in Britain at the turn of the century[5] and in the United States from the 1930s onwards.[6]

The aims that bring single actors and environments in the entrepreneurial world to propose or accept practices and institutes of integrative participation are chiefly two: to raise workers' motivation for greater commitment in the discharge of their tasks, and – closely connected to this – the need to achieve collaborative, confident relations between employees and management. These two fundamental, recurring aims tend to be viewed as preconditions for social cohesion among those acting inside the firm; in a number of situations this can imply, more or less openly, the consideration of these practices and institutes as an effective deterrent, to influence trade union action or even to prove its redundancy.

In recent years, this combination of aims has been linked to managerial attempts to innovate and refine human resource management, and to shape – better than before – the nature of industrial relations and their evolution. The application of integrative participatory forms is often viewed as a strategic option adequate to legitimise management rights and duties fully and verifiably, to limit the shortcomings of standard wage systems (by attracting workers with supplementary economic benefits), and to render capital accumulation processes more transparent and less exclusive (by involving workers through ownership quotas in the firm).[7]

To complete this picture of participation, three features need to be emphasised.

Its manifestations are in fact hardly homogeneous, especially as to the key aspect of trade union representation during the application of integrative institutes and practices.

These have spread – though at first at different times – to many capitalist countries, in Europe and more notably in the United States and Japan. This is a major difference, compared with most other participatory experiences, generally proposed and implemented in a far smaller number of countries. The emphasis given to this feature does not warrant the belief that integrative participation may arise without the support or influence of its actors' industrial relations traditions and orientations. In the case of the United States and Japan, for instance, it has certainly been favoured by strongly decentralised collective bargaining. This does not change the fact that, at least since the 1990s, it has had ample opportunities of success in clearly different environments. This phenomenon appears linked (though not exclusively, of course) to the variety of connections established with previous industrial relations arrangements and with trade union action.

The phenomenon is greatly facilitated by the venue of integrative participation, which is typically a corporate group, a firm or its parts. Its manifestations may share common traits and be favoured by legal provisions of support and regulation; in any case, they reflect the character and specifications of single groups and firms.

The integrative participatory model comprises the direction of *economic* participation and that of *cultural-organisational* participation.

The main objective of the former is to interest workers in the firm's performance by offering them the benefits of its results.

The latter is based on workers' involvement in the purpose and mission of the firm and its constant need for innovation, assuming motivations shared by the different actors involved in it.

These two directions cannot be placed on the same plane. While instances of the former are evident and verifiable, the latter is a more complex and latent phenomenon. The former reflects well-defined, clear-cut participatory forms; in the latter, instead, the participatory dimension is a precondition for a range of processes related mostly to the firm's organisation. The former can be activated without the latter, while the latter can hardly survive in the medium-to-long term without economic concessions. Another difference can be envisaged between these two directions. The latter is more prone than the former to view single workers or specific groups of workers (rather than workers as a whole) as the recipients of participatory messages and implications. In practice, however, this tendency does not always arise.

119

The fundamental differences, which will be outlined in greater detail in the course of the chapter, can be summarised as follows:

a   economic participation provides workers with tangible benefits, asks them to take an interest in the firm's performance without touching the criteria and decisions that oversee its functioning, and can be applied in traditionally-structured firms and in more advanced ones;

b   cultural-organisational participation does not provide for explicit economic advantages for workers, who are asked to identify with the firm's organisation (marked by increasingly integrated programmes and processes) and give it their consensus and contribution in view of its objectives of innovation and advancement.

2 Forms of economic participation

This direction is expressed mostly by two forms: *profit sharing* (which includes institutes and practices which, on top of fixed wages, allocate workers a variable proportion of their salary, related to the firm's results as calculated by special performance indicators) and *employee ownership* (which includes institutes and practices that allow workers indirect benefits from the firm's results, by access to share capital).

Besides these two main forms, there exist other less typical forms of profit sharing and, in past years, other devices for involving workers in economic benefits. This calls for a clear approach to any evidence of this participatory direction, especially as regards its profit sharing form.

This may in fact be approached from two viewpoints: on one hand, as an integral part of economic participation; on the other, as an instance of the old tradition of using incentives to favour workers' commitment.

The first of the two approaches is undoubtedly more relevant in this context, as it comprises recent and present instances and takes into due account the participatory qualities of a form that reaches beyond the traditional confines of incentivation devices.

The second approach cannot be entirely overlooked, however, in consideration of the following facts: monetary incentivation is always a problematic motivator of workers' attitude and effort; traditional incentives – and above all individual piece-work – are among the most prominent and exploited exceptions to the standard employment relationship in capitalist firms, alongside others exceptions, either with (e.g. wage indexation) or without participatory traits;[8] there are some types of wage indexation, such as specific group- or collective-schemes, that do not appear clearly distinct from certain modes of economic participation.[9]

Profit sharing exhibits three salient features: its collective dimension regards all the firm's employees or segments of these (middle and top management); it rests not on workers' performance and output (as in the case of traditional incentives) but on results achieved by the whole firm and/or its success (e.g. meeting budget targets);[10] and it unfolds in a high number of ways, classifiable according to their greater or lesser "depth".

The first case (low depth) refers to schemes that tend to involve workers by reference to indicators reflecting their contribution. The standard indicator in this area are *productivity* gains, which relate to *gain sharing* schemes.

The second case (high depth) refers to schemes that involve workers by reference to indicators reflecting the firm's *overall results*, but leaving aside any consideration of their contribution. These schemes, known inclusively as "participation in profit", are the real-term equivalent of profit sharing.

The degree of depth allows us to keep gain sharing separate from profit sharing. The two have various points in common, especially in their implementation, but cannot truly be merged.

The term gain sharing was originally applied to traditional incentivation systems.[11] In the United States and Europe it is now referred to productivity-linked profit shares, and in particular to the different variables that reflect it (use of plant, scrap recovery, attendance rates). These incentives are not usually linked, therefore, to labour productivity alone (the amount of work per product unit).

Profit-sharing schemes include "participation in profit". As observed above, this expression is too vague and signals the need to identify more specific modes of implementation,[12] in the past as well as today. The main modes (not always clearly indicated in agreements or even in literature) regard:

i   added value (total sales *less* purchase of intermediate goods and depreciation);
ii profit (profit *less* tax and allocations).[13]

These modes *directly* relate shares distributed according to the firm's results, to whatever occurs *immediately* after their observation.

Other modes, on the other hand, involve *deferred* payment, such as:

a   a percentage of profit placed in funds and invested on the workers' behalf;
b   certain wage items frozen in accounts inaccessible to workers for a given period;
c   shareholdings proportional to profit, frozen in a trust account for a given period.

As mentioned earlier, the crucial feature of profit sharing is the fact that a share of workers' remuneration varies according to the firm's results. This raises the problem of ensuring that workers enjoy the benefits of results achieved with their contribution (though individual effort is far more diluted here than with traditional incentives); another problem is the cost workers may have to sustain if the firm achieves no positive results.

The last problem is at the forefront of the current debate on the viability of economic participation and has extended to the employee ownership form.

It is normally noticeable in the fact that workers accept the risk and consequences of fluctuations in the firm's performance, with considerable changes in the conditions of traditional employment.

Many authors, even authoritative scholars such as J. Meade,[14] argue that all forms of economic participation share the inevitable consequence of dividing earnings and losses between workers and capital; although remedial measures can be activated – especially under profit-sharing schemes – to limit the repercussions of losses on workers. Such correctives are harder to apply when schemes of "full participation in profit" [15] are introduced, whereby no fixed salary is provided and all labour is remunerated with a given share of the firm's profit or earnings. This scheme has been notably analysed extensively with reference to M.L. Weitzman's proposal.[16] It does not require as much coherence, if applied in less radical terms (as Weitzman himself argues) – i.e. stating that workers should earn a greater proportion in fixed wages and a smaller one as a share in profit or earnings.

Later in the chapter we shall reconsider the issue of risk and other aspects of profit sharing schemes, with the aid of the two above-mentioned authors.

The second form of economic participation has been defined as the possibility for workers to benefit indirectly from results achieved by the firm, by access to shareholdings in its capital. This participation is *indirect* insofar as it relates to the firm's overall profitability rather than balance-sheet indicators, thus enabling subjects involved to reap the full benefit of the firm's growth.

The said participatory form rests on employees' access to ownership. This qualitative change in their status is one of the recurring issues in the slow progress of participatory proposals and experiences, and especially of those tending to establish economic democracy solutions or perspectives under the antagonistic rationale.

This type of workers' access to ownership appears highly different both historically and institutionally. Its effects in terms of company control are much slighter – being proposed or accepted by employers, often even with approval or support (especially by tax concessions) from a moderate political environment – and it introduces correctives than generally have little influence over workers' actual conditions.

This form of economic participation should not be confused with other forms implying a different approach to shareholding. The difference can be easily noted by looking at the alternative ways whereby it unfolds, ranging from individual to collective shareholdings, both inside and outside the firm.

Employee ownership proper occurs within the firm, as it represents a participatory form that seeks to involve workers in the firm's "fortunes" – under the rationale of the integrative model.

Proposals and solutions outside the firm do not concern this involvement, but rather the condition of workers as citizens or as organised groups confronting capital ownership.

The first case – individual ownership, normally known as "popular capitalism" – brings to mind European public companies resulting from the privatisation of State concerns (in Britain, France and now also in Italy). It involves citizens and their families as a whole; it does not seek to improve the employment relationship or its conditions; and its influence on firm structures and management may be irrelevant. The rapid increase in the number of individual investors is certainly not irrelevant, but has little significance for the rationale of participation.

The second case brings to mind the Swedish experience of investment funds (Chapter 2), whose political and macroeconomic objectives lie outside the sphere we assigned earlier to economic participation.

This is realised inside the firm by the employee shareholding form, with traits that always allow a sharp division between individual and collective shareholdings. Its recipients are single workers but in practice its provisions affect all the firm's workers or entire groups of them. Sometimes single workers can decide whether to join the scheme offered (choosing whether to invest in the company that employs them), an aspect that highlights the difference between employee shareholding and deferred profit sharing with a distribution of share quotas, as referred to earlier. The practical experience of this type of shareholding is varied and diversified, partly because of its complex technicalities,[17] which do not need to be recalled here. However, they can be subsumed under one of the following modes:

1   a quota of shares is reserved for employees, generally at preferential conditions (lower costs, right of pre-emption in public purchase offers, deferred payment) or at special conditions (e.g. for high-seniority workers);

2   a quota (even considerable) of shares is destined to the creation of shareholding schemes, under which they are not moved directly into workers' private accounts but into a fund where they normally remain tied up for a given period.

The first of these modes can take on the traits of fully-fledged individual participation in ownership.

The second mode, as observed in the important case of ESOPs (Employee Stock Ownership Plans) in North America, often functions as a form of pension saving.

3 Instances and results of economic participation

The following pages will simply outline the general traits of this phenomenon and its occurrence in a few countries. Such instances are relatively recent and, above all, their outcome is unclear. Economic participation is highly diversified within the same country, even if it addresses motives that altogether tend to be homogenous.

The most striking difference concerns its degree of diffusion and recognition. In Europe, the two countries with the highest level of economic participation are Britain and France, though their industrial relations are traditionally distinct; in other countries, instead, diffusion is lower and greater problems are encountered. This scenario confirms that economic participation is associated with conditions marked by significant innovations, notably in the orientation of the actors involved in these relations.

This participation is known to involve prevalently the initiative of employers and managers. However, it has been favoured considerably by public measures and has relied, in certain cases, on a reduction the unions' power, and in other instances on their collaboration.

But the initiative is not generalised: it concerns especially certain productive segments, as in France,[18] or specific types of employer, as in Britain;[19] both forms are widely present in Italy, while in Germany, for example, employers have supported only employee-shareholding plans.[20]

More in general, many employers appear to be wary of economic participation schemes and waver between tradition and innovation in personnel policy and in the use of labour, between constraints due to collective bargaining and participatory solutions that may somehow interfere with their prerogatives, between the advantages of flexible wages and the costs attached to greater worker-involvement.

In economic participation, as in other participatory forms, the public actor has a prominent role; to the point that its extent may be related to the spread of the phenomenon. Compared with other participatory forms, two important differences can be observed.

The first is that under economic participation, State action does not aim to favour perspectives and institutes proposed by labour nor is it due only to pro-Labour political conditions and governments. Conversely, in some countries – such as Britain – State intervention started at the end of the 1970s, as the Conservative Party came into power.

The second difference is that the public actor provides resources (tax concessions) to ensure the success of the phenomenon. This is an unusual option for participatory experiences in the firm, with notable precedents always associated with the introduction of concertation-type agreements.

In the EEC area,[21] public policies exhibit varying degrees of encouragement and support.

Both differences are prominent in Britain and France; in the latter this dates back to the country's direction at the end of the 1950s.

In Germany, shareholding has been constantly supported by legal provisions that from the 1960s to our day have marked a shift away from the objective of greater distribution of wealth among citizens and workers to that of greater worker-participation in the ownership of company capital.[22]

In other countries, such as Italy, a wide debate has developed, but only with minor measures or even none at all. In some of these countries, this has partly been a result of the new dilemma between experiences in single firms and more general instances, in the wake of perspectives such as workers' investment funds or solidarity funds (Chapter 2).

Notably, public measures consist above all of tax concessions and incentives which, despite their marked diversity, have been implemented not only in France and Britain but also in several other countries (Germany, Belgium, Holland and Denmark), often right from the early post-war decades.

Even in the United States, generous tax concessions are the chief factor behind the diffusion of ESOPs, with several benefits also for firms (i.e. the provision of low-priced capital, an internal share market, pension-fund savings).[23]

The decisive role of fiscal measures – especially in the United States, France and Britain – in the success of different modes of employee shareholding means that greater costs may eventually have to be placed on the State budget.[24] This arrangement is justified in the sphere of economic policy and under the rationale of economic democracy, as it seeks to encourage saving among workers. On the other hand, it raises a number of questions on the participatory rationale proper, as it tends to dissolve exchange (connected to non-antagonistic participation forms) and prevents the assessment of actual changes in wage systems with concessions to the firm because of workers' involvement in its capital.

As for the trade union actor, the prevalent orientations in Europe were at first diffident or hostile, even in traditionally collaborative environments. This may be due to ideological reasons, to fears related to the functions of workers' collective representation, to their difficult compatibility with other on-going participatory experiences. Such orientations have recently been scaled down in favour of a more pragmatic line; as in the case of Italy, for example.[25]

In practice, trade union orientations and actions appear hardly homogeneous, especially in consideration of the features of national industrial relations systems.

Britain, partly similar in this to the United States, has heard various trade union statements in favour of employee shareholding, but the unions remain basically unfavourable to profit sharing.[26] On the other hand, trade union involvement reaches a high at the signing of agreements.[27]

In France, trade union or works-council involvement is quite frequent in profit sharing practices (*intéressement*), whereby the law obliges employers to negotiate.

In Germany, trade union structures have had no serious difficulty in restraining the spread of profit sharing, given their preference for wage policies compatible with productivity. Some unions, on the other hand, have opposed employee ownership legislation, invoking the need to safeguard the persistence of codetermination.

In Italy, decentralised bargaining has been employed for a gradual correction in the country's conflict-based and highly claim-driven tradition, with motives and results adapted to firms' requirements. Recent years, in particular, have seen the spread of negotial solutions that highlight the connection with economic indicators, especially as they regard leading industrial groups.[28]

These brief notes on the diversity and evolution of trade union orientations and actions confirm our argument at the start of this chapter that, being free to arise without mediation by trade union representatives, economic participation can in fact be applied either with or without them – and the first case is by no means negligible or unusual.

This means that economic participation, especially by profit sharing accords, is highly adaptive to different contexts, includes potentialities likely to emerge in the future, and can enrich negotial solutions verifiable in industrial relations systems.

These real or potential qualities do not normally cancel its unique traits.

Unlike industrial democracy and despite trade union presence, economic democracy does not seek to establish formal bodies charged with the definition of working conditions or even business decisions.[29]

Unlike collective bargaining, economic participation overcomes the restrictions of the pluralistic system and the sharp division between the functions and interests of each side involved. These features preserve their interests if, as often happens, its realisation rests on bargaining practices with the "natural" actors of collective bargaining, considering that the latter may expect concrete opportunities and objectives of the participatory type.

Is the use of such opportunities an explicit qualitative leap for the negotial-bargaining method, or does it belong to an intermediate phase that will sooner or later be replaced by traditional bargaining and its standard wage systems?

Our view is that we are confronted with a qualitative leap in this method, for the reasons at the root of the phenomenon and the said features, because bargaining has to compete with participatory solutions that occur even in the absence of workers' representatives.

On the other hand, this is not an alternative to less innovative bargaining practices (as in many other participatory forms in the firm) nor a generalised phenomenon; it can spread at times and does not normally extend, in its venue, to all areas of employment regulation.

These observations should be related to its diffusion, as illustrated by the evidence below. Our data is taken largely from the 1980s and is not, therefore, always up to date. In certain cases it may be overestimated, as the same subjects can take part in different schemes, and these are not available to all the firm's employees nor do all workers accept to be involved in participation. Such data [30] concerns both forms of economic participation, without considering their disaggregation into a host of implementation modes.[31]

Two overall considerations should be made at this stage: in Europe and the United States the phenomenon has spread steadily, whether more rapidly (as in France) or more slowly (as in Italy), but always less so compared to Japan; its incidence in terms of workers' income and benefits is generally weak. The proportion of wages affected is generally under 10 per cent, and at times well under the same figure. The quota of shares reserved for workers is seldom more than 5 per cent of all shares issued.

In France, profit sharing (*intéressement*) reached 5,000 agreements in 1990.[32] While *participation à la croissance de l'entreprise* agreements appeared in 12,000 firms.[33]

In Great Britain, profit sharing expanded rapidly, and by 1987 it covered 50 per cent of manufacturing firms. Employee shareholding was implemented in more than 30 per cent of large concerns.[34]

In Germany, profit sharing is found in 5 per cent of manufacturing firms. Employee shareholding is available in 1,600 firms.[35]

In Italy, 25 per cent of large concerns are estimated to employ wage systems related to business performance indicators. Employee shareholding is not common.

In the United States, 32 per cent of firms were providing profit-sharing schemes by 1988. Shareholding consisted mostly of different ESOP schemes affecting over 10,000 firms.[36]

In Japan, economic participation expanded far more than in the West, but the comparison is not fully pertinent because: in Japan, the linking of a portion of wages to the firm's performance was by no means a novelty and is firmly rooted in the country's industrial relations [37] system, of which it is part, with deep participatory motives and widespread practices.

This contributes to the peculiarity of the Japanese case, where allowances, extra-wage bonuses (amounting to several months' pay, even in non-manufacturing sectors, and linked to parameters of seniority and merit) [38] and the profit-linked quota are not always clearly distinguishable. The quota varies from firm to firm,[39] its incidence is often comparable to European countries and is never estimated to top 10 per cent of workers' total earnings.

What about the results of economic participation? Extensive literature is available on this topic, centred on empirical research carried out mostly by economists.[40] Despite this contribution, often marked by the use of sophisticated techniques, our knowledge of the outcomes of economic participation still appears sketchy and is a good reason for caution.

Altogether, such outcomes appear to this day doubtful and contradictory. They reflect significant context-related differences but at times also highly different environments. These concern equally the domain of such events, as briefly illustrated below.

Prevalently positive effects are observed in France, Britain and Germany as regards workers' motives. They are more sensitive to profit sharing than to employee shareholding, as they wish to enjoy freely the benefits attained. For the United States, the estimate is more uncertain, as diversified outcomes have been attained with the first form,[41] and diversified attitudes with ESOP schemes.[42]

The broadest agreement on the positive effects of economic participation – and of profit sharing in particular – is observed in the field of productivity. This view may be countered by the argument that such effects are due prevalently or significantly to the fact that only profit-sharing schemes tend to be introduced exclusively by firms in good shape.[43] This observation applies also to European countries. In the United States some observers even deny any positive effects on productivity, also because firms have activated profit-sharing practices chiefly as an anti-union deterrent.[44]

We have found no certainties, on the other hand, as to the effects of economic participation on wage flexibility. The information available raises a number of doubts on the real extent of flexibility in Western countries and even in Japan. Such countries, especially those with gain-sharing practices, have protective clauses and weighting devices that reflect the reluctance of employers and trade unions to apply the profit-sharing rationale in a consistent manner.[45] Employers probably fear a wage spiral; trade unions tend in fact to view this participation as an additional measure rather than a substitute of traditional wage systems.

Another area of investigation, for some authors, are the effects of this participation on employment levels. Unlike wage flexibility, however, this is not a precondition for participation and should not be considered crucial to its activation, although its observation may provide insights into possible effects in the macroeconomic sphere.

Most of the empirical research on this subject has been carried out in Britain. Some researchers have noticed a significant correlation between participation in profit and employment levels. Others have found higher employment in firms applying this form of participation than in others, though this is attributed mostly to increased productivity. It has been argued – in this case – that overall employment does not increase, as firms with new wage systems may gain greater shares of demand at the expense of other firms, without demand rising in the economic system.[46]

4 Economic participation and the share economy

The phenomenon of economic participation is still not clearly defined, scarcely influential and rather controversial in its outcome; despite being widely investigated and involved in intense theoretical debate. Among possible reasons for so much interest, the following deserve mention: its forms allow a reduction of restrictions in pluralistic practices, without changing the institutional character of the firm; such forms are an exception to the typical employment relationship and offer an important opportunity to change workers' status; economic participation directly addresses requirements voiced by firms, but at the same time it has been investigated – as noted above – for its potential benefits on macroeconomic and social results.

We have so far discussed economic participation with reference to its two forms: namely profit sharing and employee ownership. Yet, despite the common purpose of interesting workers in the firm's performance, these forms exhibit a number of differences at the level of their participatory rationale and – more in general – of their potential benefits. In our view, the first form is more prominent and significant, at both levels, than the second. The considerations leading us to this conclusion arise from the following comparison:

a   the former can be easily classed with industrial-relations processes and continual negotiation practices, while the latter appears more removed and prone to favour situations where economic participation is used as an anti-union deterrent;

b   the former seems more suited to the fundamental aims of participation (i.e. raising workers' motivation levels to achieve greater commitment and collaborative relations among the firm's actors) while the latter seeks to involve workers in an area that is less relevant and only loosely linked to their performance and to relations in the firm;

c   the former can involve subjects and their representatives more actively and directly than the latter, as to the definition of participatory content and procedures, with their respective implications for the firm's functioning;

d   the former provides a commodity (income) at the heart of workers' need for protection and consideration in the present as in the past, while the latter concerns a commodity (shares) that under present conditions tends to appear as an extension of workers' citizenship within the firm;

e   accordingly, the former is likely to meet with the approval of subjects and to raise their expectations, also in consideration of the full independence they preserve in the use of the commodity proposed. Conversely, there is little evidence to suggest that the latter form – apart from when it serves specific purposes – is a priority for many workers.

It may be objected that our assessment of employee shareholding overlooks or underestimates its great potential, which is proved in fact by recent exemplary cases. The two most prominent cases, between 1991 and 1994, are United Airlines (which signed an agreement with the trade unions whereby the majority of shares will be transferred to its employees) and Air France (offering employees the freedom to opt for a pay cut in exchange for company shares). Both cases seem to imply a wide range of applicative options with this form of participation, under a number of uncommon conditions. These are due mostly to economic problems experienced by single companies – as proven by the decision to cut or freeze wages, which is familiar to the rationale of economic participation. Differences between the two, nevertheless, appear considerable.

At Air France, access to capital may be said to lie within the bounds of employee shareholding, even if the mode envisaged is seldom employed. The meaning of this initiative is not irrelevant, as it concerns the contribution made by workers to the firm's high requirements and the fact that the benefits provided are deferred in the medium-to-long period.

At United Airlines, instead, the arrangement is far more innovative. It lies well outside the said bounds, with a solution similar to the cooperative. But in this case the significance is due to the firm's considerable size and to its presence in a sector highly exposed to domestic and international competition.

Similarly, literature on this subject focuses on the first form and points out various problems, though some also extend to the second form. Such problems – mentioned earlier in the chapter – can be expressed in question form:

i   is the legitimation of economic participation sustainable without adequate participation at the decision-making level?
ii are workers willing to accept an amount of risk alongside their interest in the firm's performance, a risk linked to the proportion of variable income and its concrete implementation?
iii can an agreement be found as to the usefulness of public intervention (tax concessions) to favour the introduction and diffusion of economic participation?
iv can the application of the first form be truly beneficial outside the domain of the firm, especially in terms of jobs offered?
v   will economic participation become a consolidated phenomenon, with ample prospects unaffected by negotial regulation by workers' representatives?

It is easy to observe that these questions cover a broader and more complex dimension that envisaged initially in the integrative model; this extension was noted earlier among the manifestations of economic participation and is prominent in "share economy" contributions.

Such contributions are characterised mainly by an attempt to establish effective relations between the micro and macro levels; i.e. between potential wage-system innovations and participation in the firm and their respective links with the economic environment, especially in the labour market.

These contributions are amply illustrated in Martin L. Weitzman's theory and the ensuing debate, as well as in James E. Meade's project.

The authors differ in many respects, and especially in the following: while Meade plans to join the modes of economic participation to institutes that recall the spirit of industrial democracy, Weitzman's objectives offer workers a sense of involvement without giving "voice" to their representatives.[47]

For Weitzman,[48] stagflation is an "ailment" caused by a wage system that assigns every employed worker a given income before its production and promises a fixed salary regardless of the firm's conditions, thus favouring unemployment and inflation.[49]

Stagflation can be conquered by leaving aside traditional wage policies and applying instead the following participation formula: workers' remuneration regulated automatically by indicators linked to the firm's performance – preferably its profit – for a proportion between 15 and 20 per cent.

With this formula, it becomes convenient for the firm to increase employment, while cutting prices to raise sales. If all firms (or a considerable proportion) were covered by the participatory rationale, there would be a balanced expansion of the economy: prices of all goods would fall, real-term wages could not be reduced in the long term and the objective of full employment would be achieved.

The abolition of unemployment improves the average worker's condition and increases the proportion of income earned by labour as a whole.

The participatory rationale brings workers to take a broader perspective than mere wage protection; in fact the appeal of trade union bargaining power rests on the delusion that workers' well-being is not dependent on the firm's economic conditions and that they can always earn a higher salary than that offered by free competition.

The participatory system is more attractive than the traditional wage system but has stricter rules. The two systems are now alternative to each other: the latter offers a fixed nominal remuneration to all employees, but no guarantee of full employment and very harsh conditions for the unemployed minority; the former offers full employment to everyone, with a variable remuneration that fluctuates (if linked to the firm's profit) according to variations in demand for the firm's products, but is normally higher that a fixed salary.

Arguing in favour of his approach,[50] Weitzman recognises that it is not easy to realise; on the other hand, it already occurs in the Japanese experience, with exceptionally good results. Two conditions are needed for its implementation in Western countries: a deep change of attitude by industrial relations actors (who when drawing up contracts should consider their effect on the economic system), and the introduction of strong fiscal incentives to make workers aware of personal benefits available under profit sharing (tax cuts due to this form of participation could be offset by revenue from higher employment).

The issue of workers' interests is raised again by Weitzman, as he addresses the objection that participation is a socially unsound device for redistributing risk, compared with wage-based systems.

Again, the author only provides an indirect answer, by shifting his analysis to the macro level: fixed wages stabilise the income of individual employed workers but not of workers as a whole, who would benefit instead from the full employment formula.

Weitzman's formula has met with a broad consensus and uncommon enthusiasm ('the best idea since Keynes'). At the same time, it has encountered strong criticism; in Italy, mostly on the part of Mario Nuti.[51]

We shall mention only three of Nuti's most important objections. The profit-sharing contract is much superior to the money-wage contract. For workers this participation transforms the probabilistic distribution of uncertain employment and certain income into a probabilistic distribution of higher average employment (given the lower cost of labour) equally variable over the cycle, with a more variable income in time. The effect of imposing participation contracts is essentially the same as imposing lower wages.

Profit sharing still meets with reluctance among workers: this can be reduced by involving them in decisions that expose them to income variability when codetermination practices and institutes are introduced.

Wietzman's formula is not capable of ensuring the objective of full employment, unless a set of economic conditions and results are introduced simultaneously: for example the abolition of traditional unemployment (due to the lack of fixed capital) and Keynesian unemployment (due to insufficient aggregate demand). The author's approach cannot be applied unless both of these conditions are met.

The criticism filed against Weitzman seems to centre mostly on the macroeconomic and social effects of his formula, which is easily understandable as it pursues the optimal objective of full employment. In our perspective, however, profit sharing arises and is applied as part of integrative and collaborative participation inside the firm, and should be viewed as such. This approach is narrower than the share economy approach, as it does not view the potential qualities of this participation as a "public commodity" in terms of greater solidarity among labour. This certainly exposes the limits of economic participation, though notably the same problems occur with other participatory forms, such as codetermination.

If should be noted, indeed, that Weitzman's approach assumes a level of solidarity among workers which is not easily attained – especially if unprompted, that is without mediation by their representatives.

Weitzman's evaluation of trade union action – which he later revised to acknowledge its compatibility with his formula [52] – offers a clear-cut picture of negotial activity as a provider of necessarily stable but excessive wage levels, overlooks the fact that collective bargaining outcomes have often been shaped by business conditions and the economic cycle.

Drawing attention to the wage system, Weitzman appears to restrict workers' need for protection to mere monetary considerations, ignoring the fact that a great part of trade union experience has depended on the demands, institutes and practices of formal regulation.

On the other hand, he interpreted an unquestionable need for substantial and effective labour-cost flexibility.

Events in recent years have emphasised this need and its link to surplus labour supply. Constraints due to competition have put pressure on inflationary trends (reducing them in many industrialised countries) but have also exposed a large fossilised layer of unemployment which can be expected to shrink only in part, even after a cyclical recovery.

This bitter novelty makes Weitzman's concern even more relevant today and enhances – though of course not exclusively – the role of trade union action, especially wherever its weight is greater. Trade unions, in fact, are now confronted with a difficult choice between protecting the employed alone and pursuing an expansion of labour demand.

In the latter case, it seems likely that the unions will be forced to moderate their claims at the national level (by category and sector), while abandoning the pursuit of a close link inside the firm between wage trends and productivity trends – if further labour saving is to be avoided.

Meade's contribution [53] offers an organic and skilful plan in both political and economic terms: a project involving changes in institutions and business organisation, centred on the use of active partnership for securing social harmony.

His plan reaches well beyond the confines of industrial relations and its multitude of participatory forms. It is mentioned here mostly because its dominant and recurring concern are the interests and economic convenience of employed workers.[54]

The changes he suggests are coordinated with market competition. The transition from strict economic participation to a varied programme of full economic democracy is free of anticapitalistic themes, though it implies highly ambitious institutional, political and cultural conditions (which are its weakest point).

At the micro level, the main novelty is labour-capital partnership, an unusual type of "limited cooperative" where capital shares and labour shares have both voting and decision-making rights. The acquisition of ownership rights by workers does not imply any real change in the distribution of wealth between capital and labour. The aim of greater equality in conditions and opportunities is pursued mostly at the macro level, in society as a whole.

At this level, a gradual shift is envisaged from national wealth to public wealth by a formula known as "inverse nationalisation", which leaves management to the private sector and transfers profits to the community in the form of social dividend – that is a basic income distributed to all citizens, regardless of their occupation.

The strong role of public ownership and the widespread use of labour-capital partnership allow workers to diversify their sources of income and, theoretically, to rely on four different sources: a social dividend, a sum paid as "labour share" dividend, an agreed amount paid as fixed wages, and income on capital shares in different partnerships or other forms of private investment, with a strong fiscal incentive.[55]

For the firm to function properly, Meade introduces the "differentiation principle", whereby a worker entering into a partnership cannot acquire a number of "labour shares" equal to those of a worker who already belongs to the firm, even if the jobs are the same. This overturns the principle of equal remuneration for equal performance (a mainstay of trade union regulation). The former principle aims to foster greater demand for manpower (as new partners entail lower costs in proportion to the extra income produced), while at the same time reducing risks for workers (similar to capital risks).

Because of the risk factor – considering that a worker should never "put all his eggs in one basket" – it is advisable not to venture too far on the road to strict economic participation, as this can increase productivity and the size of the cake and thus the average share per worker, but it also raises the risk of fluctuations in the size of the workers' overall share.[56]

Similarly, the workers' demand to participate in the firm's decision-making power is a natural factor in this proposal; yet the implementation of their demand may hold back innovation in techniques and products and, more in general, the needed level of efficiency.[57]

In this manner, Meade tends restrict the difficulty of relations between workers and the firm, by focusing on the macro level, on the presence of favourable external conditions, and on institutions consistent with the partnership system, namely: strong distributive intervention by the State, changes to the ownership structure (by fiscal policy and hereditary transfer) and fiscal burdening of socially undesirable events (such as advertising).

Meade's contribution has all the charm of a broad reformist proposal, as it seeks to define institutional alterations capable of overcoming social costs and conflict inherent in capitalist economies.

In our view, however, the leap necessary to realise the advocated economic and social changes is too great. Meade imagines a voyage to the island of Agathotopia – "the good place to live in" – after failing to find the island of Utopia, "the perfect place to live in". But his island is close to another and its metaphorical distance from the mainland formed by advanced capitalist countries is enormous.

Regrettably, we cannot move to his island. Out of excessive realism, perhaps, we fail to see the conditions for the appearance of (individual and collective) social actors so keenly bent on the common good.

Meade himself is contradictory on this basic point. His representation of workers' feelings is hardly encouraging: they appear excessively fearful, obsessed with the idea of risk (as if this were avoided, without economic participation)[58] and willing to overcome their reluctance only after the introduction of various economic and institutional compensating measures.

In Meade's view of workers, the Agathotopian plan suspiciously embraces their needs and expectations, which brings to mind the remark made many decades ago by Selig Perlman[59] on the traditional political-ideological frameworks for their liberation.

This is not Meade's case, of course, given the economic basis of his proposals and the sophistication of their social implications. There is no doubt, however, that such proposals extend outside the domain of industrial relations and hinge on the regulation of social relations at the level of society.

This inevitably raises the question of what conditions are needed to ensure political consensus for the economic and institutional changes advocated, including the development of will, State administration with extensive public property, and the need to reconcile efficiency with a highly expensive system (in Meade's opinion) leading to high levels of equality.

Finally, a word about the problems attributed to economic participation.

It is always risky to make predictions about phenomena related to labour relations; however, we cannot overlook evidence showing that this participation is not a passing "trend".

First of all its link to recent and current changes in the arena of competitive economics and productive sectors, extending to countries previously marked by wide differences in industrial relations and participatory experiences.

The second important point is that this participatory direction has acquired an uncommon level of acceptance and legitimation in the history of participation. Its forms have met with widespread consensus from two industrial relations actors (employers and the State), with the trade union actor gradually moving closer, though often critically and of course sensitive to the presence of anti-union intentions or to the consequences for the instruments and institutes of protection it represents.

Another important point is that the forms of economic participation, despite their late development, concern themes that are deeply rooted in the past of labour regulation and valuation. The tie between performance remuneration and results is known to be one of the most frequent exceptions to typical criteria for the use of employed labour. The modes of economic participation have strongly renewed this tie, but without causing a split. This is true of profit sharing in particular.

Now let us turn to the problems. We believe that unless adequate rules are provided, economic participation should not normally be supported by public money. The prominent advocates of the opposite belief (involving tax concessions) point to the functions of this participation (effect on employment and savings formation) that are collateral to its basic functions.

The issue of concessions is often invoked in conjunction with the risks that workers are said to incur. Without denying the existence of this problem, we feel it has been unduly emphasised in economic literature, which has equated the relation between employees and the modes of economic participation with a utilitarian choice made by an economic subject within a system of preferences;[60] this underestimates the fact that employees act in a collective dimension and a well-structured interactive context, where they have a fairly limited range of choices.

As Meade himself acknowledges,[61] the overall rate and type of risk to workers is certainly not lower in the presence of traditional wage systems and in firms lacking participatory institutes; this is even more true today that a large layer of unemployment is fossilised and employment is no longer guaranteed in large concerns as it was in the past.

Once the rationale of economic participation is accepted, the problem is how workers should contribute to its implementation and control. Among the options available, the soundest provides for profit-sharing negotiation, with the intervention of workers' representatives. In practice, this participation can exist even without the requirement of negotiation; yet its qualities are freer to surface and above all to persist, if such representatives intervene both *ex ante* and *ex post*, provided the employer is far-sighted enough to respect this condition.

For many observers,[62] such participation implies – to be consistent – the presence or workers and their representatives in the firm's decisions. The problem is, what decisions?

The requirement of negotiation involves the implementation of the collective bargaining method or the action of co-managerial bodies (as defined in Chapter 4). Moreover, it increases the opportunities to introduce information and consultation practices concerning the firm's policies and strategic decisions.

On the other hand, the involvement of workers' representatives in decisions on the functioning of the firm and its bodies is, in our view, both unnecessary nor inappropriate. Unlike more intense forms of industrial democracy, economic participation does not require the optimal condition of completeness in codetermination institutes. This does not exempt collective bargaining from its duties of protection and formal regulation; the presence of workers' representatives in modes directly concerning the variability of their income should be ensured by the said decision-making bodies; workers are keen to work in firms that function effectively, with managers whose prerogatives are unhindered and equal their responsibilities.

The consistent application of economic participation with no extension to codetermination calls for a remark on a recurring object of our study: namely the relations between participatory forms and pluralism.

In the case of codetermination, the degree of deviation from pluralistic frameworks concerns institutes producing participation, the recognition of interests shared by workers and the firm, and a potential or actual demise of the traditional division of responsibilities between the two sides.

In the case of economic participation, the degree of deviation appears more contained in its institutes, similar and more explicit in the recognition of common interests, and clearly inferior in the demise of divided responsibilities.

Altogether, economic participation exhibits a more limited departure from the pluralistic framework compared with codetermination and, thanks also to certain traits, it appears more easily and widely applicable.

Notes

1   Cf. G. Della Rocca and L. Prosperetti (eds), 'Introduzione', in *Salari e produttività. Esperienze internazionali ed italiane*, Angeli: Milan 1991.

2   P. Santi, 'Economia della partecipazione e relazioni industriali', *Giornale di diritto del lavoro e di relazioni industriali*, No. 43, 1989, p. 446.

3   Cf. F. Vito, *Introduzione alle Encicliche ed ai Messaggi Sociali. Da Leone XIII a Giovanni XXIII*, Vita e Pensiero: Milan 1962, Chapter 2.

4   G. Geroldi and S. Caselli, 'L'economia partecipativa: idee e problemi per lo sviluppo di una nuova impresa', *Prospettiva sindacale*, No. 82, 1991, § 2.

5   Cf. M. Poole, *The Origins of Economic Democracy: Profit-sharing and Employee-shareholding Schemes*, Routledge: London 1989.

6   Cf. D. D'Art, *Economic Democracy and Financial Participation. A Comparative Study*, Routledge: London 1992.

7   Ibid., preface by K. Thurley.

8   Cf. M. Nuti, 'Democrazia economica: mercato, politica e partecipazione', in M. Carrieri et al., *Il progetto "Democrazia Economica"*, CESPE Papers: Rome 1991, No. 3.

9   See G.P. Cella, 'Gli incentivi nelle relazioni industriali italiane', in G.P. Cella (ed.), *Il ritorno degli incentivi*, Angeli: Milan 1989; and S. Negrel-

li, 'La contrattazione decentrata delle retribuzioni nel settore privato in Europa: tre metodi e quattro modelli', in CNEL (ed.), *Retribuzione, costo del lavoro, livelli di contrattazione,* Rome 1991.

10   Cf. G. Della Rocca, 'Relazioni industriali e incentivi', *Il Progetto,* No. 27, 1985.

11   A. Marsh, *Concise Encyclopedia of Industrial Relations,* Gower Press: Portsmouth 1979, p. 121.

12   In this light, a highly useful approach is provided by M. Uvalic, 'La partecipazione finanziaria dei lavoratori nei paesi membri della Comunità Economica Europea', *Politiche del lavoro,* No. 14, 1991. This contribution is based on M. Uvalic, *The Pepper Report. Promotion of Employee Participation in Profit and Enterprise Results in the Member States of the European Community,* EEC and EUI, Florence and Brussels 1990.

13   Both modes rely largely on definitions made in J. Meade, 'Forme diverse di economia della partecipazione', in F.A. Grassini (ed.), *Salari e partecipazione. Un dibattito sulle tesi del Premio Nobel Meade,* Il Mulino: Bologna 1987, pp. 28-29.

14   Ibid., Chapter 2.

15   Ibid., p. 26.

16   M.L. Weitzman, *The Share Economy. Conquering Stagflation,* Harvard University Press: Cambridge, Mass., 1984.

17   See, among others, Camera di Commercio di Milano, *L'azionariato dei dipendenti,* Milan 1993.

18   Cf. J. Moreau-Taddei, *L'intéressement, element de competitivité des entreprises,* CIPD, Paris 1991.

19   Cf. M. Poole, 'Factors Affecting the Development of Employee Financial Participation in Contemporary Britain: Evidence from a National Survey', *British Journal of Industrial Relations,* March 1988.

20   Cf. M.A. Gurdon, 'The Politics of Property in the Federal Republic of Germany', *International Labour Review,* No. 5-6, 1991.

21   Cf. M. Uvalic, 'La partecipazione finanziaria dei lavoratori nei paesi membri della Comunità Economica Europea', op. cit.

22   M.A. Gurdon, 'The Politics of Property in the Federal Republic of Germany', op. cit.

23   See, among others, R.A. Dahl, *A Preface to Economic Democracy,* University of California Press: Berkele, 1985, Chapter 3.

24   P. Santi, *Economia della partecipazione e relazioni industriali,* op. cit.

25   Cf. M. Ambrosini, M. Colasanto and L. Saba, *Partecipazione e coinvolgimento nell'impresa degli anni '90,* Angeli: Milan 1992.

26   M. Poole, *The Origins of Economic Democracy, Profit-sharing and Employee-shareholding Schemes,* op. cit.

27   'United Kingdom: ESOPs. A New Share Ownership Option', *European Industrial Relations Review,* February 1989.

28   See, among others, M. Biagioli and S. Cardinaleschi, 'La diffusione di voci retributive legate ai risultati d'azienda: una ricerca empirica sulla recente esperienza italiana', *Politiche del lavoro*, No. 14, 1991; M. Ambrosini, M. Colasanto and L. Saba, *Partecipazione e coinvolgimento nell'impresa degli anni '90*, op. cit.

29   Contradicting the opinion of D. D'Art, *Economic Democracy and Financial Participation*, op. cit.; and D.J.B. Mitchell, 'The Share Economy and Industrial Relations', *Industrial Relations*, Winter 1987.

30   Information on this topic may be found in particular – among sources quoted here – in the contributions by M. Uvalic, P. Santi, G. Geroldi and S. Caselli.

31   See, for example, P. Terzoli, 'L'azionariato dei dipendenti in alcuni paesi Ocse', *Industria e Sindacato*, No. 12, 1992; and Camera di Commercio di Milano, *L'azionariato dei dipendenti*, op. cit.

32   'France: Reform of Profit-sharing and Financial Participation', *European Industrial Relations Review*, May 1990.

33   P. Terzoli, *L'azionariato dei dipendenti in alcuni paesi Ocse*, op. cit.

34   'United Kingdom: ESOPs. A New Share Ownership Option', op. cit.

35   J. Cable, 'Produttività, salari e *performance* delle imprese: indagine empirica nella Germania Federale', in G. Della Rocca and L. Prosperetti (eds), *Salari e produttività. Esperienze internazionali ed italiane*, op. cit.

36   See, among others, J. Blasi and D.L. Kruse, *The New Owners: The Mass Emergence of Employee Ownership in Public Companies and what it means to American Business*, Harper Business: New York 1991.

37   Cf. G. Bonazzi, *Il tubo di cristallo. Modello giapponese e fabbrica integrata alla Fiat Auto*, Il Mulino: Bologna 1993, Chapter 1.

38   K. Yamaguchi, 'Lavoro e relazioni industriali', *Il Progetto*, No. 63-64, 1991.

39   Cf. M.L. Weitzman, 'La partecipazione ai profitti come strumento di politica economica', *Politica ed Economia*, January 1986, pp. 51-52.

40   Refer, among others, to the authors quoted under footnote 30 in this chapter.

41   Cf. D. D'Art, *Economic Democracy and Financial Participation*, op. cit., Chapter 2.

42   Cf. P. Dewe, S. Dunnt and R. Richardson, 'Employees Share Option Schemes. Why Workers are Attracted to Them', *British Journal of Industrial Relations*, March 1988.

43   Cf. D. Wallace Bell and C.G. Hanson, *Profit Sharing and Profitability. How Profit Sharing Promotes Business Success*, Kogan Page, 1987.

44   Cf. D. D'Art, *Economic Democracy and Financial Participation*, op. cit., Chapter 2.

45   Cf. G. Della Rocca and L. Prosperetti (eds), *Salari e produttività. Esperienze internazionali ed italiane*, op. cit., pp. 15-16.

46 Cf. P. Santi, *Economia della partecipazione e relazioni industriali*, op. cit., pp. 436-437.

47 See, among others, R. Dore, *Taking Japan Seriously. A Confucian Perspective on Leading Economic Issues*, Athlone Press: London 1987, Chapter 8.

48 M.L. Weitzman, *The Share Economy. Conquering Stagflation*, op. cit.

49 M.L. Weitzman, 'L'economia della compartecipazione: replica a Nuti', *Politica ed Economia*, April 1986.

50 M.L. Weitzman, *La partecipazione ai profitti come strumento di politica economica*, op. cit.

51 Refer to M. Nuti's contributions: 'Codeterminazione, partecipazione agli utili e cooperazione', in B. Jossa (ed.), *Autogestione, cooperazione e partecipazione agli utili*, Il Mulino: Bologna 1988, Chapter 8; 'L'economia della compartecipazione: critiche al modello di Weitzman', *Politica ed Economia*, January 1986; 'Partecipazione e pieno impiego; controreplica', *Politica ed Economia*, April 1986; 'Partecipazione ai profitti: lavoro certo contro salario certo', *Politica ed Economia*, September 1987.

52 M.L. Weitzman, 'L'economia della compartecipazione: replica a Nuti', op. cit.

53 J.E. Meade, *Agathotopia: The Economics of Partnership*, Aberdeen University Press: Aberdeen 1989.

54 Cf. F.A. Grassini, 'Introduzione', in F.A. Grassini (ed.), *Salari e partecipazione*, op. cit.

55 See the effective presentation by E. Morley-Fletcher to the Italian edition (Feltrinelli: Milan 1989) of J.E. Meade, *Agathotopia: The Economics of Partnership*, op. cit., p. XIV.

56 J. Meade, 'Forme diverse di economia della partecipazione', op. cit., Chapter 2.

57 Ibid., Chapter 3.

58 Cf. N. Andreatta, 'Occupazione e partecipazione al reddito d'impresa', in F.A. Grassini (ed.), *Salari e partecipazione*, op. cit.

59 S. Perlman, *A Theory of the Labor Movement* (1928), Macmillan: New York 1949.

60 Cf. M. Salvati, 'Economia e sociologia: un rapporto difficile', *Stato e Mercato*, No. 38, 1993.

61 J. Meade, 'Forme diverse di economia della partecipazione', op. cit., Chapter 2.

62 See, for example, D.J.B. Mitchell, *The Share Economy and Industrial Relations*, op. cit.

6 The integrative model as cultural and organisational participation

1 The total quality perspective

Cultural and organisational participation is founded on workers' involvement in the firm's objectives and on a constant need for innovation. It is expressed especially by the programmes and instruments of total quality, which assume shared motivation by its actors.

In our approach, it forms one of the two directions in the integrative participation model. At the start of the previous chapter we presented the rationale that supports this model and the features shared by both directions. The differences, however, are not irrelevant.

The essential difference has already been illustrated:

a   economic participation offers economic benefits to workers in exchange for their interest in the firm, with no responsibility for the criteria and decisions that oversee its functioning;

b   cultural-organisational participation does not entail explicit economic advantages for workers, who are asked to identify with the firm's organisation and show a high commitment in the pursuit of its aims.

This difference leads to another aspect: cultural-organisational participation, unlike economic participation, does not imply visible exchange solutions in favour of workers; it does not envisage monetary benefits for them; it is more interested in the firm's needs, which have to be met with no additional labour costs.

Two other aspects are unique to this type of participation and unprecedented in the long history of participation.

The first is the fact that it proposes and experiments a link with a new production mode, in firms with increasingly integrated programmes and

141

processes, by means of far-reaching organisational innovations in the use of labour. It therefore provides a participatory line that is considered both necessary and functional to this type of production.

The other aspect is that, according to its advocates, this participatory line is not entirely new but has already produced brilliant results in the Japanese experience, often cited simplistically or misleadingly.

Cultural and organisational participation exhibits a further peculiarity. It does not reflect participatory forms with clear, specific traits and institutes; rather, it appears almost as a compulsory element in broader global programmes and processes, lacking as such its own well-defined domain. This feature, combined with the others mentioned above, does not help the assessment of its participatory significance and confines; and, as we shall see, it can ensure an operational flexibility that allows it to co-exist with economic participation and consolidated industrial relations systems.

Total quality appeared rapidly in the early 1980s, first in the United States and later in Europe, in conjunction with changes in the international economic arena and especially with the challenge of Japanese competition. It was introduced by manufacturing firms but extended soon to the tertiary sector.[1]

Total quality can be defined as a set of cultural, organisational and productive choices aimed at: flawless products obtained with high productivity; a gradual reduction of production costs; a collaborative and conflict-free business atmosphere; all centred on full customer satisfaction.

These choices embody the belief that success in competition is reserved for firms whose concerned mainly with human resource mobilisation. This implies far-reaching organisational changes which limit traditional hierarchical rules, abandon over-bureaucratic schemata and encourage arrangements more sensitive to the external environment.[2]

The total quality perspective hinges on the involvement of every person and position in the firm, but its qualifying feature, of course, is the attitude and quality of management,[3] as it offers a new leadership system extending from the cultural sphere to managerial matters; this is achieved primarily by supplying the tools needed to improve labour use and efficiency.

All these features are observed[4] in the variably consistent shift away from Fordist or Taylorist models, which dominated the mid-1900s, to a new production mode.

Fordism was modelled on the assumption that the efficiency of a production system is proportional to its output of standard, long-life products capable of resisting market variations.

Taylorism involved "one-best-way" production processes, imposed optimal practices (i.e. with no involvement or contribution of employees) from the top, and viewed any departure as a flaw.

Under the new production mode, strictly consistent flexibility is pursued in production arrangements; checks become standard practice in every production step; in particular it rejects a merely imperative and detatched style of personnel management, in favour of highly responsible – and generally more qualified – workers.

Essentially this new mode aims at three advantages: a varied range of products easily adaptable to market variations, a reduction in time taken from the design stage to the realisation of new products, and a tendency to constant quality improvement.

The total quality perspective, whose results rely on the optimum use of human resources, appears far more ambitious and extensive than other perspectives aimed at enhancing the functional value of these resources.

Among past esperiences, it may be compared to the human relations movement founded by Elton Mayo in the 1920s, which spread from the United States to Europe in the following decades, with a minor presence also in Italy during the 1950s.

Mayo's crucial emphasis on the "human factor" [5] marked a deep renewal in the approach to subordinate labour: he criticised the traditional view that employees can only be motivated by economic incentives; he discovered the importance of relations between people and informal groups to workers' behaviour and efficiency; he observed that satisfaction and productivity at work depended more on group rewards than on rewards provided by managers; this implied adequate consideration of human resource management, within a collaborative model of society and of the firm.

The reasons behind the approach taken by Mayo and his followers are shared by the advocates and the applications of total quality. Their approach depends mostly on the need to lessen the practical and theoretical rigidity of Tayloristic production.

It could not, however, attempt to alter its organisational structure and – compared with total quality production and management processes – it is a form of superstructural intervention, an additional corrective measure and a vehicle of good manners providing some extra respect for the worker and greater advantages to the employer.

In more recent times, the comparison can be made with attempts to "humanise" work and its perspective by job-enrichment practices, within a "neo-artisan" vision of employment, as it is tellingly called.[6]

Its advocates aim above all to legitimise implicit "stratagems" used by workers to adapt work to their own pace, and to retrain labour. Management lays down the overall programme, then it assigns discretionary operative areas to independent groups of workers. Objectives and working hours are bargained on the fringe of such areas and entrusted to shop-floor workers, like a by-water whose control is handed over to employees.

But if this is feasible for firms managed in the Fordist tradition, it is no longer possible in an integrated firm. The neo-artisan version tends to emphasise workers' self-organisation of product flow, while in the integrated firm labour performance follows a better-defined route: personnel acquires greater responsibility without increasing its independence accordingly.

The two perspectives outlined above concern shop-floor workers. Instead, total quality programmes extend to all employees in the firm, with a greater proportion of clerical jobs, and tends to overcome the traditional distinction between production workers and other employees. In particular, it seeks to counter the diffuse administrative Taylorism that – even after the introduction of major innovations in production – may persist in the hierarchical-functional structure and surface in everyday behaviour at the workplace,[7] in manufacturing firms and even more in the service sector.

2 The integrative model and the Japanese experience

This landmark experience for the sponsors of total quality is typified notably by a collaborative atmosphere among the firm's actors, with marked differences to Western forms of the collaborative model (Chapter 4).

It contains and predates many features of the integrative model, and especially of the total quality perspective, but its significance is far wider and greater for two principal reasons: because the origin and development of such features predate and surpass the current organisational needs of competitive firms; and because the same features involve relations between firms and employees, in an economic system that forms as a whole a specific variant of the capitalist set-up.

Significantly, the effects of these two reasons have brought the Japanese experience to confront problems that were either ignored or underestimated by many total quality supporters in the West; such issues include the macroeconomic regulation of wage dynamics and, notably, profit sharing.

On the other hand, analysts have not always favoured this experience, as it raises problems about its feasibility in Western countries, which lack important aspects of Japanese capitalism and follow different labour employment criteria.

These observations show that no discussion of the Japanese way of production or of social relations inside the firm can overlook the overall nature of the "Japanese system". In the current chapter we shall simply focus on this connection, with the aim of some observations made by an expert investigator of the system such as Ronald Dore.[8]

Confirming a widely accepted view, Dore notes that Japanese workers are strongly committed (especially in terms of product perfection), have good qualifications and training, and appear highly collaborative (e.g. in their loyalty to the firm and direct contribution to quality circles).

The attainment and preservation of this satisfactory condition are associated to and favoured by a combination of factors, e.g.: managers are more oriented to production results than influenced by shareholders' interests; the implementation of income policy – an essential means of regulating distributive processes – on a year-to-year basis;[9] a public administration ensuring stability in economic policy; and a school system based on strict selection and merit.

The "Japanese system" is favoured by two other key features: its high level of productive efficiency, so that the right decisions can be made because everyone has done their duty, tending a the constant improvement of products and services offered to customers; a sense of fairness that requires the acceptance of compromise in transactions among individuals and interest groups and leads to great moderation in the use of market power by each economic and social actor.

The nature of this system is most evident and marked in relations between firms and workers and in industrial relations, which all share three main features:[10] the permanence of workers in the same firm until retirement age;[11] the prevalence of company unions, common to both shop-floor workers and clerical workers, responsible for bargaining, consultation and control; a composite wage policy, whereby pay is linked to seniority, qualifications, attitude to work and family conditions.

These relations apply to what Dore terms the "community" firm, clearly separate from the typical joint-stock company firm. In the latter shareholder rights are paramount, directors and managers act as their trustees, and employment relations inevitably display antagonistic traits; while the "community" firm is for all those employed in it so that shareholders appear as a group of outside subjects; group loyalty brings all internal components to make the firm prosper and top management requires wide recognition of its professional and moral legitimation.

The "community" firm is superior (compared to the traditional firm) in terms of innovation, competitiveness and satisfaction of all those involved. It has opened the way to industrial democracy, which in Dore's view is destined to develop also in other capitalist environments, taking into account two fundamental achievements of the Japanese experience: a new balance of interests and control between workers and shareholders in favour of the former; the total reliability of its top management, resting on trust (90 per cent) and only partly (10 per cent) on evidence that the trust was well placed.

Its application to other contexts, whose history and socio-cultural features differ from Japan, inevitably requires major alterations – as Dore himself accepts, stressing that the Japanese lesson should be taken seriously but not merely imitated.[12]

Caution is necessary not only with this aspect, but also when considering the author's presentation of the Japanese experience, which – as Michele Salvati rightly points out[13] – tends to be idealised and referred to a system where, for good and for bad, everything is consequential.

In effect, certain points are inconsistent even in Japan. Apart from general features, such as the contrast between the country's wealth and quality of life, other aspects more directly related to the world of employment should be recalled: the difference (not only in terms of wages) between those employed in large concerns and small firms or in the service industry; a rapidly-ageing population supported by a scarcely generous welfare system; current tensions in the labour market undermining the fundamental institute of lifetime employment.

In this context, of course, it is essential to consider workers' (not only monetary) conditions – a point that Dore tends to overlook. The question to address is what benefits and costs the Japanese experience entails for workers, with reference to "community" firms and their widespread participatory implications.

We shall answer this point with the valuable help of Giuseppe Bonazzi's sharp analysis,[14] which makes use of the extensive literature on production modes and other relations within the firm.

Japanese workers are subject to structural pressures, which force them to accept greater responsibilities the surpass the confines of their specific tasks, and to cultural pressures demanding their full availability.

This happens in production processes, whose most typical organisational feature is the just-in-time process, a solution ensuring a constant and perfect correspondence between the supply of goods and market demand.

For this solution to function, several key principles need to be implemented, starting from workers' involvement, which is observed in: the "autonomation" principle (i.e. the right and duty of employees to stop the production line if they notice any anomaly or flaw and to intervene with suitable corrections); workers' mental ability and skilfulness employed not only in routine tasks; the use of horizontal coordination as a more effective alternative to hierarchical coordination; the ability of each department to identify and handle problems in view of objectives consistent with the firm's overall purpose.

Another key principle is provided by total quality control. This assumes: an adaptive flexibility of programmes to market demand; the provision of technical tools (such as devices for avoiding unintentional errors), methods (for example, statistical production control) and social means (notably, quality circles; the abolition of tasks that produce no added-value content and of stock-keeping;[15] the extension of production workers' duties to servicing and control.

Production processes thus arranged and their successful management (total-quality management) require, therefore, a highly collaborative company atmosphere and a very dedicated workforce.

In this context, is work more intelligent or only more demanding and concentrated, or both things at the same time?

The question is unavoidable, as Bonazzi argues, because of the ambiguity inherent in the condition of labour in the typical Japanese firm; here many investigators have noticed that work is more responsible but also more demanding, more flexible but also more disciplined, more collective but also more controllable, less bureaucratic but equally binding for internal relations.[16]

This ambiguity lies at the root of strongly diverging judgements, as reflected in another issue: that is whether the experience of the Japanese firm can be replicated in the West, and what adjustments may be required. Clearly diverging opinions are voiced by favourable and hostile observers.

The former believe that work benefits from greater intelligence, as human skills are employed to the full. In their view – often with an apologetic note – the constant effort to improve task performance is both respectful of human dignity and a source of self-esteem and great self-realisation for employees. If this is true, the results can only be positive, and its introduction in the West is feasible.

For the latter, work does not become more intelligent but only harder. Some view the Japanese firm as an extreme version of the Taylorist-Fordist production mode; others take for granted the obsolescence of this mode but stress in particular its new de-humanising aspects. In this light, the success of Japanese firms in forcing workers to internalise an obsessive work ethic [17] depends chiefly on the 1950s trade union defeat and on an industrial relations system shaped by firms alone. The Japanese experience is thus incompatible with European industrial relations systems.

Somewhere in-between, more problematic observers emphasise the ambiguities of this experience and possible adaptations that may limit its most disagreeable effects in the Western world

As for its historical development, they recognise the importance of the antagonistic trade union line, but claim that employers showed restraint in their victory. They had enough political intuition to understand that often worker' claims could be freed of their revolutionary content and turned into valuable collaborative factors. This produced "a long-term social agreement whereby the right of free enterprise was associated with revolutionary concessions in typical capitalist terms, such as job security for workers, equal treatment for shop-floor workers and clerical workers, a wage structure linked to seniority and merit parameters, constant vocational training and growth, and the acquisition of managerial duties";[18] all this under the control of company unions, whose prominent action has often produced collective identification with the firm's fortunes.

Under this arrangement workers are tied to productive requirements, but the firm's success depends largely on their willingness to cooperate.[19] The firm is interested in an industrial relations set-up capable of ensuring the active consensus and responsible dedication of employees. The functioning of its organisational structure does not depend on unilateral instructions but on negotial adaptation and on a trade union role compatible with the country's culture and history.

This implies the recognition that employment has not been "unrestrained" in Japan (as claimed by the opposite side) and the need to verify whether it is adaptable to the West without necessarily reshaping its local industrial relations systems.

3 Total quality in a European context

In Western countries – mainly the United States, but also Europe – the total quality perspective is dominated by an increasingly vast amount of literature and journalism, at times repetitive or emphatic, that ranges from enthusiastic tributes to the total quality "philosophy" and the operational details of its implementation; there is always a common reference to the Japanese experience. Such literature focuses on: the different functions of quality;[20] the stages of its implementation;[21] the implications of the crucial shift from product to process rationale; and the benefits available, especially the opportunity to combine higher productivity and higher quality levels.

Among the conditions for its success, there stands out a need to pursue quality without imposition but by consensus, to introduce deep changes in business management culture, and to rely on employees who, at every level of the firm, identify with its overall purpose and with specific programmes. This implies a strategic decision to employ human resources to the best effect, as they constitute the most important factor.[22]

The firm's actors require recognition; their effort must be acknowledged before results, as a parent would do with his or her children. This recognition is not monetary but consists of rewards that seek to build trust and give workers support and satisfaction for their actions.

Among these rewards, human resource management serves not only as a top-down process, but is equally a bottom-up process, whereby an employee can act on his or her superior.

Involvement and recognition play a part in the preparation and implementation of numerous devices and techniques – ranging from quality promotion initiatives (the diffusion of company policies and creed, regular information on the outcome of actions taken, campaigns on important objectives) to the promotion of individual suggestions (sometimes with minor economic benefits), from the CEDAC system (whereby a group identifies the causes and suggests solutions to avoid waste) to the famous quality circles (formed by small groups that voluntarily oversee their organisational unit – which allows staff more participation and freedom, promotes constant training, and improves the leadership and managerial qualities of middle management as a link between operative and managerial work).

The organisational and managerial messages, stimuli and guidelines in such literature and in related business-consultancy have been highly popular in managerial circles in search of quality. We do not wish to underestimate their progressive role for the counterpart and for business management. In our case, however, their value should be referred to relations between the quality perspective and the treatment of workers, between workers' involvement and the requirements of participation.

Our assessment will focus on two points, which differ only in their presentation: the view of the Japanese experience and the role given to industrial relations.

Point one: this literature has illustrated and praised the experience only for its results, technical-organisational solutions and high consideration of human resources, but has essentially overlooked its policies and institutes favourable to employees. In other words, it portrays Japanese workers as actors who identify with the firm's objectives only thanks to the "good manners" of superiors and to job enrichment.

This literature assumes *a priori* the irrelevance of monetary rewards, ignoring the Japanese experience of exchange, which affects not only salary and income but mostly job security.

It presents interactive processes in the firm and relations among its actors as if they lacked regulation and representation of workers.

It tends to portray the firm as a community, but does not consider the elements inherent in a "community" firm, which not only arises from converging motives and objectives but especially from a long-term agreement limiting the shareholders' role and the space and unscrupulousness of financial capitalism (compared to the West).

Undoubtedly, these omissions make it easier to market quality-based "recipes" and to convey the appeal of the Japanese experience. However, Western entrepreneurs should be warned that the mere repetition or inspiration of the same experience may be beneficial but is also a great challenge.

Point two: the literature in question normally claims that it is possible to achieve quality and firms equipped for the objective, without confronting – also in a Western context – the issue of industrial relations.

It avoids any consideration of relations between the application of total quality and its impact on the nature of such relations. Trade unions, conflict, collective bargaining and workers' representatives are not addressed, nor are they a source of problems to tackle and solve. Apparently, the quality firm is a venue without collective regulation, where trade unions are neither accepted nor opposed, because they are absent. Workers must be involved only directly, individually or in small groups, with no collective representation or mediation of their needs and interests.

There is no doubt that in a number of cases the firm does not need to confront workers' representatives. This is possible in sectors (such as data processing and wholesaling) that do not belong to the typical industrial sectors, and in certain contexts in the United States, where much of the literature comes from. But in European countries, the problem of industrial relations and of this comparison are not normally avoidable. European contributions in the field overlook the significant difference between (recent) widespread North-American situations and European situations.

In Italian literature, for instance, there is no notable difference between translated and domestic contributions, as if the realisation of total quality erased the local past and present of employment and industrial relations. In such contributions, history can be practically said to have no place.

However, the range of literature on quality is not totally uniform.[23] Even in the United States, some observers stand out for their departure from the prevailing approach.

Among these, Sydney P. Rubinstein [24] advocates trade union presence in quality processes because, alongside technicians and management, the trade unions are one of the firm's institutional centres. In his view, business systems tend towards instability, if participatory democracy (quality circles) is introduced without representative democracy (trade unions).

The total quality perspective has no fixed outcome and cannot be confined to a path with no alternatives. This is true not only at the level of interpretation but also on the plane of actual experience.[25] As for the latter, we have focused on the European approach to quality, especially in connection with two aspects: the impact of quality firms on the industrial relations set-up; and the reasons why workers should be willing to get involved in quality schemes.

Though certainly marked by the cultural hegemony of the Japanese experience, the European approach to total quality has been implemented with considerable adaptations. This is the case on the plane of technology and organisational factors, where it is typified by a gradual, experimental use of processes and "hybrid forms" merging the Japanese approach with others. Even Western firms explicitly seeking to counter the threat of Japanese competition, have chosen selectively among its constitutive elements.

As for human resource management, research [26] shows that European firms have employed softer strategies (compared with Japanese practices) in their use of manpower. They are often forced to introduce technical-organisational innovations to avoid the mere intensification of human work. The determinism of just-in-time processes is limited by their effect on human resources; such processes are emphasised from different fronts both by advocates and opponents of the Japanese experience.

The preference for quality objectives, especially in the motor industry (Fiat, Ford, Renault, Peugeot, Volkswagen, Opel) exposes – alongside the clear differences – a number of common features, and especially the search for agreements with unions for the consensual involvement of manpower.

This important aspect not only proves there is no violent impact on the industrial relations set-up but also confirms that a departure from the Japanese experience is possible. Unlike the latter, in Europe such agreements have not followed a dramatic trade union defeat; instead they have taken hold in environments where organised labour is firmly rooted, with trade union roles and recognition normally surpassing company level, with representatives at the workplace always involved in the regulation of employment, and yet – more recently and diffusely – adapting to new economic and productive conditions.

As for specific Italian cases,the agreements signed in 1991 and 1992 at Fiat introduced cash prizes for improvement suggestions and set up joint committees in charge of devices for involving work groups, alongside an innovative variety of profit-sharing bargaining. Many other firms in different manufacturing sectors have evolved over the last ten years forms of in-plant bargaining similar to Fiat's (profit sharing and bonus systems for contributions to quality) or, more often, collective accords with wage quotas linked to production targets combined with quality targets.

As for the reasons why workers should be willing to provide a dynamic, continuing and reliable performance, we do not have enough information on the firms applying such schemes as a whole. It is significant that workers have reached a substantial consensus in firms implementing negotial practices but the same may also have happened in others.

It may be overambitious to attempt an explanation of this outcome, due certainly to dissimilar reasons. However, three types of consensus can be assumed (though not sharply distinguishable), which we shall refer to as identification, exchange and convenience.

Identification consensus is due to subjects who in practice share the functions and merits attributed to total quality by managers and management literature. They seem aware of the difficulties experienced by firms trying to hold their market position and of the need for everyone's effort to improve competitive capacity. They are aware that the need to improve the firm's competitiveness implies an enhancement of the contribution provided at different levels in the firm: this concerns many employees in the vast and varied world of "white-collar" workers as well as "blue-collar" workers whose role is greatly revalued.[27]

Exchange consensus is shown by subjects who judge the correspondence between the commitment required and the advantages attainable.

This type of consensus can arise in conjunction with: economic rewards to individuals, groups or collective actors; increased professional competence (a commodity that permits a better position within the firm's organisation and is expendable on the employment market);[28] an improvement in the environmental and ergonomic conditions of the place of work and above all a reduction of effort.[29]

Convenience consensus – which involves subjects less actively – can be due to overall conditions (the political scene, declining conflict, workforce fragmentation, etc.), to guarantees (however scarce they may appear) offered by trade union presence, or to the natural fact that it is worth paying a price to be employed in a reliable and innovative firm. This last type is in fact a form of minimal consensus,[30] a kind of "unspoken consent".

4 The effects on production and the participatory capacity of total quality

The 1980s were the heyday of total quality programmes and their management. In the United States and Europe, this way of organising production was introduced by many firms and large concerns – not only in the manufacturing sector – and lies at the root of the ambitions and attitude of the latest generation of managers.

More recently, however, a wide debate has developed around the virtues attributed to total quality and has analysed the results it was expected to achieve – suggesting an outline of its future development as well as corrective measures, or even its replacement.

This debate is supported by specialised magazines such as the *Harvard Business Review* or prominent business papers (like the *Wall Street Journal*) in English or in other languages (for instance, *Il Sole-24 Ore* in Italy) and is sponsored by business consultancy firms and by entrepreneurs with an experience of quality programmes.

In these pages it is unnecessary to retrace the debate, because the motives and solutions prospected have not so far reached a level of "dignity" equal to that of the total quality perspective, and because – if we are not mistaken – it exhibits no significant novelty in its management and consideration of human resources.

The voices in this discussion have different accents: besides those claiming that quality should be better applied, with greater attention to the use of such resources,[31] there are others that attribute its modest results to a flawed or excessive implementation of the Japanese experience.[32] The most critical voices [33] highlight by empirical analysis its scarce effects on profitability, the stalemate in many programmes and the choice of overambitious objectives. One of the corrective measures suggested is a focus on customers' real needs, still overshadowed by the rhetoric of "customer satisfaction", while firms appear to pursue a self-defined variety of quality.[34]

As for human-resource management, the great majority of observers uphold the assumptions and guidelines found in literature in favour of total quality, namely the minor weight of economic incentives as motivators, personnel training and job enlargement, the provision of procedures and devices ensuring everyone's active and creative contribution to strengthen the firm's market position.

The debate on total quality and its revision do not imply any great change in human resource management or in the contribution expected from employees. The idea, in fact, is that firms – especially large competitive in manufacturing and other sectors – cannot revert to previous modes of production. Organisational and commercial strategies may change, but the firm will nevertheless remain subject to the its to cut costs, integrate processes, achieve higher levels of efficiency, and adapt to the changing nature of the market.

The European firm in particular will have to confront the consequences of harsh international competition, as its labour costs and its regulation of industrial relations are both greater. It will have to enhance flexibility in production (product-market relationship) as well as in labour (employment criteria and costs), often integrated by numerical flexibility (revision of employment levels).

If such predictions are well founded, to what extent is the active involvement of employees possible – or at least their willingness to participate?

The modes of production and organisation in this type of firm submit employees to constant improvement of performance, to multiple constraints due to the efficiency-quality connection, and to strict checks in view of complex and detailed objectives. In very plain terms, workers are not more exploited, they work in more comfortable and civilised production areas, but are kept under pressure either explicitly or practically.

The factors that can be said to offset this situation are those attributed to the Japanese experience. In the West, the factor most often mentioned is the centrality of labour and greater consideration for its providers (in terms of respect and value); this has led many trade unions to abandon their scepticism towards the principle of total quality programmes. Another factor is the possibility to graft the use of labour in the integrated firm on the character and functioning of industrial relations systems.

The opposite case should also be considered, however: the tendency to reduce regulations and institutes for collective settlements with employees, in the face of problems invoked by firms when they depart from the employment and labour-cost criteria used in other centres and contexts.

Moreover, attempts to involve workers have been and will be disrupted by the progress of numerical flexibility, which has even shaken the solid "Japanese system".

We shall now come back to the question introduced earlier and recall the three types of consensus presented.

With identification consensus, it is not easy to discuss participation, especially as it is viewed in this study. This depends not only on the lack of a collective dimension, but above all to the fact that every worker's active and reliable performance seems to function as a kind of "gift",[35] a reward, a donation presented to the firm; in other words, a contribution which is offered but not explicitly specified in the wording of contracts.

It is ultimately a contribution with no exchange, if not in the long term and provided the firm is increasingly profitable and well positioned on the market. This is not easily accepted by employees as a whole, while it may interest individuals gaining personal benefits in terms of professional competence or career, and symbolical or tangible rewards (such as the pride of group loyalty, involvement in a productive environment desirable to outsiders, and the enjoyment of supplementary benefits).

With convenience consensus, there is no participation as subjects do not provide their commitment and remain alien to the involvement required, with the reintroducion of separate objectives and duties for labour and the firm; whose avoidance is notably a precondition for any form of participation (with the exception of a few forms belonging to the antagonistic model).

This type of consensus may persist, unless exogenous factors or events intervene in the firm's life – one of the most likely being the development of cycles of strong trade union struggles and initiatives. The latter, in particular, are highly likely to occur with the implementation of numerical flexibility requirements.

The manifestations we have attributed to exchange consensus are hardly homogeneous. Some of them, such as the attainment of greater professional competence, involve individuals or specific groups of employees and can be tied to motives typical of identification consensus.

Others, far more significant and consistent in terms of actual participation, pertain to the collective dimension and are observed in the negotiability of the total quality implications of labour practices and in the distribution of benefits attained. As already experienced in many European instances, it is now necessary to reconcile the regulation of employment subject to later revisions with the concrete pressure of flexibility, to ensure workers a share of income related to results (by means of economic participation schemes and institutes), and to strongly innovate industrial relations systems without losing the main traits of the European labour-inclusive tradition.

Within the negotial rationale, or even in the lack of explicit bargaining practices, exchange consensus may become more consistent if job security is considered and defined. On this ground, the firm's objectives acquire greater legitimation an may include an objective that workers consider highly important. This is crucial, ultimately, also to the persistence of two other types of consensus.

Notes

1   Cf. V.A. Zeithalm et al., *Delivering Quality Service*, Free Press: New York 1990.
2   M. Crozier, *L'Entreprise à l'écoute*, Inter Editions: Paris 1989.
3   See, among many others, F. D'Egidio and C. Möller, *Vision and Leadership. Per un cambiamento culturale teso all'eccellenza*, Angeli: Milan 1992.
4   Cf. G. Bonazzi, *Il tubo di cristallo. Modello giapponese e fabbrica integrata alla Fiat Auto*, Il Mulino: Bologna 1993, passim.
5   G. Baglioni and B. Manghi, *Il problema del lavoro operaio. Teorie del conflitto industriale e dell'esperienza sindacale*, Angeli: Milan 1967, pp. 409ff.
6   G. Bonazzi, *Il tubo di cristallo*, op. cit., passim.
7   Ibid., Chapter 2.
8   R. Dore, *Taking Japan Seriously. A Confucian Perspective on Leading Economic Issues*, Athlone Press: London 1987.
9   Cf. M. Salvati, 'Introduction' to the Italian edition (Il Mulino: Bologna 1990) of R. Dore, *Taking Japan Seriously. A Confucian Perspective on Leading Economic Issues*, op. cit.
10 Cf. K. Yamaguchi, 'Lavoro e relazioni industriali', *Il Progetto*, No. 66, 1991.
11 Cf. G. Brunello, 'Profit sharing e politiche del lavoro', ibid.
12 R. Dore, 'Un modello utile per l'Occidente?', ibid.
13 M. Salvati, 'Introduction' to the Italian edition (Il Mulino: Bologna 1990) of R. Dore, *Taking Japan Seriously. A Confucian Perspective on Leading Economic Issues*, op. cit.
14 G. Bonazzi, *Il tubo di cristallo*, op. cit.
15 T. Ohno, *Toyota Seisan Hoshiki*, Diamond: Tokio 1978.
16 G. Bonazzi, *Il tubo di cristallo*, op. cit., pp. 40ff.
17 Cf. M. Revelli, 'Introduction' to the Italian edition (Einaudi: Turin 1992) of T. Ohno, *Toyota Seisan Hoshiki*, op. cit.
18 G. Bonazzi, *Il tubo di cristallo*, op. cit., p. 42 [our translation].
19 Cf. N. Oliver and B. Wilkinson, *The Japanization of British Industry*, Basil Blackwell: Oxford, 1988.
20 For example in A. Galgano, *La qualità totale*, Il Sole-24 Ore Libri: Milan 1988.
21 Cf. J.M. Juran, *Quality Control Handbook*, McGraw-Hill: New York 1979.
22 See A. Galgano, *La qualità totale*, op. cit., Chapter 8.
23 See, for instance, G. Del Mare, 'La grande sfida della qualità totale', *Quale impresa*, No. 7-8, 1992.
24 S.P. Rubinstein, *Participative Systems at Work. Creating Quality and Employment Security*, Human Sciences Press: New York 1987.
25 Ibid., Part II.
26 Cf. G. Bonazzi, *Il tubo di cristallo*, op. cit., pp. 47ff.

155

27   A. Martelli, 'Qualità totale. Un mito da riaccendere', *Mondo economico*, 8 May 1993.

28   Cf. M. Piore and C. Sabel, *The Second Industrial Divide. Possibilities for Prosperity*, Basic Books: New York 1984.

29   Cf. G. Bonazzi, *Il tubo di cristallo*, op. cit.

30   Cf. G. Cerruti and V. Rieser, *Fiat: qualità totale e fabbrica integrata*, Ediesse: Rome 1991.

31   A. Martelli, 'Qualità totale. Un mito da riaccendere', op. cit.

32   Cf. A. Plateroti, 'Crolla negli Usa il mito di Tokio', *Il Sole-24 Ore*, 17 November 1993.

33   R. Abravanel, 'Le delusioni della qualità totale', *Il Sole-24 Ore*, 18 June 1992.

34   Cf. G. Uggeri, 'Cadono i dogmi della Total quality', *Il Sole-24 Ore*, 24 November 1993.

35   Cf. G. Akerloff, 'Gift Exchange and Efficiency-Wage Theory: Four Views', *American Economics Review*, May 1984.

7 Participation and the political democracy method

1 A rich tradition of shared connections

At the beginning of this research it was argued that the problem of workers' participation raised two fundamental issues: its relationship with political democracy and with the firm's working. Though both issues have already been discussed, they are at the centre of this and the following chapter.

Participatory proposals and experiences often appeal to and pursue strong ties with political democracy. A clear and lasting demonstration of this is provided – as known – by the success of terms like "economic democracy" and "industrial democracy".

Such terms are rooted in the key features of modern democracy. This is essentially a pluralistic democracy, insofar as it draws from the existence and variety of initiatives by agencies and intermediate organisations – normally composed of territorial institutional structures incorporated into the state's laws and mostly of collective bodies sponsored by social groups, with the greatest weight so far going to those formed by employees.

In capitalist environments, in particular, a process of "democratisation" has taken place. This produces bodies, institutes and procedures that enable those involved to participate in venues with aims different to the political sphere, where social status counts more than citizenship.[1]

The increase of venues and actors in a democracy is regarded since Tocqueville[2] as a positive event, a requirement for the consolidation of political democracy whereby the political sphere penetrates the social tissue pervasively. The perspectives and solutions involved in the pursuit of this objective are not exactly coherent. They range, very briefly, from the tradition of liberal thinkers to various positions critical of the political and economic outcome of capitalist societies. In the first approach, the democratisation process may multiply and complete the quality and venues of democracy but is wholly and primarily legitimised only by political democracy and by the proper working of the state's laws.[3] In the second approach this objective cannot be limited to the mere existence of democratic laws regarding the form of government (formal democracy). Democracy is wholly legitimised only if its outcome is productive and allows venues that favour economic and social equality (substantial democracy).

Many of those who support participation in theory or in practice accept or emphasise the distinction between formal democracy and substantial democracy. Some, however, argue that substantial democracy can only be realised through deep structural and institutional (i.e. antagonistic) changes to the capitalist system; others instead believe in the introduction of formal and procedural corrections to the market economy and its institutions (an option that does not rule out proposals and experiences with actual antagonistic implications). Both sides, however, share the assumption that achieving economic and social conditions of greater of real equality calls for the political democracy method, also in venues unlike those of political democracy, and even outside the political-institutional sphere.

On this assumption, democracy is such if it enables and co-exists with economic democracy or, in a narrower sense, with industrial democracy. These involve two related functions of crucial importance: the need to foster the action and especially the implementation of the duties of political democracy and the need to expand democracy in productive relations, as its absence is unacceptable and even undermine the survival and development of political democracy.

The connection between participation and democracy is evident in the first stages of employee labour and it reaches into recent times.

In the first phase, perspectives that tend to pursue "workers' influence and control over economic events" (Chapter 2) assume that the advent of "real" democracy is incompatible with the persistence of a capitalist system. Theories and experiences of workers' control show a common feature, namely the attempt to bring about structural and institutional change in order to achieve a new industrial order where firms are controlled, in part or entirely, by workers' representatives.

The Swedish investment fund project is itself aimed at giving workers an economic standing equal to the social status they have long enjoyed in the political and social sphere.

The explicit use of the democratic method for managing productive processes and selecting employment criteria is the most notable feature of cooperative and self-management initiatives.

Subsequently, in connection with instances of advanced capitalism, a consistent number of those who support participation are normally included in literature on "the political limits of democracy",[4] which emphasises especially the non merely economic nature of power in large companies and the influence exerted over democratic life by economic concentration.

Among such authors literature, only a few claim that democracy requires deep institutional changes in the capitalist system in order to function correctly. One of them is Rainer Eisfeld (Chapter 4), who suggests socialising firms through control from below.

A larger number of authors highlight obstacles to the achievement of a pluralistic democracy and propose formal and procedural corrections to the market economy.

Charles E. Lindblom argues that alongside the constant and marked influence of entrepreneurs on political decisions, managers' choices in the productive sector evade the sphere of democratic decisions on technology, plant sites, organisation and discipline of the workforce, selection and remuneration of staff. The union's action mitigates but does not neutralise the authoritarian nature of firms.[5]

Starting from the assumption that the notion of democracy has not yet allowed a triumph of democratisation processes, Robert Dahl (Chapter 6) finds one of the most poignant instances of this anomaly in the inequalities of income and of status originated by firms. As an alternative he suggests setting up collectively owned firms managed democratically by all subjects involved in them, thus appealing to the equality of voting rights.

Carole Pateman also attracted a great deal of attention with her "participatory theory of democracy" whereby firms are viewed as a political system and are therefore guided towards industrial democracy which – in her perspective – entails the direct participation of all interactants, from the lowest to the highest level of management. Complete participation occurs wherever the imbalance in decision-making power is decreased, as the transformation poses no insurmountable obstacle to efficiency-oriented criteria and requirements.[6]

The complex link between participation, democratic method and the realisation of political democracy loses importance if set against the rationale and experiences of economic participation.

When the qualities and inherent potential of participation are considered, its latent significance appears less important than its actual effects; the actors' mutual gains and the obligations they submit to are underlined. These notions are widely present in actual experiences, not only as the result of entrepreneurial or managerial initiatives. The same notions are upheld by believers in the "share economy" (Chapter 5).

Some authors,[7] on the other hand, reintroduce an approach based not only on the functions and utility of this type of participation, presented instead as an extension of democratic ideals. Normally, however, its supporters refer their proposals to contexts interpreted in strong adherence to political democracy, aiming at the establishment of laws and the achievement of objectives offering greater fairness, more stable socioeconomic arrangements and a lower rate of inequality.

This relates, for instance, to the complex contribution of the reformer James E. Meade, who envisages considerable changes in the institutional set-up and in business organisation and yet strives to combine social equity with an efficient economic system and respect for compatibility, which are both unavoidable issues even in view of contexts that transcend traditional capitalism.

The appeal and observance of democracy is not normally underlined in the programmes of cultural-organisational participation (Chapter 6). Innovations in relations between actors operating in firms, coupled with the renewal of traditional criteria for the application of authority and responsibility, contain certain elements that contribute to the advancement of democratisation processes (consensus, trust, identification, confrontation), yet without creating suitable institutes and rather often with an instrumental use of such elements.

The connection between participation and the democratic method has led to interesting exceptions in the field of industrial democracy, since it was not conceived or implemented as an extension of this method to relations among the firm's actors. Themes and institutes inspired by democracy are present, but seldom aimed at achieving a close resemblance to the working of political democracy.

The term "industrial democracy" originates from the title of an influential volume [8] published in 1897, by Sidney and Beatrice Webb. The authors – in their attempt to legitimise trade union activities in the face of efficiency and economic science [9] – refer to the development of workers' organisations as a history of democratic method: after the first stages of "primitive" democracy (e.g. the use of referenda) they have reached a "typically modern democratic form" (with elected representatives, executive committees, trained officers). [10] The same authors also tend to argue that political democracy can succeed if it takes into account union regulations and accepts that organised labour should not employ the means of political democracy to pursue structural and institutional changes in the economy and in firms.

Hence two major assumptions in the authors' theoretical contribution, namely that industrial democracy is equivalent to union democracy (relations within workers' organisations and how they are governed) and that industrial democracy must remain within this sphere and not extend to the management of firms. The latter assumption rejects as unrealistic the tentation of making unions the principal decision-makers in productive settings:[11] entrepreneurs or "managers" are expected to decide what to produce and how to produce it, taking into account the opinion of workers' representatives – that is union negotiators – as far as working conditions are concerned.[12]

Several decades later, Ralf Dahrendorf reintroduced the term "industrial democracy" without suggesting connections or comparisons with political democracy (Chapter 4). He outlines a broader domain for industrial democracy – from the sphere of trade union democracy to institutes and practices regulating collective labour relations and conflict – but, like the Webbs, he does not include business management as it requires an authority structure to function properly and because potential restrictions are imposed by workers through the negotial-contractual method involving pluralistic practices.

Actual experiences of codetermination never stress the need to support or legitimise the role of participation by appealing to the political democracy method, although in a few intentions and perceptions it is viewed as equivalent to the democratic order of society.

This is true also in the German experience. Trade unions always focus their attention on the composition of supervisory boards but do not try to win a majority of seats in them. Their preference for equal representation, regarded as the best objective, is consistent with the assumptions of a type of participation that accepts the viability of joint decision-making alongside those who hold management duties, in accordance with business constraints and with safeguards protecting and enhancing labour. These reasons rule out an unconditional reliance on the rationale of representative democracy. Furthermore, codetermination does not represent the sole form of representation for workers, who can also count on works councils, contractual practices and a body of legal requirements upholding their rights and interests.

The same condition is found in Sweden, even more clearly than in Germany; here codetermination was established in a period of radical union demands for economic democracy (Chapter 2) and yet allows only minority representation for workers (who are given control duties) on the boards of directors of firms.

2 The problems of participation through the political democracy method

The connection between participatory experiences and the political democracy method – widely upheld in the past and even quite recently – leads inevitably to a fundamental question: is the method of political democracy applicable to participation and relations among actors in the firm? Can participatory processes develop on the basis of this connection? Is it possible to employ a method borrowed from the political-institutional sphere also in the sphere of production?

The matter has always been disregarded by those who were or still are in favour of using this method, either because they believed in an economic order different from capitalism or because they were not sufficiently concerned about its implications for productive environments and economic processes.

Among the few who have addressed it we shall mention Robert Dahl,[13] who claims that objections to the prospect of extending democracy to the management of firms are strikingly similar to dated criticism of democracy when applied to national government. This view is characterised by an "evolutionary" faith that disregards (surprisingly) the inherent difference between the functions of political-institutional rules and business rules.

Other authors,[14] on the other hand, argue that such objections are certainly relevant, as the actual implementation of participation through the political democracy method creates great difficulty to the duties and roles of actors in the firm.

Before focusing on these difficulties, we shall challenge the basis of participation through political democracy.

Our thesis is that such foundation does not exist and is not accountable. Various forms of participation may certainly include – as will be seen – a host of democratic features but not an extension of the political democracy method to industrial relations.

The participation of employees observed in forms of economic democracy and industrial democracy should be viewed only as part of the democratisation process: it may have increased the degree of correction to the market due to economic policy and notably improved social and economic relations inside firms, however these important tasks have not been performed in any stable or widespread manner – nor is this theoretically conceivable – on the assumption of applying the political democracy method.

The thesis outlined above is based on a distinction between the notion of democracy and the process of democratisation in its various forms.

Political democracy and democratisation are historically intertwined in the development of pluralistic democracy but remain distinct – and not only because the latter is conditionally dependent on the former.[15]

Political democracy applies to a well-defined sphere – that of decisions by the state and public institutions – under different constitutional solutions, whose authority is always supported and legitimised by the free will of citizens.

The democratisation process has an unspecified domain, occurs in collective organisations and venues often parallel to public institutions, and exhibits a variety of forms which can be summarised as follows:

1   instances whereby actors interested in the aims they have set themselves establish organised associate bodies in which they make decisions (or legitimise those charged with taking them) that concern only themselves and the use of authority in their organisations. This type is clearly inspired by collective bodies such as workers' unions, employers' associations and professional associations;

2   instances whereby the actors concerned use their own organisations or are present in official bodies representing their needs and interests be-

fore other actors and in venues established by others; these venues have well-defined aims and are managed by decision-makers whose authority is not legitimised by the actors concerned. This type can be found in many venues (e.g. educational institutions) but in our case, of course, it refers to the firm.

Differences between the two groups indicate that the democratic method is applicable to associate bodies in the first group, while it is not to organisations and venues in the second group. The crucial point is that in the first case the actors concerned are responsible for decision-making and for delegating authority (like citizens in political democracy processes);[16] while in the second case the same actors express their needs and interests but have to confront those already given decision-making authority in venues where they can hardly follow the normal criteria observed by associate bodies and representative institutions.

Our thesis is more concerned with ways and means for meeting participatory demands rather than with the objectives inherent in such demands, even if the two are not unrelated.

Moreover, it should be noted that our thesis does not apply indifferently to all forms of participation. In particular it is not relevant to cooperatives and self-managed enterprises where workers hold the right to make decisions and delegate authority. These two forms have different problems (Chapter 2), however the legitimacy of the democratic method is never questioned.

Our thesis may be rejected (as used to happen) by those who pursue participatory objectives in an antagonistic perspective. They are not expected to respect the firm's formal and organisational arrangements, whose substantial legitimation they do not recognise. In this perspective the democratic method applied to business management is not in contrast with their goals. The problem is how to realise conditions for achieving such goals – which accordingly has hardly ever occurred.

On the other hand our thesis appears quite feasible, compared with certain intentions still voiced in political and trade union circles and not least in literature emphasising the "political limits" of democracy, as both groups pursue participation through the political democracy method in a market economy.

Coming back to the issue introduced at the start of this chapter, we shall now try to discuss in greater depth the nature of the impossible connection between political democracy and the motives and objectives of participation.

The definition of democracy will first be examined. With reference to the major interpretations of "classical" theory – inspired by political philosophers in the seventeenth century and later developed into many versions by liberal-democratic countries – democracy may be defined as a form of government aimed at the common good, supported by citizens in equal conditions as to political rights, who by their vote select representatives legitimised to take decisions in accordance with the majority principle.

This definition admits both a descriptive use of democracy (unlike other forms of government) and a prescriptive use of democracy (its preference to such forms).[17]

Over the last few decades the debate has centred not only on these two uses but at the same time on the actual working of democratic political systems. This study does not attempt to trace its development;[18] only a brief mention will be made of those traits or theories that relate most directly to the issue here addressed.

The previous paragraph looked at the approach shared by those who condemn the gap between formal and substantial democracy. It appears that a certain degree of quality of equality (not only in the juridical sphere) has been partly achieved by democratic political systems; yet this notion seems to disregard the important results of economic policies and of the democratisation process. This is confirmed by the ample literature focusing on the "social limits" of democracy, based on the fact that by creating favourable conditions for the growth of interest groups and for greater expectations an "overload" of demands is placed on public institutions, thus creating great problems of governability;[19] this is accepted also by authors with a Marxist background.[20]

An interesting approach to the functioning of democratic systems, overcoming the traditional division between formal and substantial democracy, is provided by the "economic theory of democracy".

This assumes that political democracy operates in a similar way to the competitive market model in economics, insofar as political leaders (like entrepreneurs) and the majority of citizens (like consumers) through their respective interests and preferences produce political decisions by "maximising" demand and granting votes.

This theory first appeared in 1943 in a well-known study by Joseph A. Schumpeter.[21] Here "democracy does not and cannot mean that people actually govern". Democracy "simply means that people are given a chance to accept or reject those who are to govern them",[22] through "free competition for electors' votes between candidates to the leadership".[23] The democratic method is "an institutional means for reaching political decisions, whereby single subjects obtain the right to decide through a competition aimed at the people's vote".[24] Moreover, using the majority principle, the people's vote may often be distorted, because "clearly, the will of the majority belongs to the majority, not to the people".[25]

Schumpeter's view and that of others after him (such as Antony Downs)[26] sharply alter the image of political processes provided by "classical" theory, whereby a number of citizens voice their political ideas which in turn are realised by representatives they select. In this approach, instead, citizens only grant or withhold their approval to political characters who enter electoral contests with the political manifesto they would implement if given a sufficient share of the vote.

Schumpeter's view allows a better understanding of the actual working and evolution of representative democracies. Democracy is interpreted as a method for arriving at the production of decisions through special institutional arrangements. Unlike "classical" theory, this method involves a reduction in the degree of active, direct citizen participation [27] and an acceptance of the fact that democracy has little in common with self-government. Because of its consistent reliance on the working of the competitive market, the relationship between society and politics outlined in this view is essentially atomistic and individualistic, it dismisses the weight of ideological, organisational and institutional factors and therefore underestimates the peculiarities of different nations.[28] After the Second World War and the subsequent extension of state duties, the context of political decisions became far more varied and structured – with a variety of intermediate bodies, the growth of various political and social organisations, and electoral results strongly affected by ethnic, linguistic and religious allegiances and identities (surpassing voters' direct concerns).

Schumpeter clearly discerns important aspects in the actual development of the political democracy method but eventually oversimplifies the involvement of actors who influence the selection of representatives and their decisions as a result of the democratisation process.

In connection with our thesis on the difficulty of providing a basis for participation through the democratic method, "classical" theory is mentioned here for the appeal exerted by its prescriptive use over many supporters of participation, and Schumpeter's theory is introduced because it highlights the actual working of political democracy; many of our arguments apply to both theories.

"Classical" theory relies on three essential ingredients:

a   equality among citizens as regards their political rights;
b   the appointment by citizens of representatives legitimised to take decisions;
c   it is based on the will of the majority.

Subjects operating in a firm do not enjoy, either in formal or actual terms, the same rights: they are not in a condition of equality. Workers are employees insofar as others are entitled to employ their services in exchange for remuneration or other assets. Several important dispensations have been granted to this unequal relationship, but they are only partial and unable to cancel its true nature. For a long time the rejection of its lawfulness has been upheld and pursued in order to further the development of an institutional and productive order basically different from the industrial-capitalist model. Within this new order, subjects can hold equal business rights through co-operative arrangements which typically make no distinction between who offers labour and who employs it.

This sharp distinction is inherent in private businesses but also appears, under various regulations, in the civil service and state companies of democratic political systems. Workers have acquired and widely experienced the use of voting rights for electing their own plant union representatives and securing greater rights and benefits from whoever employs their services, but without trying or managing to overturn the inherent nature of the employment relationship.

Workers are not entitled to designate those legitimised to take decisions. Even in actual instances of "strong industrial democracy", participation in decisions simply involves the inclusion of a number of workers' representatives alongside those legitimised previously and elsewhere.

Unlike political processes, firms do not allow for all subjects active within them to share in the process of reaching common decisions. Of course common decisions are not simply preordained, as they normally issue from many factors and actors (Chapter 8); yet they are not obliged to comply with democratic constraints.

Citizens have no counterpart: they personally select those responsible for taking decisions and retain the right to confirm or replace them. Workers, on the other hand, have a legitimately established counterpart which they cannot replace, although they may influence the way it exerts its authority and – at certain times and conditions – can strengthen or weaken it by granting or withholding their confidence.

In democratic political systems, the basis for legitimacy and for the legitimation of decision-taking power lies firmly within the extent of consensus from voting citizens. In a firm, the employees' consensus is a major factor, an ideal requirement, but is not strictly necessary; and even if it is indispensable at higher and intermediate levels in the business hierarchy, the same claim cannot be extended to other employees.

The underlying reasons why consensus is not strictly necessary to the functioning of a firm are as follows: the allocation of decision-taking authority originates mainly from sources that exclude consensus, i.e. ownership, the legal system, managerial positions and skills; proof of this authority is provided above all by economic achievements rather than the degree of consensus from those involved in the firm.

The results of action by political institutions can be judged by several yardsticks, among which the consistency between stated objectives and their actual implementation is only one and often not even the most notable instance. While in firms, even if various secondary yardsticks (occupational levels, induced local development, promotion of professional skills and jobs) do appear, profitability (capitalisation, profits, investment, research and innovation, market share) remains the decisive factor.

Political institutions interact with the economic sphere first of all by supplying public commodities, distributing resources, and regulating economic activities; in these processes effectiveness does not always go hand in hand with efficiency, especially in the case of goods and services that cannot compete on the market or enter its rationale. In a firm, on the other hand, effectiveness must match efficiency so that product type and quality meet market demand at a competitive price.

Decisions cannot be taken in a firm according to the will of the majority, that is the majority of those working within it. The majority principle is tightly linked to two other key components of political democracy, which – as mentioned above – are not relevant to the nature of a business enterprise.

According to this principle the outcome of competition, once that the rules of the game have been set, usually entails the victory of one side and the defeat of the other. In a firm, even assuming the same type of competition, one of the two sides cannot lose without forfeiting in practice its ownership rights and managerial responsibilities. Indeed, relations between workers and their counterpart never embody – except for exceptional cases – this type of competition: if the latter party cannot be defeated, the former cannot prevail as it cannot enjoy the consequences of being a majority.

After the space devoted to "classical" political democracy theory, less needs to be said about Schumpeter's theory. His view of democracy as a decision-taking method with little space for idealism may seem more easily applicable to relations between actors in a firm. However this is not the case. The essential components of this theory can be listed as follows:

a   citizens (or the people, in Schumpeter's words) are only free to accept or reject candidates who aspire to govern them;
b   such subjects achieve the authority to take political decisions by competing for people's votes;
c   political decisions are not taken by the people but by a majority, even assuming that the people's will is a clear and tangible entity.

In the firm, there are no candidates to government. Certain subjects detain the right to manage the firm or to nominate, confirm or replace those charged with the task. Workers' appreciation of this behaviour may strongly affect the selection of managers (as in Japan), but decisions are not their prerogative. The process exposed by Schumpeter is partly present in certain sectors (to what degree, is yet unknown) such as the press, where journalists have the right to confirm or not the appointment of a new editor. Sectors in this class are unique, as a journalist's role is not limited to the terms in his contract, but even his rights fall short of acceptance/rejection of ownership.

With very few exceptions, those exerting authority do not compete in this area, even when they aim at a broad consensus among members of the firm's community; the outcome of whatever competition does arise is independent of the workers' will; and anyhow their will has no vote, which instead is a requirement of all democratic procedures.

As for the functioning of these processes, Schumpeter's emphasis on the primacy of majorities adds even more weight to our remarks on its inapplicability to relations among actors in the firm.

3 The political and the social basis of participation

Our critical discussion on the basis of participation in the light of the political democracy method ought to render inadequate the terms "economic democracy" and "industrial democracy".

However these terms can be considered inadequate only if we assume or expose a connection between this method and participatory events. In the development of participation, they have in fact been used with reference to different forms and aims tending to alter or improve working conditions for employees and as such they are also employed in this book, bearing in mind the need to establish their nature and domain.

Most of the directions and forms of participation are instances of economic democracy or industrial democracy but we know that other more recent forms and directions cannot simply be included among them.

At this stage the question is whether it is possible to find a basis for participatory events, and of course a basis unlike the one discussed earlier.

This basis – illustrated in general terms – can enable participation to act, at different depths, in the sphere of equality among the firm's actors.

This basis does not concern the method as much as the purpose of participation. As for its method, participation may largely differ – as we shall see – from the basis mentioned earlier and yet it shows close connections with democracy in terms of values and themes.

Modern democracy is known to rest on the condition that all citizens enjoy equal political rights and on the acquirement of new rights and liberties, and at the same time it is expected to stand out especially in themes concerning the reduction of social and economic inequality.[29]

Political-institutional means for implementing these values and themes still differ considerably and in the prevailing liberal-democratic setting have taken a direction whereby: for the themes of democracy, results are too few and doubtful if associated with the use of individual rights or liberties, and should instead be pursued through political measures with distributive effects (on wealth, income, social opportunities, and other useful or desirable resources); measures leading to less inequality and to a better distribution of the same liberties. This direction clearly applies to decisions taken over many decades in economic policy, with the important contribution of the democratisation process. The overall results are remarkable but too few for those seeking social conditions of real equality.

It is not our intention to discuss here what "amount" of equality is attainable in capitalist democracies. Alongside these expectations of actual equality, it appears that complex societies with a high social division of work are constantly producing new inequalities, that the aims of equality should be related to the social structure and obtain a sufficient degree of political consensus, and that such aims are constrained by their compatibility with institutional and productive action and with the motives of individuals and groups. There is no doubt, however, that equality remains a burning issue at the centre of debate and conflict in the political arena and of normative theories on the social order. Such theories are now less concerned with the "reasons" of equality – namely its extent and implications – than with its content.[30]

A major area of investigation is no doubt the firm and relationships between its actors. Within this sphere, workers are not entitled to conditions of equal rights.

Employees cannot act in the firm as citizens do in the political arena. They have gradually acquired a number of rights, especially those concerning the recognition and free initiative of their representatives, but such rights do not stem from a condition of equal rights.

These limits should not be viewed as evidence of incomplete democracy. They are due to constraints on the firm's activities and to the different, legitimate rights of other actors.

Nevertheless in the area of workers' interests and concerns, the opportunities to realise themes linked to democracy for the reduction of social and economic disparities are not absent, even if they require methods other than political democracy.

At this level are found today both the nature and potential of participation, which even in lesser contexts than political democracy may depend on structural and organisational conditions equally instrumental to the realisation of the same themes. The firm, in fact, can satisfy the common or converging interests of both sides; here distributive implications involve a venue that is a typical producer of resources. Opportunities for positive intervention by actors and their representatives have been widely tested.

The reduction of inequality has always produced attempts to alter or correct the asymmetry inherent in the employment relationship. Altogether, the dispensations introduced by collective bargaining and legal measures point in this direction. Participatory proposals and instances at different levels of institutionalisation, have normally pursued objectives of higher quality than protection based on such dispensations, aiming therefore at conditions of greater equality.

169

In their long history, the "ingredients" of participation have arisen under many different arrangements, often unaware or suspicious of the qualities and potential mentioned above.

Though more radical in terms of equality, antagonistic forms and orientations in favour of the political democracy method have produced very few results, except in special occasions and places. Different forms of collaborative model have opened up – especially under the institutes of industrial democracy – new perspectives for reducing inequalities in the status of employees, allowing their representatives to define and control their condition as part of a recognised role. The rationale underlying the integrative model plays down and softens the need to correct the imbalance inherent in the employment relationship, as workers' economic or professional involvement becomes a necessary option.

On this long road, participatory solutions advance slowly in a movement that may be defined as the passage from a "zero-sum game", where actors have opposing interests and the gain of one side entails the loss of the other, to a "non zero-sum game" whereby actors acknowledge an area of common interests and can achieve mutual gains through exchange institutes and practices.[31]

Participation has a good chance of realising the themes assigned to democracy if it uses different methods from those of political democracy.

Which method, therefore, is applied in the case of the participatory forms involving employer and employees in the firm?

The question can only be addressed by introducing two generalisations:

i the methods and rules of participation appear very diversified, compared with its objectives and context. They display a degree of adequacy – insofar as they allow the operation of participatory processes and institutes – related to the requirement that calls for their acceptance by the actors involved;

ii in forms that include this requirement, the methods and rules of participation display important connections and similarities with those widely experienced in industrial relations and especially in collective bargaining.

Collective bargaining is usually typified by the following features: negotial agreements between the parties, formed by individuals and/or representatives with unequal rights and roles whose interests seldom coincide; the outcome of these agreements is affected by a number of factors, such as the unique factor known as availability of the resource "conflict"; acceptance of the agreement follows a rule similar to unanimity (the sides convene on the outcome), without which no agreement would be possible.[32]

Clearly the three elements listed above do not constitute the essential components of political democracy and centre around the negotial method, in line with a pluralistic harmonisation of interests.

Among participatory events they appear very close to the procedural traits associated with collective bargaining, namely the directions of collaborative participation (especially industrial democracy) and economic participation (unless it reflects unilateral initiatives taken by the employer).

These depends mostly on the negotial method. The major differences from bargaining (Chapter 1) do not concern method, though it is distanced from tradition by the "quality leap" inherent in participatory culture and exchange. Changes include a less frequent use of the resource "conflict" and the growth of institutes that make negotiations more predictable and procedural (i.e. information and consultation, joint commissions, reference to strict indicators, etc.).

Other directions of participation, on the other hand, are not based on the negotial method: these include explicitly antagonistic and integrative participation with "total quality" programmes.

The first direction, at least in its initial phase, involved conditions in which this method could hardly be relied upon, as workers had no (fixed) right of organisation or recognition of their representatives. If applied consistently, the will of the majority would have prevailed (a criterion not adequate and generally not applicable to relations in productive settings).

Conversely, the second direction may involve negotial means but in its more orthodox versions does not call for negotial legitimation, taking it for granted that actors in a firm share the same interests if human and professional resources are well managed. One could say that in this perspective, unlike the previous case, the will of the minority does prevail (a criterion incompatible with the nature of participation).

Finally, the negotial method should not apply to cooperative firms, whose essential features calls for the method of political democracy, but not without implementational problems due to the prevailing will of the majority: here, unlike the political arena, there are no winners or losers because the members of a cooperative are like citizens in a firm but their loyalty extends beyond formal rights and commits them to their professional tasks, and because the spirit of a cooperative is built on the cohesive power of consensus and identification. For these reasons, therefore, cooperatives should tend to follow unanimity principle. And indeed the persistence of problems in day-to-day and long-term management is mostly due to this powerful constraint.

Notes

1   Cf. N. Bobbio, 'Democrazia/Dittatura', in *Enciclopedia*, Vol. 4, Einaudi: Turin 1978.

2   Cf. R. Aron, *Les étapes de la pensée sociologique*, Gallimard: Paris 1967.

3   G. Sartori, *Democrazia. Cosa è*, Rizzoli: Milan 1993, Chapter 1.

4   Cf. A. Baldassarre (ed.), *I limiti della democrazia*, Laterza: Bari 1985, Introduction.

5   C.E. Lindblom, 'Il potere di mercato come potere politico', in A. Baldassarre (ed.), *I limiti della democrazia*, Laterza: Bari 1985.

6   C. Pateman, *Participation and Democratic Theory*, CUP: Cambridge 1970.

7   See for instance D. D'Art, *Economic Democracy and Financial Participation. A Comparative Study*, Routledge: London 1992.

8   S. and B. Webb, *Democrazia industriale. Antologia degli scritti*, UTET: Turin 1912.

9   G. Baglioni and B. Manghi, *Il problema del lavoro operaio. Teorie del conflitto industriale e dell'esperienza sindacale*, Angeli: Milano 1967, pp. 44ff.

10 S. and B. Webb, *Democrazia impossibile. Antologia degli scritti*, edited by G. Berta, Ediesse: Rome 1984, Introduction ('I Webb e lo studio del tradeunionismo'), pp. 46ff.

11 Ibid., p. 53.

12 Ibid., p. 265.

13 R.A. Dahl, *Democracy and its Critics*, Yale University Press: New Haven 1989, Chapter 23.

14 ILO, *Workers' Participation in Decisions within Undertakings*, Geneva 1981, pp. 29ff.

15 G. Sartori, *Democrazia. Cosa è*, op. cit., Chapter 1.

16 Cf. G. Romagnoli, *Contro la legge ferrea. Organizzazione e rappresentanza nel sindacato*, Rosenberg & Sellier: Turin 1992, pp. 25ff.

17 Cf. N. Bobbio, *Democrazia/dittatura*, op. cit.

18 Refer among others to C. Pateman, *Participation and Democratic Theory*, op. cit.; L. Bordogna and G. Provasi, *Politica, economia e rappresentanza degli interessi*, Il Mulino: Bologna 1984.

19 Cf., for instance, E. Granaglia, 'I limiti dell'intervento pubblico', in V. Castronovo and L. Gallino (eds), *La società contemporanea*, UTET: Turin 1987, Vol. 1.

20 Such as P.A. Baran and P.M. Sweezy, *Monopoly Capital*, Monthly Review Press: New York 1966; and J. O'Connor, *The Fiscal Crisis of the State*, St. Martin's Press: New York 1973.

21 J.A. Schumpeter, *Capitalism, socialism, and Democracy*, Allen & Unwin: London 1954, Part 4.

22 Ibid., Chapter 23.

23 Ibid., Chapter 23.

24   Ibid., Chapter 22.

25   Ibid., Chapter 22.

26   A. Downs, *An Economic Theory of Democracy*, Harper & Row: New York 1957.

27   Cf. C. Pateman, *Participation and Democratic Theory*, passim.

28   L. Bordogna and G. Provasi, *Politica, economia e rappresentanza degli interessi*, op. cit., pp. 89ff.

29   N. Bobbio, *Democrazia/Dittatura*, op. cit., p. 531.

30   A.K. Sen, *Inequality Reexamined*, Oxford University Press: Oxford 1992.

31   Cf. H. van den Doel, *Democracy and Welfare Economics*, Cambridge University Press: Cambridge 1979, Chapter 3.

32   Cf. G.P. Cella, 'Inattese instabilità della rappresentanza', in G.P. Cella and U. Mückenberger (eds), *L'esperienza tedesca: modello sociale in trasformazione. Il futuro della società e del lavoro*, Angeli: Milano 1993, p. 10.

8 Participation and the functioning of the firm

1 Current factors affecting participation

This chapter will deal with an issue introduced at the beginning of the volume and taken into account in each chapter. It concerns the relationship between the implementation of participation and the functioning of firms.

We shall start by looking at three questions.

1   Under the present conditions of the economy and of capitalist societies, especially in Europe, what factors play in favour of or against the participatory perspective?

2   Alongside the political and social basis, is there an economic basis?

3   Assuming the existence of a tenable connection between these two bases, what forms and processes can be considered truly viable?

Let us review the current factors that bear upon this perspective. Naturally they are set within the bounds and trends of capitalist countries as a whole; and yet the weight of previous experiences and the uniqueness of each national context are destined to remain prominent.

This condition is explained by the simple fact that many factors are in fact contradictory, as they may lead to conditions that either increase or decrease opportunities of participation. Even factors which are classifiable as favourable or unfavourable are very seldom free of ambiguities.

The road ahead of participation is by no means straightforward and this has always been the case in relations between employers and employees; in many instances actors have a great freedom of choice and action to demonstrate, in Pareto's terms, their "instinct for combinations"; economic and productive facts or constraints do not imply, to a large extent, forced decisions.

Certain structural factors seem to be mostly unfavourable. They include the growing importance of phenomena such as the move from traditional to multiple forms of employment relationship, the growth of mixed types of employment (with traits and provisions of self-employment), and a sharp rise and projected increase in the turnover of employed workforce.

The problem of unemployment – which affects a high proportion of people everywhere and is only partly due to economic trends – has a strong impact on the prospects of participation, especially during restructuring phases that involve cuts in employment and seriously hit the manufacturing sector and many large concerns. This tendency undermines participatory events, especially when they rely on the adherence to converging objectives by workers and employers (cultural-organisational participation). On the other hand, this tendency may also imply a strong degree of joint responsibility on the part of workers' representatives and may produce instances of co-decision. Volkswagen provides a fitting example, in its effort to limit job cuts by redistributing positions and sacrifices.

As for the effects of "globalisation", many observers[1] predict a reduction in welfare funding, an erosion of collective labour protection and a sharp increase in mixed forms of labour. These changes should not be viewed too severely, as if the whole world were a huge single market. They may affect a proportion of firms, mostly in vital sectors of the economy; but these will cohabit with older productive environments marked by national and sub-national features.

In either case the motives of participation will not necessarily cease to exist, as it will depend increasingly on decisions taken within the firm rather than on overall structural and political conditions.

This view recurs when we look at the factors expected to favour participation in the future. They derive from its expansion in the service industry, a richer variety of jobs and the provision of greater satisfaction and remuneration to attract workers; but above all from management's tendency to acknowledge that the human factor is central to the firm's survival and growth.

The last factor, which appears prominently in literature and in total quality programmes (Chapter 6), is addressed more systematically in a recent contribution by Michael Crozier[2] which proposes a business strategy based on effective cooperation between actors in the light of technical and economic constraints.

As for the key importance of the human factor, this does not depend on the implementation of participation but rather, in our view, on the critical issue of participation itself.

According to Crozier participation should be based on interaction between actors in the firm, viewed as an arena for competition with different powers, roles and rewards; it should be scarcely formalised and oriented to problem solving; it is not obliged to recognise any form of representation.

In the real world there are many instances of participation that approximate the author's description, considering the great differences present within and between capitalist countries. It is clear, however, that opposite instances are possible and not always associated with the past (Chapter 5).

Crozier's approach disregards the impact between the firm's strategic and organisational requirements on one side and the institutional and negotial context of industrial relations on the other, i.e. the nature and functions of trade union representation.

As the presence or absence of representation affects especially the type of participation, we cannot omit to mention its "state of health".

In Europe, following a period of obvious but not unvaried withdrawal during the early 1980s, trade unions have shown that they can still command considerable numbers, though with national differences dating from previous periods.[3] This fact, however, is attended by great problems due to structural changes (e.g. declining employment in the manufacturing industry), public intervention policies (hardly ever aimed at producing or reproducing protection for staff), and the employees' waning interest in trade union organisations.[4] Especially in the private sector, union action can no longer be based on the security and organisational means of the past, nor can it count exclusively on the resource "conflict" or on the connection between the action of a few subjects and progress for everyone.[5]

Special problems occur and will occur in the preservation and legitimation of representation, not only in terms of overall labour protection. Workers' interests appear today typically multidimensional (income, working conditions, workplace, welfare and social security),[6] often in contrast with each other and not always held together under union protection. These problems, which are already partly verifiable and partly with long-term effects, co-exist with union actors and their activity in many business situations and (in some countries) also in the political-institutional sphere; yet the trade union experience is not on the decline and predictions for the future are unwarranted, also because of its ability to adapt and innovate so often displayed in the past.

Two aspects, however, deserve further attention as they alter the traditional nature of union action.

First of all the growing social and organisational fragmentation of unions, the degree or division and diversity in their behaviour and objectives, and further decentralisation.[7]

Secondly, the greater opportunities available to organisations and representatives competing against confederated unions and their structures, to specialised or local bodies (for groups of workers), which in single firms may not appear as openly as trade unions.

Ultimately, participatory schemes and experiences will often have to confront the collective nature of workers, though this may take on organisational aims and features different from the past.

2 The economic basis of participation

The second question at the start of this chapter regarded the likelihood of finding the economic basis of participation; in other words, whether participation is compatible with the firm's functioning and, more importantly, which of its forms and means are so.

This question has to be addressed for the following reasons: participation is a phenomenon with a political and social basis but naturally it also acts at the economic level; given its latest forms and the ensuing debate, it is clear that participation cannot be legitimised only or mainly on this basis; throughout our research we have tried to trace its compatible forms and means and to highlight the problems involved in those lacking the same essential requirement.

In our search for the economic basis of participation, we shall refer to a major direction in economic theories of the firm over the last few decades. Of course the following pages do not propose to illustrate such theories but merely to quote some of the major findings, which reveal whether they contain explicit or implicit evidence in favour of participation.

The theories under investigation are normally known as "neo-institutionalist" and have produced a paradigm which differs in various points from the prevailing neo-classical paradigm. They first appeared in 1937 in a seminal paper by Ronald H. Coase [8] and were boosted by the prominent work of Herbert A. Simon. Their claims and the ensuing developments were upheld by other authors and in the extensive work of Oliver E. Williamson.[9] Thus our references will centre on Williamson and Simon.

The following pages propose to: highlight differences between the neo-classical and the institutional paradigm, illustrate briefly the major results of the above authors' contributions, and interpret these through the rationale of participation.

For institutionalist economists such as the neo-classicists, the yardstick for measuring a firm's functioning is unquestionably its efficiency.

Neo-classicists claim that the firm operates in a context of perfect competition and, more importantly, they assume certain knowledge of the facts and factors affecting it. Thus the firm appears technically as a connection between needs and resources, leaving hardly any option to the behaviour of its actors and assessing results through its pricing system. In this light the firm seems, therefore, to be a predetermined and necessarily efficient unit. Those active within it seek to maximise their benefits and are able to choose in wholly rational terms.

The unquestionable theoretical and paradigmatic success of the neo-classical approach hardly translates into an equal explicative capacity and indeed it has often been the target of direct empirical attacks.[10] Though attractive, its assumptions do not take into account the evidence, as they fail to describe the procedures employed by actors in the firm to take decisions in complex conditions.

The overall impression gained when comparing institutionalist contributions is that they provide an *inside* view of the firm,[11] seen as a complex and imperfect transformer rather than a unit operating in a conclusive and necessarily efficient way.

Competition, again, is considered crucially important as for the neo-classicists, but its analysis must take into account the institutional context (a body of political, social and legal rules providing a basis for production, exchange and distribution) and institutional adjustment (due to the behaviour of the economic operator) in order to expose how production units can co-operate or compete with each other.

The key question that arises with reference to the institutional context and institutional adjustment, is what structures should govern the firm, what activities should be organised within it, and why and how they can be organised.[12] This question involves the degree of efficiency achievable through *possible organisational forms*: alternative organisational arrangements directly affect the firm's objectives and may shape its functioning more than other factors (e.g. technology-related factors).[13]

The efficiency of possible organisational forms involves an essential element that differentiates institutionalists and neo-classicists: the former, unlike the latter, assume that economic agents live in a complex environment of *great uncertainty*: intrinsic uncertainty (such as that due to natural events) and extrinsic uncertainty (due to the behaviour and decisions of other actors). Over the last few decades institutionalists and economic theorists have focused their efforts on the attempt to master the uncertainty factor intellectually.[14] Consideration of this factor highlights the importance of administrative and organisational procedures and behaviours; the existence of a firm hinges on its capacity to decrease the degree of uncertainty; the attainment of efficiency requires an adequate organisation. Thus the behaviour of actors in the firm is an area of major empirical events which calls for an explanation.

From the evaluation of uncertainty stems the critique of a key component of neo-classical theory, i.e. the rationality of the economic operator's decisions. Institutionalists stress the vital need to overcome the assumption of total rationality and of optimisation of behaviour in decision taking. Instead they argue in favour of *limited rationality*, in agreement with Simon's approach – which allows a more realistic definition of decision-making processes.[15]

Indeed, organisations established as governing bodies can be considered a "device" that accounts for man's limited ability to understand and calculate in the face of complexity and uncertainty. Within these organisations, the economic actor seeks a *satisfying* solution to the amount of information needed for making decisions, taking into account both their cost and the unavailability of complete information.

In the light of these facts, it is clear that actors in the firm enjoy considerable *discretionary powers*, which may be considered a precondition for the firm to function. Such actors operate in a context that allows different options in decisions about institutional arrangements, hierarchical structures and relations, and decision-making processes. This is especially true about large firms, where for decades there has been a sharp distinction between owners and managers.

The structures governing a firm employ margins of discretionary power, adjusted to the level of efficiency and to objectives achieved, which do not always depend merely on the maximisation of profit; moreover, they employ a wide range of instruments of control, primarily in order to restrain opportunistic behaviour among subjects and to foster and achieve great commitment on their part.[16] The economic man of institutionalist theory is hardly unrelated to the utilitarian ethic of neo-classical thought; however, its application produces none of the coherent and optimal results envisaged.

In order to define the firm's confines and explain its organisational and functional processes, Coase and Williamson introduced the analytic notion of *transaction costs*.

This denotes a way of coordinating economic activity and viewing relations between economic institutions that differs from the market.

When the market functions properly (as when prices are not distorted by monopolies), coordination is a spontaneous event, relations and agreements between actors are free of friction, and decisions are taken inductively after the economic activity has actually occurred. In effect transaction costs are nil.[17]

When conditions are different – a most common instance in the real world, with its "transactional failures" in market behaviour and its limits due to limited rationality – it is preferable to replace the market with the firm's internal organisation and the behaviour of its hierarchy. In this way coordination takes place within the firm's confine, in a better structured enterprise whose organisation "internalises" and absorbs its economic activities – in view of a reduction in the weight of the uncertainty factor, greater efficiency in information collection and, at the same time, a curtailment of transaction costs.

This type of coordination confirms the potential for considerable discrepancies in the firm's working and results, due to the direction and quality of its organisation, characterised primarily by the way it manages transactions affecting its actors as a whole. In fact the firm depends on a network of contracts between actors, which establish complementary relationships with different roles and opportunities to orient decisions and actions. But these *contracts* may be *incomplete*, insofar as the parties in a transition do not agree *ex ante* by contract on actions to be taken or on the use to be made of assets in every possible situation that may occur in the future. Such actions and assets are not definable in unambiguous and verifiable terms, and the lack of "verifiability" is proportional to the complexity of actions and products and to their lack of "materiality".[18]

Contractual incompleteness often tends to demotivate the commitment of the above actors, also because of their diversity. Hence the major problem of productive processes – namely how to increase their wealth and welfare, attain a balance between incentives offered by organisations and participants' contributions to their resources, and allow for surplus management involving more symmetric criteria and bargaining practices for participants.[19]

In this network of contracts, a prominent position is taken by contracts with employees, where incompleteness is at its highest.

Employment contracts are a major instance of the explicative inadequacy of market-coordination of economic activities. Apart from other considerations, they cannot be attributed to this form of coordination as they rely on a relationship that is no longer between market agents but between the authority of employer and employees.[20]

Simon discounts as abstract the traditional economic theory whereby, after selling their labour at a set price, employees become an utterly passive factor of production and are hired by the employer to maximise his profit. Simon redresses traditional theory by examining especially the uniqueness of employment contracts, compared with other types of contract.

In sale contracts, for example, the buyer pledges to pay a fixed sum and the seller promises in exchange a fixed amount of a certain commodity. While in an employment contract such detailed specifications are missing: certain features of the worker's behaviour are fixed by the clauses of the contract, others are committed to the employer's authority and some are left to the worker's decision as he carries out his tasks. After delivering the commodity, a worker – unlike a seller – is concerned about the tasks he is given and how to perform them. Moreover, he ought to share in the distribution of the firm's results, in which he plays an active role.[21]

Williamson argues that the structures governing manpower should be selectively harmonised with the features of transactions affecting them and act with great care according to the level of skill of the human resources employed. High skills will require more frequent changes in employment contracts and call for procedural safeguards aimed at a fair balance between services rendered and rewards, prompt assessment of complaints and continuity in the employment relationship (an additional source of value)—without forgetting that the workers' contribution is often far more subtle than business accounts, especially when their replaceability is low.

Such needs, which may be connected to the uniqueness of employment contracts, justify the use of bargaining between contractual parties and recognition of the action of workers' organisations. These provide representation of workers' needs and preferences but they may also be viewed as an essential component of governing structures – which restrains "opportunistic bargaining" (typical of small groups), cuts bargaining costs, rationalises the wage structure according to the objective features of different tasks, and encourages collaborative commitment.[22]

Conversely, when workers are obliged to accept unwelcome or unnegotiated conditions rather than develop their own collaborative commitment (active attitude to service, enterprising skills, functional use of intelligence), they may offer only formal collaboration (working only to rule and providing the lowest acceptable level of service), as their contracts are normally incomplete and the power of each party may be confined to using or controlling opportunism.[23]

After outlining the main claims of recent theories of the firm, we are now ready to expose the economic basis of participation. Though resting on assumptions and empirical evidence on the functioning of firms, this basis also includes the legitimation and adequacy of key features in the political and social foundation of participation.

The economic basis rests on the use of the efficiency criterion. In the above theories one of the main concerns is the search for conditions and institutes that foster effort and commitment in the firm's population. Despite its utilitarian features, mainly consisting of opportunistic leanings, this is not an unchangeable "natural condition".[24] Such leanings can be corrected, in the institutional setting and nature of each context, by policies aimed at equity in the distribution of tangible and non-tangible rewards, by reconciling different interests and by a relationship of mutual trust and recognition.

Clearly, this approach differs from almost all traditional proposals (not only past ones), where the importance of the labour factor in terms of efficiency appears, if not entirely lacking, a mere addition to workers' rights and political and social arguments.[25]

Altogether the above options pave the way to the development and implementation of the participatory rationale. They belong to the component that directly supports its economic basis. We refer to the plurality and variability of organisational forms affecting the firm in a context of uncertainty and limited availability of rationality, and thus of ample margins of discretionary power in actors' decisions – especially of those in authority who take the decisions. The decisions are therefore modifiable, often unstable, testable and aimed at curbing transaction costs.

According to the above theories this objective advises the search for a balanced relationship between incentives offered by the organisation and by participants' contribution to its needs. Though generic in its wording, this statement gives validity to and embodies the potential of many non-antagonistic participatory proposals and events.

These proposals and experiences are clearly confirmed by looking at employment relationships and contracts.

Owing to the uniqueness and incompleteness of such contracts, workers are granted recognition of a certain degree of initiative, if not autonomy, in the performance of their services and of their expectations for the distribution of benefits attained.

These concessions outrun the initial terms of the contract and are legitimised by negotiations between the firm's actors, which may involve individuals or their representatives. In neo-institutionalist texts, the presence of a collective dimension is implicit or explicit. In the second case – as for Williamson – it is found in the action of trade union organisations, and especially in collective bargaining.

This presence, alongside the functions assigned to trade unions as part of the firm's governing structure, may be more fittingly ascribed to the sphere of participation. Participation in fact increases actors' collaborative tendencies, reduces the incompleteness of contracts, and lays the conditions for workers' representation to play in favour of the interdependency network within the firm.

3 Currently viable participation

This closing paragraph will address the third question we first put at the beginning of the chapter, concerning the participatory forms and processes that may be regarded as viable in the present day. Before answering this question it is necessary to recall an overall opinion of participatory functions and spaces, whereby participation is not destined to occur generally.

As these pages are about currently viable forms and processes, a choice is made between the many participatory instances known to us. As in the past, and perhaps even more than before, we are confronted with a great variety of highly diversified forms, each with potentially different means of implementation; as noted earlier, the selfsame factors affecting participation are in many respects ambiguous.

All this helps to explain, though just partly, why participation is not likely to be applied in a generalised fashion.

Participatory events are widespread and significant but they cannot aspire to become a standard and constant means of regulation in relations between the firm and its staff. Its role, at least in the medium term, will not be similar to that played so far, for example, by collective bargaining, and not only because the two can cohabit.

Even if factors favourable to participation were to prevail, its extension would not be very great as it is more likely to be promoted and implemented in the presence of special political-institutional conditions and in certain economic and productive settings. If this claim is realistic, the participatory perspective, despite its unique and innovative role in labour relations and employment, will from now on be unable to outline a complete and stable "system", even in a context limited to Europe.

Our attempt to define its current forms and processes will have to rely on elements in the sociopolitical basis of participation that have permitted a connection with claims about its economic basis.

This type of convergence is explained by two factors: on one side by the gradual shift in workers' and representatives' participatory demands towards arrangements that acknowledge an area of interests shared with the firm, with the mutual benefits this entails; and on the other side by the fact that the theoretical interpretation of the firm's functioning upholds the utility and legitimacy of participatory motives and institutes, in the light of the special nature of employment relationships and contracts.

Convergence can result in a potential union between the qualities of participation viewed as a means of equity and the firm's need to coordinate its activities, and especially to enhance the commitment of its actors.

With these points in mind, the question above will be addressed in the light of the following assumption: under the present conditions of capitalist economies and societies, participation can be realised and become desirable if it is succeeds in being compatible with and somehow in providing a positive contribution to the firm's efficiency needs and objectives.

This assumption supplements the notion of participation illustrated in the introduction, which claimed, among other things, that: participation works when it can rely on the converging intentions and mutual interest of the parties concerned (it cannot simply be an "achievement of workers" or a response to the firm's needs); it reaches a fair degree of stability and continuity through mutual obligations and exchange mechanisms between those concerned, including the bargaining method and the recognition of workers' representative structures (not necessarily within the trade union movement); it should be characterised by a high sense of equity (rewards distributed in proportion to contributions, actors' renunciation of maximisation of personal benefits, careful use of power) and by the social and cultural preconditions necessary to achieve shared productive efficiency objectives.[26]

Our concept of participation assigns the same ideal and practical status to its response to workers' interests and expectations and to the firm's needs as related to its functioning and worker involvement.

It should be stressed that this notion differs sharply from two other opposing interpretations considered in this book. The first interpretation, which occurs in proposals and in a few experiences, shows a tendency to underestimate: the need for employer consensus and benefits, the firm's search for efficiency, and its difficulty in reconciling the use of entrepreneurial prerogatives and participation in decision taking (Chapters 2 and 7). The second interpretation, which is more recent, emphasises the firm's needs and suggests a participatory "climate" capable of fostering and enhancing workers' qualities and contributions, but limits the exchange inferences and disregards the role of workers' representation (Chapter 6).

We shall now pass on to the following issues: what participatory forms are today relevant and applicable; and what venues and procedures may be used to implement and verify them.

3.1. What forms?

We shall list those forms that, ranging from the latest instances, to notable experiences of the past, appear today of special significance. They are reconsidered without further specifications, as they were analysed in detail earlier in the book (Chapters 4 to 6):

a   cultural and organisational participation, which relies on workers' involvement in view of the firm's objectives, its mission and constant need to adapt, applied chiefly to planning by the means of quality control. However, this form may be viewed [27] in broader terms with reference to the firm's organisational coordination which overcomes the hierarchical tradition of management and favours decision-taking at lower levels, innovating the collection and use of information, with a variably marked division of tasks;

b   economic participation in results, whereby workers are involved in the firm's functioning without affecting the criteria and decisions that regard its conduction, which translates into the institutes and practices of profit sharing;

c   participation associated with workers' access to ownership, which normally belongs to the sphere of economic participation but in theory and in practice may include strategic control of the firm, related to the size of holdings and the desire to exert such control; [28]

d   collaborative participation, which can be traced back to the "strong industrial democracy" tradition, applied to the firm's decision-making processes and workers' representatives in its institutional bodies.

No further mention will be made here of two other significant and differing forms: the cooperative firm, which has a special place in the development of participation, and financial participation, which has grown rapidly over the last few decades and still has more potential.

As for the cooperative, suffice it to say that it provides an institutional alternative to the capitalistic firm, since workers are not subordinate or dependent on others for the firm's ownership and management. There is no need (at least in the "pure" cooperative, where all members are also workers in the firm) to pursue converging aims and mutual benefits among actors whose interests are initially dissimilar. Its great difficulty in achieving a suitable degree of efficiency is due – as stressed again in recent times [29] – to the features inherent in this type of firm and not to differences in status and rights between its actors (Chapter 2).

In financial participation the distinction exists, hence the need to reach converging intentions and mutual benefits among actors. But difficulties are certainly fewer compared with other forms, as they do not involve the firm's organisational processes and financial participation is normally able to reconcile economic-oriented means with its clear social aims (Chapter 3).

In addition to the four forms listed above, adequate attention should be given to a problem associated with employment, which normally evades the range of participatory proposals and experiences and yet involves one of the most sensitive and truly influential issues bearing on workers' conditions. We refer to:

e   the likelihood of awarding "voice" and rights to workers or their representatives in the face of processes at work in the "firm market" (firms' lifetime and allocation, ownership allocation, and firm control).

This market is normally set beside the institutions and rules that oversee its functioning. In our perspective the point is whether at firm or corporate group level the recognition of workers' presence and intervention is viable, and whether the processes in this market may become – to a certain extent – an object of negotiation and participation.

Taking into account the main claims of the political-social basis and the economic basis, it is clear that participation should also include such processes. These affect workers' conditions – often even their occupational and professional prospects – more strikingly than other processes within the firm. If the firm, which at heart is an economic entity, is not merely such, then evidence of the fact should appear in conjunction with decisions and changes affecting the prospects of its actors.

Workers' conditions cannot remain independent of the firm's behaviour on the market and its economic results; however workers are entitled to know how far such implications are due to objective factors and events rather than the behaviour of owners and managers who do not "love" their firms but buy them and sell them as real estate, or fail to take strategic decisions concerned with profitability and consolidation of their market position.

This problem is certainly among the most difficult to match with suitable arrangements and adjustments that may together further workers' interests and offer the firm adequate results in business terms. In our perspective this problem uncovers the aspect of labour employment in the capitalist firm least legitimised at present, as it leaves workers vulnerable to events that can dramatically affect their condition and, at times, their very prospects; this occurs – despite relief offered by welfare provisions – even in firms with strong trade union protection.

On the other hand, trends in ownership and entrepreneurship allocation play a key role in the level of efficiency of an economic system and the need for technological and organisational innovation in its firms.[30]

This fact is regarded as vital and beneficial at the macroeconomic level, in the medium to long term.

Yet it may involve high social costs in the firm over the short to medium period: can its implications pass "over the employees' heads", especially in times that stress the human factor's centrality and require the collaborative involvement of all actors?

A few considerations will now be made on the implementational aspects of the forms listed above.

First of all, it should be remembered that they do not always occur separate from each other. They can cohabit or partly overlap. Some may also extend beyond their original bounds: this is true, for example, in the case of information and consultation rights (originally coinciding with industrial democracy) and of the means of cultural-organisational participation.

Secondly, attention should be given to methods of activation. As observed earlier (Chapter 7), these appear heterogeneous and highly diversified. Major experiences coupled with our notion of participation, call for the *negotial* method, which provides for the workers' presence in its collective dimension and for representative structures. In fact, other methods have been and will be employed, in which management initiative prevails over confrontation with the workers' will and its representatives.

Thirdly, the role of trade union organisations must be reconsidered: it appears commonplace and crucial to negotial method, even if bargaining arrangements with non-union types of representation may be used. This role surfaces in contractual action (when it takes on participatory themes and practices), in the tasks assigned to trade unions in firms by legal provisions or agreements between parties drawn up at higher level, and in the formal or factual appointment of workers' representatives within the specific institutes of participation.

Even taking into account current difficulties met by organised labour in promoting representation and the variety of different national settings, it clearly appears that the union's role and presence are destined to remain with participation in the future. Moreover, by their political and negotial action, trade unions have been able to represent the workers' "voice" (sometimes not only in defensive terms) in the face of the implications of crises and reorganisations in the "firm market".

3.2 What venues and processes?

Establishing what venues and processes are associated with participation is a key purpose of this study.

As participation includes qualitatively significant exceptions to the standard employment contract and in various degrees allows jointly for workers' rights, interests, objectives and expectations affecting the firm's functioning, reference to the firm's governing structure is necessary in order to establish participatory venues and processes.

In a deliberate simplification (confirmed by other authors), these venues involve both *strategic control* and *hierarchical control*.

The first of these concerns the right to use the firm's capital, its assets and relations, and thus the access to "political" decision-taking (re. investment, plant localisation, transfers and acquisitions, management decisions, product types, etc.).

The latter includes activities whereby such decisions are implemented by the hierarchy that manages the firm's organisation, detains authority, and initiates authority relationships within the firm.

The distinction between these venues mirrors the difference between ownership and management typical of present-day corporations – a major point in the theory of the firm from Berle and Means onwards – whereby ownership delegates to management the running of the firm. In many firms, however (not only family concerns), the two venues are not sharply divided, and notably this can happen even within corporations because of the degree of freedom and the range of tasks taken on by managers, often exceeding the limits of hierarchical control.

In our approach the above distinction is preserved, so that potential instances of "cross-contamination" are not taken into account.

It is well known that, as a firm functions, its governing structures can rely on a wide margin of discretionary power and can put into action a great range of means of control related chiefly to its organisational qualities and type.

Thus the coordination occurring within the firm's domain and its relations with the institutional setting translate into decisions involving the venues of strategic control and hierarchical control.

As for participation, only decision-making processes due to strategic control will be taken into account although the most frequent and varied implications concern decision-making processes assigned to hierarchical control; these are of two types, namely *organisational decision-making processes* and *distributive decision-making processes*.

The first type refers to processes involved in the attainment of the firm's objectives (return on capital, sound assets, market position, innovative capacity, reputation, limitation of transaction costs), through the direction and action of its organisational arrangements and the use of internal resources – chiefly human resources – in compliance with the efficiency criterion.

The second type refers to the body of themes, acts, rules and institutes that by contributing to the (incomplete) definition of the contractual relationship make available additional assets to actors operating in the firm.

Our view of distributive processes embraces a wider sphere than that normally attributed to them: besides monetary benefits, we include other assets such as later benefits, professional qualification and enhancement, recognition of rights, and token rewards. In other words this sphere should include any opportunity that can further contribute to reducing the asymmetry of subordinate employment, without questioning the firm's institutional arrangements.

3.3. Theses and proposals

Having defined the venues and processes that confront the current prospects of participation, five theses are now introduced which further develop the notion of participation at the heart of this book.

1   Participation involves hierarchical control but also strategic control.

The former instance appears more acceptable and practicable, because hierarchical control consists of ways of using and enhancing subordinate employment and – despite its innovative and renewed arrangements – shows continuity in results, compared with union and legal regulations.

In the latter instance the implications of participation appear more difficult and dubious, and of course alien to the antagonistic rationale. And yet their feasibility may also be assumed, as strategic decisions often affect workers' conditions and prospects too deeply to be considered not liable to correction, mediation and negotiation.

In the short term participation can usually rely on the converging interests of workers and employer, but it acquires real qualities when it includes a broader perspective which reconciles the firm's and its workers' objectives (chiefly in the area of employment).

This perspective does not intend to disregard the lawful responsibilities of those exerting strategic control in virtue of their ownership right to limit risks in the provision and use of capital and in the pursuit of sound assets for the firm. Instead it is supported by the fact that in its "political" decisions and in tackling the uncertainty of economic action, firms take into account risks affecting workers' conditions and prospects (for reasons mentioned above in connection with the "firm market") by turning to adaptive solutions that to a certain extent can reduce social costs without weighing on vital competitive requirements.

2   Participation does not directly apply to organisational decision-making processes.

In order to function in a competitive market, the firm undeniably needs to depend on the functional element in task division and on the "proportional" element in authority and subordination. Both elements should be present also in firms and organisations such as public bodies, not subject to competitive restraints in the pursuit of their purpose. These two elements imply that, in order to fix and curb transaction costs, the holders of hierarchical control should be able to make organisational decisions and take on the duties attached – decisions that the other actors accept and may be partly shared if reached in agreement and believed to favour the firm's functioning. This means that – within a precise institutional setting and in compliance with the rules established and accepted by such actors – holders of hierarchical control can reach the right level of efficiency if they are free to carry out managerial duties, exert authority (though by different ways and means) and employ the qualities and skills of the firm's population with a great degree of independence.

Limiting participation to the threshold of organisational decision-making processes – a thesis rejected or simply undervalued in most participatory proposals – is a vital requirement for the firm to function properly; its importance is now even greater, if the participatory firm is to compete against other firms and face the challenge of productive environments with less regulation and lower labour costs.

3   Participation as such applies directly to distributive decision-making processes.

The exclusion of organisational decision-making processes is countered, from the viewpoint of workers' interests and expectations, by the opportunities inherent in distributive processes.

Participation finds its proper place within the latter processes because they reconcile the needs of the firm – with its institutional features and organisational restraints – and the benefits available to its staff: in terms of (real or potential) financial, professional and "citizenship" benefits.

Within these processes participation is founded chiefly on the following principle: after assessing *ex ante* and investigating *ex post* what assets and benefits are to be distributed and how to allocate them, the firm's functioning and the actions of its hierarchy are expected, in the intermediate phase, to unfold normally (barring unforeseen events) without too much hindrance or opposition, procedural complications or recurring tension.

Distributive processes may thus be subjected to decisions shared between holders of hierarchical control and employees; the latter are entitled to intervene in such processes, so that holders of hierarchical control significantly limit an authority which is instead their prerogative alone in the sphere of organisational decisions. In effect, it is a matter of improving the workers' status and their range of rewards, while at the same time complying with the firm's operational needs.

4   The application of participation to distributive rather than organisational decision-making processes must not be viewed in narrow terms and, as often happens with social phenomena, it is not destined to result in straightforward events.

In this light, at least two corrections deserve our attention: the initiation and outcome of participation imply in practice indirect "retroactive" effects on organisational decision-making processes. Assets, procedures and institutes in the participatory perspective give rise to implications which are not uninfluential in organisational choices and for the behaviour of those making them; the extent of such implications should not be considered uniform across different participatory forms. It is more modest when participatory forms involve clearly defined assets offering tangible benefits (such as economic participation in the firm's results) or the offer of benefits that do not normally interfere with the firm's functioning (such as financial participation). It is greater in the case of participatory mediation confronting strategic decisions and seeking to reconcile the firm's objectives with workers' objectives and prospects.

5   The achievements of participation rely on a trade-off between the firm's interests and workers' interests and expectations.

Their maximum stability and full legitimation depend on freedom of initiative for the parties involved (through negotial practices), on the formalisation of institutes and procedures, and on safeguards provided by actually acknowledged exchange arrangements.
The implications of these theses for the features of listed participatory forms will be now be considered.

Cultural and organisational participation This form is proposed for firms capable of constantly innovating both their managerial action and their organisational and functional structures; it stresses the enhancement and mobilisation of the human factor.
The emphasis placed on the notions of delegation, decentralisation, reduction of hierarchy, and resolution of different problems within the firm could give the impression of a participatory perspective affecting decision-making processes.

However this is not the case, if not to a small degree. It is not the case for strategic control, both because it does not allow for workers' participation in institutes and procedures and because their involvement in the firm's mission implies above all confidence in its leaders and a strong commitment to their objectives, as well as encouragement to adjust production to the market.

Instead it is the case – to a modest degree – for hierarchical control. Without underestimating innovations in organisational decision-making processes affecting workers and accordingly a better use of their talents and skills, it seems appropriate to claim that, for a great part of staff, participation in such processes does not normally extend beyond a certain limit, a threshold that avoids harming hierarchical arrangements.

Distributive processes are a different matter. As we know, they highlight job enlargement and recognition, greater consideration for employees' dignity and individual traits, and often the assessment of their merits and contribution.

The weakness inherent in this participatory perspective over the medium to long period (i.e. its lack of clear exchange arrangements) combined with the "threat" of restructuring and its negative effects on employment (a disastrous event in this light), may be offset – as has actually happened – by negotiating and formalising participatory events (especially in conjunction with other forms, and namely economic participation) or by offering safeguards through adaptive and renewed bargaining rules (especially for the numerous components of flexibility).

Economic participation in results This involves workers directly, by means of a variable wage share proportional to the firm's results and calculated on special performance indicators. It functions according to clear exchange mechanisms: financial benefits for workers, flexible retributive criteria allowing for potential fluctuations in remuneration, and direct involvement of workers in the firm's good running.

The perspective clearly lies outside decision-making processes, as shown by its results. This is true not only when it is selected and directed by entrepreneurial action but also when it translates into negotial practices. The negotiability condition is made necessary by two separate requirements: the provision of guarantees to workers on the selection and inspection of benefits and risks at stake; and the completion of protection covering non-economic aspects of service, when workers' representatives are confronted – as in many other instances – with hierarchical control.

Both requirements confirm that, given its chiefly distributive nature, this form has very strong links – unlike industrial relations systems, which centre almost invariably on remunerative assets.

This form has the advantage of easy implementation, since its content is well-defined and is not exposed to conflicting interpretations and meanings.

191

It moves toward the firm's major needs and at the same time involves employees' interests directly. As mentioned earlier, it can appear in conjunction with other participatory forms or also with regulation, as in the bargaining tradition. Its weight is due to collective variations in a portion of remuneration and yet hinges on the dimensions of this portion and on two important conditions: transparency in the criteria informing this institute and consistency in its application (real term variability).

Share-ownership participation Like the previous one, this form normally belongs to economic participation. Its potential, however, may be more significant as it involves the symbolic asset of capital shares, may alter workers' status (by an employment relationship that is no longer merely wage oriented) and commit them to the firm's "fortunes" (involving an extensive time-outlook). On the other hand, this participatory perspective is rather indirect, with limited scope for workers' initiative, and has often proved alien to the arrangements of industrial relations.

In this form, workers' opportunities to influence decision-making processes do not appear realistic. Given the object of participation, the venue for this influence to occur is strategic control; but this is hardly viable because the transfer of shares to employees remains within limits that never threaten owners or holding companies. Only under special conditions will employee ownership of shares have any effect on strategic decisions – as for instance when they are called to help the firm overcome a difficult phase by buying its shares so that part of their wages or other forms of remuneration are withheld or delayed.

This form does not apply to the use of hierarchical control: its rationale implies that workers' involvement in the firm's "fortunes" should take place without interfering with its functioning, as they are rewarded *ex post* by benefits related to its achievements. Wherever the unions are present or the form does not appear potentially hostile to unions, it becomes an additional, almost residual arrangement, compared with contractual protection.

On the other hand, the same form contains a number of distributive rewards: not only the enjoyment of dividend, but also special conditions for the purchase of shares, ample tax concessions and (though less verifiable) workers' satisfaction with their new status.

It may extend beyond the field we allocated to economic participation, if implemented by collective arrangements through shareholding schemes associated with high stakes.

These arrangements have allowed shareholder workers to aspire to seizing strategic control, by striking alliances with management or through their own direct representatives. Strategic control can be achieved even if employees are encouraged to acquire the majority or a high stake of shares in their company during a severe crisis.

In either case, these arrangements resemble the cooperative (meaning an "imperfect" cooperative, where not all members are employees). Yet their development differs greatly from a cooperative, not for the lack of antagonistic motivation but rather because the firm is not established by the workers' initiative. Instead, the firm's functioning problems are rather similar and concern (Chapter 2) capitalisation, the appointment of managers, the discontinuous coherency of interests among employee members and, above all, their tendency to interfere with decision-making processes under hierarchical control – which often implies an increase in costs and conditioning even for those charged with strategic control.

Participation as industrial democracy This participatory perspective based on codetermination dates from the "strong industrial democracy" tradition and is typified by two essential features: its application to decision-making processes and the presence of workers' representatives in the firm's institutional bodies.

It used to be the only widely tested instance of collaborative participation aimed at actually influencing the firm's decisions and functioning.

Its most prominent and convincing version is found in Germany, where legal provisions and widespread implementational practices enable workers' representatives to "codetermine" strategic decisions within such bodies but do not allow their direct intervention in organisational decision-making processes. Today even more than in the past this version can be adequately applied only to firms with solid and disciplined industrial relations, by combining effective safeguards on working conditions (chiefly works councils) with full mutual recognition and a collaborative attitude on all sides.

In the German instance the presence of workers' representatives in the firm's bodies notably involves a venue preceding the board of directors (whose functions in Germany are comprehensive of hierarchical control), i.e. the supervisory board. This arrangement seems preferable because the supervisory board functions as a "clearing house" where sides confront each other before hierarchical control, whose weight depends on its ample duties and – to no lesser extent, perhaps – on the "moral authority" provided by internal consensus, as is normally the case in the German experience.

Under this arrangement the supervisory board includes representatives of shareholders and various staff groups; its composition may also provide for an equal representation of shareholders and workers, but the former are formally enabled to prevail (e.g. their chairman is allowed a double vote) to avoid stalemates.

The supervisory board also appoints and repeals the board of directors, oversees its action and exerts the right of proposal on strategic decisions.

The other arrangement is close to the Swedish experience as it provides for workers' representation on the board of directors. It may be considered equivalent to the previous scenario, insofar as workers' representatives sit in a body – the board of directors – which takes strategic decisions that will be implemented by management (in charge of hierarchical control).

In our view this arrangement appears less adequate and realistic, as it lacks the dialectic character of the previous venue (i.e. the supervisory board) in its strategic decisions and makes it harder to avoid undue confusion between the making and implementation of such decisions.

If this arrangement is adopted, we advise that workers' representatives should be a minority, in order to safeguard ownership rights and undertakings and so as not to overcharge such representatives with direct and indirect responsibilities.

In line with the last observation, workers' representatives could be allowed only advisory voting. Effective voting is not necessary to those who remain a minority. The weight and effects of their contribution depend on whether they represent the workers' "voice", on the nature and soundness of their contribution, on their ability to interpret representatives' expectations and anxieties without forgetting the firm's needs and problems.

Both of these two arrangements – and the first one in particular – rely on the workers' freedom to influence their firm's strategic decisions without directly interfering with organisational decision-making processes. Confrontation with those exerting hierarchical control lies within the sphere of distributive processes and is due to the action of works councils and other forms of industrial democracy (e.g. information and consultation rights, and co-decision institutes and procedures).

Other notable distributive features may occur in codetermination, especially influence over decisions with implications for employment or staff turnover.

These supplement the qualitative (recognition, "citizenship", rights) and the indirect (combining contractual protection and potential access to forms of economic participation) distributive features of codetermination.

The firm market and participation A consideration of relations between this market (allocation and lifetime of firms, allocation of ownership and control of firms) and the search for participatory spaces is needed, because here, more than elsewhere in capitalist economies, market performance may have striking implications for employees' conditions and even their prospects.

Although no one should underestimate these implications, it is very difficult to outline a participatory scenario. We are confronted with a contradiction between the need to enable this market to function (which occurs physiologically, in a competitive context) and the employees' rightful need to react to its consequences; these are not necessarily negative but, nevertheless, may strongly alter the professional, occupational and existential position of workers.

The difficulty of this participatory perspective can be mostly overcome by codetermination (via the supervisory board), thanks to the presence of workers' representatives in the venue of strategic decisions. We know, however, that codetermination developed in a historical period different to ours, in an exiguous number of countries with solid and disciplined industrial relations systems. No insurmountable obstacles prevent its use in the present, but admittedly it does not appear in the agenda of economic operators and politicians, or even trade union actors, outside the above countries.

Other solutions, such as those mentioned below, are neither conclusive nor easy to apply. Obligatory consultation of workers (legally enforced) in view of new arrangements may be highly significant but nothing more, if its outcome is not binding. If, on the other hand, it were binding, market activation would be strongly constrained, with repercussions on the firm's value and desirability and considerable limitations to the use of ownership rights.

Even less applicable appears an arrangement capable of solving the above problem at the root, by introducing measures aimed at altering the balance of interests and control between workers and shareholders in favour of the former.[31] Actual adjustments of this balance are both feasible and desirable, provided the sides are allowed negotial freedom. The widespread prevalence of workers over shareholders, ensured by legal rights, is a prospect that recalls obsolete scenarios of economic democracy and, ultimately, would overturn the institutional and functional order of capitalist economies.

Relations between the firm market and workers' rights remain a vital issue which can be tackled by specific measures such as: legislation ensuring transparency in the acquisition, transfer and control of firms; action by state agencies monitoring labour market trends and changes; safeguards for workers guaranteed by unions, in conjunction with new corporate arrangements (as actually happens during a crisis); welfare provisions, reorganisation of human resources, policies fostering the development and employment of labour; and finally the hope that employers may always be far-sighted enough to acknowledge that the firm as an economic unit is not necessarily incompatible with its inherent human and social dimension.

Notes

1   M. Albert, *Capitalisme contre capitalisme*, Editions du Seuil: Paris 1991.
2   M. Crozier, *L'Enterprise à l'écoute*, Inter Editions: Paris 1989.
3   Cf. G. Baglioni and C. Crouch (eds), *European Industrial Relations. The Challenge of flexibility*, Sage Publications: London 1990.
4   Cf. J. Visser, 'Mutamenti sociali ed organizzativi del sindacato nelle democrazie occidentali', *Giornale di diritto del lavoro e di relazioni industriali*, No. 62, 1994.

5   Cf. G.P. Cella, 'Inattese instabilità della rappresentanza', in G.P. Cella and U. Mückenberger (eds), *L'esperienza tedesca: un modello sociale in trasformazione*, Angeli: Milan 1993, p. 14.

6   C. Offe, 'La rappresentanza degli interessi economici e di lavoro. Forze e limiti dell'azione collettiva', ibid.

7   C. Crouch, 'Afterword', in G. Baglioni and C. Crouch (eds), *European Industrial Relations. The Challenge of Flexibility*, op. cit.

8   R.H. Coase, 'The Nature of the Firm', *Economica*, 1937.

9   See, for example, R.C.D. Nacamulli and A. Rugiadini (eds), *Organizzazione e mercato*, Il Mulino: Bologna 1985.

10   Cf. M. Salvati, 'Economia e sociologia: un rapporto difficile', *Stato e Mercato*, No. 38, 1993, pp. 198ff.

11   P. Mariti, 'Presentazione' to the Italian edition (Il Mulino: Bologna 1991) of O.E. Williamson, *Economic Organization: Firms, Markets and Policy Control*, Brighton, Wheatsheaf, 1986.

12   O.E. Williamson, 'Il dialogo tra la nuova economia istituzionale e le altre scienze sociali', *Stato e Mercato*, No. 40, 1994.

13   Cf. C. Trigilia, 'Economia dei costi di transizione e sociologia: cooperazione o conflitto?', *Stato e Mercato*, No. 25, 1989.

14   F. Ranchetti, 'Impresa, incertezza, informazione. Il punto di vista della teoria economica', in G. Sapelli et al., *Il divenire dell'impresa*, Anabasi: Milan 1993.

15   See H.A. Simon, *Casualità, razionalità, organizzazione*, Il Mulino: Bologna 1985, Chapters 11 and 12 in particular (a selection of studies compiled for the Italian edition).

16   O.E. Williamson, *Economic Organization*, op. cit.

17   See the article by G.P. Cella and W. Santagata in *Stato e Mercato*, No. 41, 1994, on D.C. North, *Institutions, Institutional Change and Economic Performance*, Cambridge University Press: Cambridge 1990.

18   F. Barca, *Imprese in cerca di padrone. Proprietà e controllo nel capitalismo italiano*, Laterza: Bari 1994.

19   H.A. Simon, *Casualità, razionalità, organizzazione*, op. cit., pp. 299ff.

20   F. Barca, *Imprese in cerca di padrone. Proprietà e controllo nel capitalismo italiano*, op. cit., p. 31.

21   H.A. Simon, *Causalità, razionalità, organizzazione*, op. cit., Chapter 2.

22   O.E. Williamson, *The Economic Institutions of Capitalism. Firms, Markets, Relational Contracting*, Free Press: New York 1986.

23   G. Provasi, *Il sindacato come organizzazione alla luce delle moderne teorie organizzative*, 1994 (MS).

24   Cf. M. Turvani, 'Introduzione' to the Italian edition (Angeli: Milan 1992) of O.E. Williamson, *The Economic Institutions of Capitalism*, op. cit.

25   Cf. F. Ranchetti, 'Impresa, incertezza, informazione', op. cit., pp. 70ff.

26   Cf., among others, R. Dore, *Taking Japan Seriously. A Confucian Perspec-*

tive on Leading Economic Issues, Athlone Press: London 1987, Chapter 1 and elsewhere.

27   Cf. M. Aoki, 'The Participatory Generation of Information Rents and Theory of the Firm', in M. Aoki, B. Gustafsson and O.E. Williamson (eds), *The Firm as a Nexus of Treaties,* Sage: London 1990, Chapter 2.

28   Cf. H. Hansmann, 'The Viability of Worker Ownership: An Economic Perspective on the Political Structure of the Firm', ibid., Chapter 8.

29   Cf. O.E. Williamson, *The Economic Institutions of Capitalism. Firms, Markets, Relational Contracting,* op. cit., Chapter 10.

30   Cf. F. Barca, *Imprese in cerca di padrone,* op. cit.

31   R. Dore, *Taking Japan Seriously. A Confucian Perspective on Leading Economic Issues,* op. cit., Chapter 8.

Glossary

Antagonistic participation

or participation with antagonistic traits comprises proposals and solutions tending to alter effectively both the imbalance inherent in asymmetrical employment relationships and often even workers' social conditions. Antagonistic participation is one of the three models of participation.

Codecision

involves several situations where institutional and/or recognised union representatives are officially chosen to protect the interests of in-plant representatives, and at the same time improve the normal working of productive structures and activities. Codecision often arises as a form of the "industrial democracy" direction in collaborative participation.

Codetermination

regards conditions where workers' representatives cooperate with the employer in taking deci-

sions which affect both labour and the firm. Such decisions are taken jointly within the firm's institutional bodies and stem from the recognition of interests common to both partners, overcoming potentially or truly their traditional division of roles and duties. Codetermination constitutes the strong form of the "industrial democracy" direction in collaborative participation.

Collaborative participation

comprises proposals and experiences that envisage an improvement in workers' socio-economic standing and a correction of the imbalance in employment relationships, without altering the institutional setting of capitalism or the firm's corporate name. Collaborative participation is one of the three models of participation.

Co-management

concerns the (unassessed) feasibility of participation in the firm's decisions, with an equal number of employees and employer's representatives within the board of directors and therefore total involvement in the firm's strategic decisions. Joint management is the strongest form of the "industrial democracy method" direction in collaborative participation.

Concertation
involves the participation of large organised interest groups (trade unions and employers' associations) in economic and social policy decisions, through collaborative practices and agreements with government based on the exchange of mutual concessions and obligations in different ways and areas. These practices and agreements involve the macro-economic and political level, with deep implications for industrial relations as well. Concertation is a direction in collaborative participation.

Consultation rights
are ensured by procedures whereby the employer informs and consults workers or their representatives in order to assess their needs and views before taking a decision, and retains the freedom to apply them unless the case calls for the consent of workers or their representatives. Consultation rights are a form of the "industrial democracy" direction in collaborative participation.

Cooperative
refers to a firm where no distinction is made between earned income and capital income, as members contribute both labour and capital and own the firm themselves. The cooperative is a form of the "explicit extension of the political democracy method to production relationships" direction in antagonistic participation.

Cultural-organisational participation
is based on workers' involvement in the firm's objectives, mission and constant need for adjustment. It does not openly envisage economic advantages for employees, who are required to identify with the business organisation and show strong commitment, on the assumption that partners in the firm are joined by the same motivation. It occurs above all as part of the schemes and means of "total quality". Cultural-organisational participation is one of the directions of integrative participation.

Directions (of participation)
are found in each of the three models of participation; they express the intentions and objectives pursued by actors and help us to comprehend the meaning, significance and implications of participation.

Economic participation
makes tangible benefits available to workers according to the

firm's functioning and results, without involving them in the policies and decisions that underlie its activity. Economic participation is one of the directions of integrative participation.

Employee ownership
includes arrangements and practices that allow workers to benefit directly from the firm's functioning by acquiring part of its share capital. Employee ownership is a form of the «economic participation» direction in integrative participation.

Financial participation
concerns instances and arrangements that favour employees' socio-economic standing at the end of their career; these have deep implications (both tangible and non-tangible) for the last part of their lives and depend on the effort and financial contribution made earlier. Financial participation usually appears in the form of supplementary social insurance funds. It is one of the directions of collaborative participation.

Forms (of participation)
occur within the directions of participation, and concern: its theoretical and tangible traits; its environment and components; arrangements, procedures, negotial tools, customs and practices.

Industrial democracy
includes instances where workers, through representatives generally appointed or influenced by trade unions, meet their counterparts in formal bodies whose task it is to decide working conditions or how these should relate to the firm's decisions, through procedures and themes which may reach well beyond the traditional confines and outcomes of collective bargaining. Industrial democracy is a direction of collaborative participation.

Information rights
state that the employer should provide workers or their representatives with data and explanations on the situation and problems of employment conditions and business, for both sides to discuss. Information rights are a form of the "industrial democracy" direction in collaborative participation.

Integrative participation
regards a number of aims and practices seeking to involve workers (not necessarily through their representatives) in the firm's operations and/or commit them to its functioning and fortunes. Integrative participation is one of the three models of participation.

Models (of participation)
offer an understanding of the rationale and fundamental motives in the development of participatory phenomena and expose the

main differences and potential similarities in real or suggested experiences.

Neo-corporatist political exchange
is a special case of concertation which involves: increasing politicisation and less independence in industrial relations; government collaboration with workers' and employers' representatives; government acceptance to negotiate economic and social policy decisions with such representatives in exchange for their readiness to agree on income policies.

Participation
involves employees and concerns the body of past or present proposals and experiences devised to alter or improve working conditions, employment relationships and often also workers' socio-economic standing in society.

Participation in public institutions
involves the presence of workers' representatives (often alongside employers' representatives) within institutions and organisations belonging to or supported by public authorities, in an advisory, supervisory or managing capacity. Participation in public institutions is one of the directions in collaborative participation.

Participatory economic democracy
signals an intention to raise the degree of market behaviour correction and widen the area of economic democracy arising from economic policy. Characteristically, participatory economic democracy: is initiated as a rule outside the political-institutional sphere, though sometimes assisted and supported by the latter; arises from the initiative of social groups and their organisations rather than the public sector or, at the most, from the joint action of such organisations and the public sector; occurs mostly at the production unit level, though it may develop at other levels.

Pluralistic political exchange
is a special case of concertation that involves: a certain degree of separation between industrial relations and their political implications; preferential union relations with a "friendly" political party; offering government resources and guarantees in exchange for the union's acceptance to avoid the full use of its bargaining power.

Profit sharing
consists of arrangements and practices which alongside a fixed salary allocate employees a variable allowance proportional to the firm's results and based on special performance indicators. Profit sharing is a form of the "economic participation" direction in integrative participation.

Self-management
occurs in firms which remunerate borrowed capital separately

from labour; every decision affecting production is taken by workers or by their representatives, so that employees secure the firm's proceeds net of production costs. Self-management is a form of the "explicit extension of political democracy to production relationships" direction in antagonistic participation.

Workers' control
involves themes and arrangements that seek to modify the capitalist economic system, first of all by establishing a new industrial order where firms are controlled totally or partly by workers' representatives. Its

forms belong to the "workers' control and influence over the economy" direction in antagonistic participation.

Workers' investment funds
were devised and employed by the Swedish trade-union movement (in the 1970s), in order to achieve high levels of economic democracy by gradually displacing part of the firm's profit to a unit trust system owned by workers and managed by their representatives. Workers' investment funds are a form of the "workers' control and influence over the economy" direction in antagonistic participation.

Index of names